KU-327-610

# IRELAND'S
# ANIMALS

# IRELAND'S ANIMALS

## MYTHS, LEGENDS & FOLKLORE

*Niall Mac Coitir*

*Original watercolours by Gordon D'Arcy*

The Collins Press

First published in 2010 by
The Collins Press
West Link Park
Doughcloyne
Wilton
Cork

© Niall Mac Coitir 2010

Niall Mac Coitir has asserted his moral right to be identified as the author of this work.

Watercolours © Gordon D'Arcy

All rights reserved.
The material in this publication is protected by copyright law. Except as may be permitted by law, no part of the material may be reproduced (including by storage in a retrieval system) or transmitted in any form or by any means, adapted, rented or lent without the written permission of the copyright owners. Applications for permissions should be addressed to the publisher.

British Library Cataloguing in Publication Data

Mac Coitir, Niall.
Ireland's animals: myths, legends and folklore.
1. Animals—Ireland—Folklore. 2. Animals—Ireland—History.
I. Title II. D'Arcy, Gordon.
398.2′452′09415-dc22
ISBN-13: 9781848890602

Typesetting by The Collins Press
Typeset in Palatino 10 pt
Printed in Malta by Gutenberg Press Limited

*Line illustration credits*
Thomas Bell, *A History of British Reptiles*, (London, 1839): lizard
J. R. G. Digges, *The Irish Bee Guide* (Dublin, 1904): bee
Richard Lydekker, *A Handbook to the British Mammalia*, (London, 1895): fox, stoat
John G. Wood, *The Illustrated Natural History, Vols. I–III*, (London, 1861): horse,
deer, wolf, pig, donkey, goat, sheep, badger, hedgehog, rabbit, cat, hare, rat,
mouse, squirrel, bat, whale, seal, otter, salmon, snake, frog
Wiliam Youatt, Cattle, *Their Breeds, Management and Diseases*, (London, 1834): cow

**Mixed Sources**
Product group from well-managed
forests, and other controlled sources
www.fsc.org Cert no. TT-CoC-002424
© 1996 Forest Stewardship Council
FSC

The paper used for this book is FSC-certified and
totally chlorine-free. FSC (the Forest Stewardship
Council) is an international network to promote
responsible management of the world's forests.

*I ndil-chuimhne ar mo mháthair, Celia*

# Contents

# Introduction

This book is about the animals that have shaped the landscape of Ireland and been important to its history. It includes not just those animals living wild in the countryside, but those living close to humans, such as the horse, cow and dog. It is neither a book of natural history nor a livestock manual. Instead, it will complement such works by looking at another important aspect to animals – their place in our folklore and myths. A key element to the book is the way it brings together stories and poems about animals that exist in the Irish tradition (all of the English translations of these poems being the author's own, bar the Donegal verse about dogs). Another purpose of the book is to rediscover the sense of wonder about animals that has been lost in the modern, more scientific approach. The medieval bestiaries, for example, while wildly inaccurate in their natural history, at least gave the animals they discussed a personality and liveliness often lacking today. The book seeks to recapture some of this spirit by jolting the reader out of common perceptions of animals, perceptions that are a hindrance to appreciating them in terms of myth and folklore. For example, the conventional approach of most books is to arrange animals zoologically, by species. This is correct when considering animals from a viewpoint of natural history. For the purposes of folklore, however, grouping the dependable but stubborn donkey with the proud and elegant horse makes little sense. A zoological arrangement can also create the unhelpful perception that species exist in a hierarchy of importance. Badgers may be more evolved than bees in terms of natural history, but in terms of folklore bees have the greater role.

Reflecting these issues, the animals in this book are arranged according to the Classical elements of fire, earth, air and water. This may seem strange at first, but it makes a lot of sense in terms of myth and folklore. The two main aspects to the arrangement are the animal's temperament and habitat. 'Fiery' animals, therefore, are those perceived to have a fierce and noble temperament, and to be swift and strong in body. 'Earthy' animals are perceived to have a passionate, sensual nature, and also to be dependable and loyal. More prosaically, they also include slower-moving animals that live close to the ground. The most obvious 'airy' animals are birds, but they lie outside the scope of this book. Other 'airy' animals include those (apart from birds) that can fly, those that live in trees, and those that are swift, fleet of foot and good at climbing. Many 'airy' animals are also perceived to have cold, intelligent and calculating temperaments, or to be at least contrary and changeable. Lastly, 'water' animals are those whose habitat is water, or close by it. They were often perceived in folklore to have mysterious, shy, wise and otherworldly temperaments. Although this arrangement of animals differs radically from that of natural history, it is not intended to overturn it. The reader will be informed where popular notions are at odds with the facts, so that sometimes-damaging myths will not be given renewed life.

The 'element' arrangement is also intended to break down another unhelpful perception, namely the rigid and often meaningless distinction between 'wild' and 'domesticated' animals. The goat, for example, is thought of as a domesticated animal, so any goats living in the wild are usually described as 'feral'. But goats have been living wild in Ireland since the Stone Age, and the Old Irish Goat is a distinct variety specially adapted to Irish conditions. It has even acquired over time a vital role in maintaining natural habitats such as the Burren. On the other hand, the deer is thought of as a 'wild' animal because of the native Irish red deer. However, the Sika deer from Japan is now far more widespread in Ireland than the red deer. It has been in the country for less than two centuries and was originally brought over as an ornamental, exotic animal before it escaped into the countryside. It would be far more accurate to describe the Sika as a feral deer, but it is never called that. The term 'feral' in theory describes a once-domesticated or captive animal that has escaped into the wild, yet it has additional unpleasant, emotive connotations of viciousness. It is much easier to speak of feral mink than feral rabbits, although strictly speaking all the rabbits living wild in this country are feral, as they were first introduced to Ireland by the Normans to be reared for their flesh and fur.

These examples show how names such as 'wild', 'domesticated' and 'feral' are too often used inaccurately, part of the misplaced human tendency to put animals into absolute categories, usually in a black or white, good or bad way. So animals are either Farmed or Hunted, Valuable or Vermin, Pets or Pests. The reality is that animals are far more intricate than these categories allow, and our interactions with them far more complex than we realise. Now more than ever, as environmental concerns become more urgent, we need to rethink our attitudes to animals and recognise that things are never as simple as we suppose. We need to treat animals with respect, without cruelty, but without excessive sentiment either. Part of our response to animals has always been emotional, so historically animals have usually been excessively feared – or excessively loved. At one level this emotion is simply because they are fellow flesh and blood creatures with which we can identify. On another level, however, it is because they affect our survival for good or ill, perhaps more than we like to admit. If we are to have a secure future, we need to face up to this interdependence with the fellow animals with which we share this planet.

## Aspects of the Folklore of Animals

We humans have always had a close relationship with the animals around us. They have provided us with food and clothing, helped hunt and herd other animals, carried goods and people, and ploughed our fields. Animals have provided for our emotional needs, too, by being companions and pets; so important is this function that pets are now regularly used to provide therapy for emotionally disturbed or disabled people. Quite apart from their many uses, however, animals are generally felt to have a certain bond with humans, sharing as we do so many characteristics. Animals feel emotions in the same way as humans, from fear and affection, to aggression and loyalty, and even love and hate. They have also the same basic physical needs and desires as people, whether it is for sex, food or the comfort of a warm fire. That they feel less inhibited about satisfying these appetites provokes both admiration and disgust. Animals, therefore, have been presented as role models for humans, in both positive and negative senses, from the earliest times. So it is that they have been bound up in our myths, legends and folk customs.

THEMES OF ANIMAL FOLKLORE

A central theme of animal folklore is the idea that animal behaviour was significant insofar as it provided moral examples (both good and bad) to humans. In Europe this notion began in the Classical world of Greece and Rome, and it has influenced Western thinking ever since. Probably the most influential and best known example of animals being used to provide a moral in this way is in the collection of animal stories known as *Aesop's Fables*.[1] These were a collection of fables (or stories with a moral) based on animal stereotypes that were allegedly the work of Aesop, a Phrygian slave who lived sometime about 620–560 BC. (Phrygia is in modern-day Turkey and Armenia.) Aesop was reputedly tongue-tied but then miraculously acquired the power of speech, allowing him to proclaim his stories for the betterment of all. The fables rely on well-known stereotypes for their effect – the fox is sly, the lion brave, the rabbit cowardly, the peacock vain and so on; but occasionally the tables are turned and the stereotype subverted, so the fables never become too predictable. The fables were hugely influential and remain so today. For example, in the fable of 'The Fox and the Grapes', the fox who cannot reach the grapes eventually gives up and walks away saying: 'Oh, but you aren't even ripe yet! I don't need any sour grapes.' The expression 'sour grapes' is still used to mean someone who makes excuses to explain away their own failure and another's success. Similarly, the fable of 'The Tortoise and the Hare', in which the two animals agree to have a race, is still quoted. The hare is so confident that he lies down and goes to sleep, only to find when he awakes and reaches the finish line that the tortoise has already crossed it. The fable stands both as a warning against complacency and arrogance and as a moral that dedicated effort can triumph over talent wasted through laziness.

There are many other fables, less well known but still entertaining and relevant. For example, the fable of 'The Crane and the Peacock' contains the moral that looks are not everything. In the fable the peacock makes fun of the crane's boring grey feathers. The crane replies: 'You may make fun of the colour of my wings, but I can rise on them high into the sky. You, on the other hand, can only flap those gilded feathers of yours down there on the ground!' The Greek philosopher Socrates was traditionally credited with first committing Aesop's fables to verse, but the stories have been found on Egyptian papyri dating to 1,000 years earlier, so there can be no doubt the fables are much older.

Another hugely influential work was the *Natural History*, or *Naturalis Historia*, written by the Roman scholar Pliny the Elder in the first century AD. This massive text consisted of thirty-seven books written on various topics to do with the natural world, including geography, botany, herbal medicine, mineralogy and zoology. Pliny drew on many earlier writers for his material, and intended his work to be a definitive compilation of the available information. His descriptions of animals in the zoology chapters (books 8 to 11) were a mix of fact and fable, but were not intended to be moralising as such. Nevertheless, the *Natural History* was so widely read that it remained the standard text on these matters until the advent of modern science. The later spread of Christianity throughout the Classical world did not change the viewpoint that animals could provide a moral example to humans. On the contrary, it was believed by Christians that God had created the natural world to provide a book of instruction to mankind. This viewpoint found expression in a work of uncertain authorship called the *Physiologus* which appeared in Greek, in Alexandria in Egypt, in the second or third century AD.[2] The *Physiologus*, a collection of animal lore, drew an explicitly Christian message from the description of the nature of each animal. It became a 'best-seller' of its day, widely copied, translated into many different languages and second only to the Bible in distribution in the Classical world.

These Classical teachings concerning animals found expression in later ages in the medieval bestiaries.[3] The bestiaries evolved largely out of the *Physiologus* and the seventh-century *Etymologiae* by Isidore of Seville, which drew upon the work of Pliny and other classical authors. Isidore believed the true nature of animals could be explained by analysing their names. Accordingly, he stated that the cat got its name from the Latin *catus* (clever) because it can catch mice. The bestiary, or 'book of beasts', was therefore a combination of moralising allegories about animals, their etymologies and the often-fantastical 'natural history' of the ancient world. Imaginary animals such as the unicorn, griffin and manticore (usually described as living 'in the East' or in 'Ethiopia') were often included alongside fantastical descriptions of real animals. Especially popular between the eleventh and fourteenth centuries, these books were lavishly illustrated so that the illiterate could be taught the character of each animal without having to understand the text. The authors of most bestiaries are unknown, but the names of a few survive, such as Philippe de Thaun, Guillaume le Clerc and Richard de Fornival whose bestiary, the satirical *Bestiaire d'Amour*, appeared about AD 1250. The bestiaries declined from the fourteenth century onwards as encyclopaedias began to appear, prefiguring the modern, more scientific approach. Tales that satirised contemporary life and events through the adventures of animals were another medieval example of animals being used to portray human habits. The most famous of these were the adventures of 'Reynard the Fox', a liar, thief and killer who always managed to win the day while others paid the price. So popular were the stories that the name Reynard remains a word for a fox to this day.[4]

Another central theme of animal folklore that was important in ancient Celtic culture is the notion of transformation into animal forms through shamanism or seer-ship. In early pagan Ireland there is evidence that poets and druids practised rituals that were essentially a form of shamanism, with the idea of gaining occult knowledge from contact with the otherworld.[5] Armed with this knowledge the seer could understand the mysteries of the past, present and future. A central feature of this process was metamorphosis or transformation, whereby the seer mystically adopted the forms of different animals to acquire extra knowledge. There are many examples of this in Celtic myths. For example, the legendary seer Fionntan Mac Bóchna was said to have lived for thousands of years, giving him detailed knowledge of past events and Ireland's lore. He achieved this feat by transforming himself into a one-eyed salmon, an eagle and a falcon before returning to his own shape. Similarly, another legendary seer called Tuan Mac Cairill was said to have owed his long life to various transformations. Originally the nephew of Parthalán, the first settler in Ireland after the Biblical flood, he survived by transforming himself in turn into a stag, boar, eagle and salmon. He was eventually eaten as a salmon by Caireall's wife, who gave birth to him and allowed him to resume human form.

The most famous example of poetic seer-ship appears in the eleventh-century *Book of Invasions* or *Lebor Gabála Érenn*, which concerns the legendary invasions of Ireland. When the Milesians, the ancestors of the Gaels, first arrive to take Ireland, one of their leaders, the poet Amairgen, becomes the first person of the Irish race to set foot in Ireland. As he does so he recites a famous and extraordinary poem in which he proclaims, through the power of his poetry, the ability to take on different natural forms and exercise various powers. In line with other tales of transformation, Amairgen describes being a stag, a hawk, a boar and a salmon. He also speaks of becoming different elements of nature such as wind and water, of his knowledge of the movements of the sun and moon, and of exercising his poetic powers of inspiration and satire. Taken as a whole, the poem is a stirring invocation of the powers of the early Irish poet, with more than a hint of druidism and shamanic powers. In fact the poem appears largely pagan in origin, with little if any Christian veneer. There have been many differing translations into English as the Old Irish is difficult and obscure; the following translation, which is the author's own, attempts to get to the original meaning as closely as possible.

## THE LAY OF AMAIRGEN

I am wind on sea
I am ocean wave
I am sound of sea,
I am stag of seven fights
I am hawk on cliff
I am sundew
I am finest herb
I am boar in fury
I am salmon in pool
I am lake on plain
I am vision of promise
I am essence of skill
I am spear bringing trophies of manly deeds
I am god who composes for noble heads.
Who heeds the warning rumble of mountain stones?
Who is it tells of the ages of the moon?
Or knows the place where sets the sun?
Who brings cattle from the House of Tethra?
Who wins a choice measure of Tethra's cattle?
Who is the god who composes,
to flay the corrupt kingdom?
Curses around a spear
Words of the wind.

Some lines needs explaining in greater detail. Tethra was the Fomorian god of death and the sea, and the cattle of Tethra (*buar Tethrach*) are the fish of the sea. In Gaelic mythology seafish were known as *buar Maighe Teathra* or 'cattle of the Plain of Tethra'.[6] The line 'to flay the corrupt kingdom' refers to the power of satire to bring unjust rulers to task. It was believed in Gaelic Ireland that the poet's satire had the ability to bring a king to ruin and misfortune, so powerful were his words. In line six the mention of 'sundew' (literally 'drop of the sun') may be a reference to the sticky secretion of the sundew plant, known as *ros solis* in the ancient world, and believed to have invigorating and nourishing powers.

Amairgen demonstrates more aspects of his powers when reciting a second poem shortly after his arrival in Ireland. Not only does he claim the ability to draw on the strengths of various animals, he also declares the ability to summon them at his command. He does this by calling up the 'cattle of Tethra', or fish of the sea, invoking the fertility of the sea to draw them into the coastal inlets and so increase Ireland's natural bounty.

THE LAY OF THE FISHES

Fish full sea
Fertile land
Upwelling fish.
Fish under waves
Flocking like birds.

Fair outpouring
Hundreds of salmon
Widespread whales.
Seaport song:
Upwelling fish
Fish full sea.

There are also numerous examples in Celtic legends of people turning into animals through magic, or being turned into animals against their will. Sometimes the changes are in the context of two individuals fighting or pursuing each other. The two great bulls that fight each other in the Irish saga *Táin Bó Cuailnge*, Donn and Finn, were originally pig-keepers who changed successively into birds of prey, fish, stags, warriors, phantoms, dragons and maggots before continuing their feud in the form of bulls. In Welsh myth the hag Ceridwen pursues the boy Gwion Bach after he tastes a drop from her magic cauldron, giving him knowledge of all the secrets of the past, present and future. Ceridwen is enraged and chases Gwion Bach. As pursuer and pursued, they take the form of greyhound and hare, otter and fish, hawk and bird. When at the last they take the form of a hen and a grain of wheat, Ceridwen swallows Gwion Bach. She later gives birth to the famous poet Taliesin, who is Gwion Bach reborn.[7] In Irish folk beliefs one of the best known examples of animal transformation was the widely held notion that witches took the form of hares to steal their neighbour's milk.

Some patterns emerge in the stories of transformation. People can turn into animals and back again, but ordinary animals cannot turn into people. Where humans have turned into animals and produced offspring, those offspring may in turn be able to transform into people (such as the Gaelic hero Oisín, whose mother gave birth to him while she was in the shape of a deer), but that is as close as it gets. Also, when people transform into animals, it is usually into wild animals such as deer or wild boar, and only occasionally into a domestic animal like a hound or a bull (most famously in the case of the Brown Bull of Cooley and his rival the *Finbhennach* or Fair-horned). There are three main reasons why people are transformed into animals in the legends. The first is the shamanic desire to harness the power of the animal concerned – achieving a longer life, for example, by transforming into various long-living creatures. The second is for the purpose of deception, such as witches turning into hares to practise witchcraft, or the story from Jocelyn's *Life of St Patrick* where the saint's power turns some of his followers into deer so that they may evade their enemies.[8] The third reason is that of punishment, or banishment, where people are turned into animals against their will. The Children of Lir, where the children are turned into swans by their jealous stepmother, is a famous example from Irish mythology. Another well-known example occurs in the Welsh tale *Math, son of Mathonwy*, where two brothers guilty of rape are turned successively into a pair of deer, wild pigs and wolves, and mate with each other in those forms.[9] An interesting example of transformation occurs in the story of the birth of the Gaelic hero Diarmaid Ui Duibhne, where the son of the steward of Aongus is transformed into a boar after being killed and has his life linked to that of Diarmaid.[10] This is a variation on the theme of animal transformation with the souls of the dead taking up residence or being reborn in animal form. This belief can be seen in folk stories portraying seals as the souls of dead fishermen, or where wizards appear as black dogs after their death.

Another feature of animal lore to appear occasionally in an Irish context is totemism – the idea of a person or tribe being spiritually or magically bound to a type of animal. The most famous example occurs in the story of Cúchulainn, where the Gaelic hero takes the place of a guard dog he has killed until a replacement is reared. The result of this appears to be that Cúchulainn's life is bound up with dogs, so that it is, for example, taboo for him to eat dog flesh. Another example appears in the story of the Munster king Tadhg Mac Céin.[11] The name Tadhg itself means 'badger' and the king appears to have a special relationship with badgers, including it being taboo for him to eat their flesh. In the story Tadhg's son was preparing a feast for his father and invoked his father's name to persuade badgers to come out of their setts, whereupon he killed them for their meat. On hearing of his son's ignoble deed, Tadhg flew into a rage and banished him. Apart from myths, animal names appear on many Old Irish inscriptions in the ogham alphabet, which date from about the fifth and sixth centuries AD and may have some element of totemism.[12] The word *con*, meaning hound or wolf, appears in many names, such as CUNNAMAQQI ('son of the hound/wolf') and CUNAGUSSOS ('hound/wolf of vigour'). Examples of other animals include BRANOGENI ('born of raven') and BROCAGNI ('little badger'). On balance, however, there is no evidence of a formalised system of totemism in early Ireland like that which existed among Native Americans or Australian Aborigines.

Another common theme of animal folklore is what might be called 'folk zoology', namely folk beliefs about animal behaviour. Some of these are derived from Classical sources, such as Pliny's *Natural History*, while others appear to be based on the speculations of country people. Perhaps 'folk zoology' is a misleading term, as they are not based upon any real observation of animals. Instead, they are often rather fanciful stories and almost invariably wrong. For example, the Roman writer Plutarch stated that hedgehogs will roll around in orchards in order to impale apples on their spines so they can carry them off to eat them, a groundless idea which nevertheless remains current today. Another widely held belief with no basis is the idea that there are two different kinds of badgers, 'pig-badgers' and 'dog-badgers', each with quite distinct characteristics. A recurring theme of these folk beliefs is the anthropomorphic notion that animals behave in a fashion similar to humans. For example, hares and hedgehogs were universally believed to steal cows' milk by suckling on their teats while they were lying down. So important was milk to the human diet that the idea that these animals would have no interest in it does not seem to have occurred. Another common story was that animals like stoats and cats gathered in groups or 'parliaments' to scheme and plot, or even to hold 'funerals' for their deceased relatives.

ANIMALS IN EARLY IRISH LAW

As befits an agricultural society, animals played a central role in the Brehon Laws of early Gaelic Ireland.[13] Animals (especially cattle) were used as units of currency, and a person's wealth could be measured by the amount of cattle they owned. Cattle had fixed values set down in law and were given in payment for goods and services and for settling fines. The basic unit of value under the Brehon Laws was the milch (or miking) cow, which was equivalent to one ounce of silver. The highest unit of value was the *cumal*, or female slave (in common with many early societies, including the Roman Empire, slavery was a feature of Gaelic Ireland). Over time it became more practical to use items of equivalent worth, so the *cumal* was later valued at either three milch cows, or a unit of land of about 13.85 hectares. Commonly used units of currency included the *sét*, worth half the value of a milch cow, and the *screpul*, or scruple, which was one twenty-fourth of an ounce of silver. The various categories of cattle were all given values, from young calves, worth only two scruples, to full-grown heifers expecting their first calf, worth sixteen scruples or two thirds of a milch cow. Male cattle were generally worth two thirds of their female equivalent, but bulls were only worth half a milch cow (twelve scruples), so they actually declined in value relative to females over time. Indeed, a well-trained ox (castrated male) capable of pulling a plough was more valuable than a bull, as it could attain a milch cow's value if it was good enough.

Sheep could be also used as currency, usually as a method of payment for lesser offences. For example, while the honour price of a *fer midboth*, or youth living on his father's land, was one yearling heifer, a youth of lower status, called a *flescach*, had an honour price of a lamb worth a bushel of grain. At the lowest rung of the ladder, an apprentice had to make do with a fleece of wool. A similar principle applied where a person removed stakes of wood from another's fence. The fine for removing one stake was a wether (castrated male) lamb, the price for two stakes a female lamb, while the price for three or more stakes was in cattle. Other animals were not in general used as currency, although horses did play a specific role in certain circumstances. For example, if a person with a claim on a piece of property could graze his horses on the land in the question for three nights in a row without being challenged, he could stake a claim.

The notion of the honour price, or *lóg n-enach* (literally the price of the face), was central to the Brehon Laws.[14] Unlike our modern legal system, there was no concept of equality before the law and so a person of high rank was entitled to a greater payment in compensation than someone of a lower rank. The most important payment that could be made was the honour price, which was the penalty for major offences. Some of these offences are obvious, including murder, theft and serious injury, while others appear strange to modern eyes, such as satire and refusal of hospitality. The honour price ranged from forty-two milch cows (or fourteen female slaves) for a provincial king, all the way down to the aforementioned apprentice who had to make do with his woollen fleece. Two of the most important ranks in Gaelic society were the *ócaire* and the *bóaire*, who were freemen but not nobles. The *ócaire*, or 'small farmer', was defined as having land worth seven *cumals* and (among other things) of possessing seven each of cows, pigs and sheep, and one bull and horse. His honour price was three *séts*, or one and a half milch cows. The *bóaire*, or 'strong farmer' (literally cow-freeman'), had an honour price of five *séts*, or two and a half milch cows. He was defined as having land worth fourteen *cumals* on which he could graze twelve cows.

For lesser offences, such as minor injury or damage to property, a range of different penalties applied. The fine for permanent leg injury, for example, was one *cumal* (or three milch cows) and the provision of a horse. A blemish to the face was regarded as particularly serious as it exposed the victim to public ridicule. A fine of one *cumal* was therefore levied for every public assembly which the victim had to endure. The fine for an illegal injury to a person's shins was three *séts*, or a milch cow and her calf. The penalty for theft was generally the honour price of the owner of the object and the owner of the property from where the object was stolen (if they were not the same). However, the Laws also state that the penalty for stealing a cow or an ox was to give back five cows or five oxen. The same rule applied to sheep, but not for pigs or horses, where only twice the value of the animal was due. The Brehon Laws also contained penalties for offences such as injury or theft carried out on domestic animals, from cats and dogs to cattle, pigs, horses and even bees. The Laws also dealt with injuries carried out by these same animals, such as injury to people or other animals and damage to property. These will be examined in greater detail in the discussion of each individual species of animal.

Apart from fines and penalties, the Brehon Laws also laid down other kinds of fixed payments including the value of land.[15] The basic unit of land in early Ireland was the *cumal* (about 13.85 hectares) which could range in price from twenty-four milch cows a *cumal* for good arable land down to eight dry cows for bogland. The Laws also lay down the obligations that a client (or tenant) had to fulfil for his lord in return for the use of the lord's land and livestock. For example, the *ócaire* had to pay his lord an annual food rent of a two-year-old bullock, while the *bóaire* had to pay a milch cow. In addition, each client had to pay a fixed amount of bread, wheat, bacon, butter, milk, onions and candles per year.

ANIMALS IN PLACE NAMES

Animals, both wild and domestic, appear in many Irish place names, with the cow and horse the most common.[16] Given its importance in Irish farming, it is hardly surprising there are numerous place names involving the cow and its various forms, such as bull, calf and heifer. The cow features in names such as Aghaboe (*Achadh Bó* – field of the cows), County Laois, Annamoe (*Áth na mbó* – ford of the cows), County Wicklow, Drumshanbo (*Droim Sean-bhó* – ridge of the old cow), County Leitrim, and Inishbofin (*Inis Bó Finne* – island of the white cow) in Counties Donegal and Galway. Regarding male cattle, it is interesting to note that oxen feature more often than bulls. The only prominent place name involving the bull appears to be Clontarf (*Cluain Tarbh* – meadow of the bull) in County Dublin. Other examples, such as Letternadarriv (*Leitir na dTarbh* – hillside of the bulls), County Kerry, are quite rare. The ox, on the other hand, occurs in quite a few place names, including Aghadaugh (*Achadh Damh* – field of the oxen), County Westmeath, and Dunaff (*Dún Damh* – fort of the ox), County Donegal. However, it should be noted that the word *damh* means stag as well as ox and that some of the place names suggest stag is meant rather than the ox. Calves also feature in a lot of names, such as Ballinalea (*Buaile na Laoi* – milking place of the calves), County Wicklow, Cloneygowen (*Cluain na nGamhan* – meadow of the calves), County Offaly, and Rathlee (*Ráth Lao* – fort of the calf), County Sligo. Heifers occasionally appear in names such as Ballyvary (*Béal Átha Bhearaigh* – mouth of the ford of the heifers), County Mayo.

The horse, too, appears in a great many Irish place names. The older Irish name for horse (*each*) features in names like Aghleam (*Eachléim* –

horseleap), County Mayo, Aughinish (*Each Inis* – horse island), Counties Limerick and Galway, and Ballinagh (*Béal Átha na nEach* – mouth of the ford of the horses), County Cavan. The later Irish name *capall* appears in Crocknagapple (*Croc na gCapaill* – hill of the horses), County Donegal, and Gortnagappul (*Gort na gCapall* – field of the horses), Counties Cavan and Kerry. Geldings feature in names like Cashelgarran (*Caiseal an Ghearráin* – stone fort of the gelding), County Sligo, and Garron Point (*Pointe an Ghearráin* – point of the gelding), County Antrim, while mares appear in such names as Cloonlara (*Cluain Lára* – meadow of the mare), County Clare, and Leamlara (*Léim Lára* – mare's leap), County Cork.

Another common animal in place names is the pig, though it may be that some of the names refer to the wild as opposed to domesticated pig. The pig gives its name to such places as Rosmuck (*Ros Muc* – headland of pigs), County Galway, Muckross (*Muc Ros* – grove of the pigs), County Kerry, and Ballinamuck (*Béal Átha na Muc* – mouth of the ford of the pigs), County Longford. Many place names are also based on the Irish word *torc*, meaning boar, and some of these may refer to wild pigs. These include Kanturk (*Ceann Toirc* – headland of the boar), County Cork, and Inishturk (*Inis Toirc* – island of the boar) and Maumturk (*Mám Tuirc* – pass of the boar), both in County Galway. Finally, a well-known place name, Bannow Strand in County Wexford, comes from *Cuan an Bhainbh* – bay of the bonham or piglet.

The other domestic animals that appear in a lot of place names are the sheep and the dog. Sheep feature in names such as Ballynageeragh (*Baile na gCaorach* – homestead of the sheep), County Down, Glenageary (*Gleann na gCaorach* – glen of the sheep), County Dublin, and Magheranageeragh (*Machaire na gCaorach* – plain of the sheep) in Counties Fermanagh and Tyrone. The wether, or castrated male sheep, can be found in names such as Ballinamult (*Béal na Molt* – mouth of the wether), County Waterford, and Clonmult (*Cluain Molt* – meadow of the wether), County Cork. The dog gives its name to places such as Glenamaddy (*Gleann na Madaidh* – glen of the dogs), County Galway, and Limavady (*Léim an Mhadaidh* – leap of the dog), County Derry, while hound (or *con*) appears in names like Convoy (*Conmhá* – plain of the hound), County Donegal, and Rathconrath (*Ráth Conarta* – fort of the hound-pack), County Westmeath.

Wild animals are also seen in many Irish place names.[17] The deer, which appears in such names as Keimaneigh (*Céim an Fhiadh* – pass of the deer),

County Cork, Drumanee (*Druim an Fhiadh* – ridge of the deer), County Kerry, and Knockanee (*Cnoc an Fhiadh* – hill of the deer) County Limerick, is probably the most common. Specific kinds of deer can also appear in place names, for example fawns in Knockanoss (*Cnoc an Os* – hill of the fawn) and Mullaghanish (*Mullagh an Ois* – height of the fawn), both in County Cork. Female deer or hinds appear in the names Cloonelt, County Roscommon, Clonelty, Counties Limerick and Fermanagh (all meaning *Cluain Eilit* – meadow of the hind) and Annahilt (*Eanach Eilit* – marsh of the hind), County Down. There are also place names involving the word *damh* which suggest that 'stag' rather than 'ox' is meant, such as Derrydamph (*Doire Damh* – oakwood of the stag), County Cavan, Derrynanaff (*Doire na nDamh* – oakwood of the stags), County Mayo, and Slievaduff (*Sliabh an Daimh* – mountain of the stag), County Kerry. Also common are place names involving the fox. Examples include Pollnashinnagh (*Poll an tSionnaigh* – hollow of the fox), County Galway, Monashinnagh (*Móin an tSionnaigh* – bog of the fox), County Limerick, Derrintinny (*Doire an tSionnaigh* – oakwood of the fox), County Cavan, and Craigmaddyroe (*Carraig Madra Rua* – rock of the fox), County Donegal. Another animal widespread in place names is the hare, which features in Ballygirriha (*Baile Giorria* – townland of the hare), County Cork, Dromgurrihy (*Droim Giorria* – ridge of the hare), County Cork, and Meenagarragh (*Mín an Giorria* – flat place of the hare), County Donegal. The badger can be found in place names such as Clonbrock (*Cluain Broc* – badger meadow), County Galway, Brockaghbeg (*Brocach Beag* – little badger sett), County Offaly, and Brocklagh (*Broclach* – badger sett), County Longford.

As we have seen with the word *damh*, it is not always clear which animal is meant in a particular place name. Other examples of this problem derive from names involving the cat, such as Carrickacat (*Carraig an Chait* – rock of the cat) County Mayo, Glennagat (*Gleann na gCat* – valley of the cats), County Tipperary, and Knockaunacat (*Cnocán an Chait* – hillock of the cat), Counties Mayo, Galway and Waterford. Rather than referring to the domestic cat, they probably refer to the pine marten, or *cat crainn* (tree cat) as it is known in Irish. But neither can the possibility that they refer to the haunt of feral domestic cats be discounted. Another source of confusion is that the pygmy shrew is sometimes known in Irish as the *luch fhéir* or grass mouse, the same Irish name as the wood mouse. Place names like Gortnaluchoge (*Gort na Luchóg* – the mice's field), County Donegal, and

Inchnalughoge (*Inis na Luchóg* – the mice's water meadow), County Clare, may therefore refer to the shrew rather than the mouse.

ANIMALS IN EARLY IRISH POETRY

Early Irish poetry is famous for its direct and lively portrayal of nature, and the imagery of animals is central to this, often made with a sharp and wry observing eye.[18] Mentions of animals in Gaelic poems range from Deirdre's lament at leaving 'Scotland of the red stags' and 'Assaroe of the seals' to Fionn Mac Cumhaill's poem about summer, when 'Bees with their little strength carry a load reaped from the flowers / the cattle go up muddy to the mountains / the ant has a good feast'. Other poems celebrate particular kinds of animals, like stags and wild boar, or treasured individual animals, like the white cat, Pangur Bán, or Bran, the loyal hound of Fionn Mac Cumhaill. These poems will feature in the individual sections on each animal. In addition, poems celebrating nature or a particular place often include a verse or two about animals. For example, the renowned story of *Suibhne Geilt* or Mad Sweeney contains many references to animals. Mad Sweeney was a king in early Ireland who later lived as an outcast in the woods, fleeing under a curse after insulting St Ronan. In the following verse he praises a wooded valley close to the sea:

> Many badgers travel its nooks
> And hares that are not slow,
> And seals with remorseful looks
> Come from the ocean below.

Another well-known example appears in the tale *The Voyage of Bran*, when Manannán, the Irish god of the sea, addresses Bran about the delights of his ocean kingdom:

> Speckled salmon leap from the womb
> Of the fair sea before you
> Like calves, like lambs, so beautiful,
> So peaceful in their harmony.

The actions of Fionn Mac Cumhaill and his warriors, the Fianna, form a major part of Irish mythology. Naturally, their adventurous outdoor life of hunting and fighting contains many references to nature and animals. A good example is a verse in a poem praising Beann Ghualainn, a place where the Fianna enjoyed good hunting:

> Martens in your mysterious woods,
> Squirrels abounding in your trees,
> Badgers that are good to hunt
> Many wild fawns running free.

Finally, one of the most evocative Irish nature poems is from the seventh century and concerns the hermit Marbán and his life in a hut in the woods, close to the trees, wild plants and animals. In a few verses Marbán describes how the animals provide him with company, speaking of them with obvious knowledge and affection.

> Hidden about
> Are herded pigs,
> Goats, bonhams,
> And wild pigs,
> Half-grown fawns, does,
> Setts full of badgers.

> Peaceful company,
> Tough, earthy crowd
> Around my house.
> To nearby woods
> Foxes come –
> Lovely that!

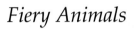

*Fiery Animals*

# Horse – Capall – *Equus caballus*

---

*T*he *horse's speed, strength, intelligence, and physical grace and beauty have made it essential to man for transport, warfare, hunting, racing and ploughing. This has made it the domestic animal probably most highly regarded and admired by man, especially by warriors and the nobility, and has been the basis of a close relationship between man and horse lasting thousands of years.*

FOLK BELIEFS AND CUSTOMS

Irish folk tradition had many curious beliefs about horses.[1] For instance, it was maintained that horses once had the power of speech and a nature very similar to humans. For this reason a horse should always be addressed as if it were a Christian. It was also said that horses had an animosity towards humans and would kill them, were it not for a quirk in their eyesight that made humans appear several times larger and stronger than in reality. Horses were also credited with the ability to see ghosts, and many stories tell of horses stopping at a certain spot and refusing to travel any further. The spot in question was invariably the scene of some tragic incident from the past. The horse had to be coaxed to continue by spreading a rug or some straw over the road for it to walk on. These stories have their origin perhaps in the horse's keen sense of smell that caused it to notice potential dangers that a human would not. Dealing with horses that were highly strung was a major concern, and the services of the 'horse whisperer' were greatly valued. These were individuals who had the gift of taming the wildest horse by speaking to it gently or breathing into its nostrils. For those who had the gift, even the most bad-tempered horse could be rendered quiet and biddable and ready for use. The secret of the horse whisperer was closely guarded, however, and seemed to be innate to the person rather than learned.

The horse was considered in general to be a lucky animal, and a favourite custom was to allow the horse to trample a little on seeds when sown to help them grow. It was also considered very lucky to have a dream that featured horses. Another Irish belief was that it was lucky to find the back tooth of a horse. Anyone who did would never want for money if they carried it about. The catch, however, was that the tooth had to be found completely by accident. Another widely held belief, in both Britain and Ireland, was that horseshoes were lucky and protective, due to their link to iron and fire – both substances hated by the fairies. To find a horseshoe was lucky, and it protected the house if nailed to the front door or threshold; the points of the horseshoe had to be pointing upwards or the luck would drain away. A horse's shoes, however, were never to be removed when it was dead, as it was said that the horse would still have need of them. The horse's halter was also believed to bring good luck, and should always be kept after the animal had been sold. It was very bad luck, though, to strike a horse with its own halter, as misfortune was sure to follow. In Ireland it was also considered unlucky to meet a man on a white horse while on the way to a funeral. The bad luck could only be averted by forcing the rider to turn back and join the procession for a few metres.

Several Irish superstitions surround the birth of horses.[2] For example, it was believed that the 'true mare', or seventh filly born in a row, was immune from all evil and that no harm would come to the person riding it. If it became a racehorse, it could never be bested. Furthermore, a four-leaved shamrock was believed to spring up at the place where the foal was born, which would bring good luck to the person who carried it. It was also thought that a horse born with a caul would become a great racehorse. In Ireland it was also believed that a foal born at Whitsuntide would either win a race or kill a man. In County Cork it was thought that a foal born without any human eye seeing it happen would have curative properties, and it is unsurprising, therefore, that the horse was involved in some Irish folk cures. For example, it was believed that a cure for whooping cough was to give the sufferer any food or medicine prescribed by a man who passed by on a white or piebald horse. It was also held that a piebald horse could cure a sufferer by merely pawing before the door of the house. A cure for ringworm, meanwhile, was to strap a horse's saddle to the back of the patient.

In Irish folklore many kinds of fairies could take the form of horses.[3] Most famous of these was the pooka, which usually appeared in the form of a terrible black horse, breathing blue flames and with eyes of yellow fire. The pooka's favourite tactic was to trick some poor unfortunate person

into getting onto its back. It would then ride madly though the countryside all night, dragging its victim through hedges and ditches. Finally, as dawn approached, the exhausted and battered rider would be allowed to dismount, and the pooka would disappear. Another kind of fairy was the Dullahan, which was generally a headless rider upon a headless black horse. What made it doubly terrifying was that the disembodied head of the horse, with flaming eyes and short cropped ears, would travel a few metres in front of its own body! Fairy horses were not all bad, however, and the people in County Clare were convinced that the many fine horses in the area were all descended from fairy horses that had emerged from the caves at Kilcorney in the Burren.

Another very common folk tale concerned the 'water horse', a fairy horse that came from the sea or a lake. Generally the horse was captured by a local man and became an invaluable worker or racer, to the great profit of the man. One day, however, the man struck the horse and it raced away back into the water. In some versions of the tale, the man's body was found floating in the lake soon after. A legend from County Kerry told of three water horses that lived in each of the three lakes in *Gleann na gCapall* (the glen of the horses), in the shadow of Mangerton Mountain near Killarney. One was snow white with a black blaze on its forehead, another jet black with a white star on its forehead, and the third was a bay horse with white spots on its forehead. They would emerge at night to damage crops and gardens in the area, until the powers of a seventh son were employed to make them stay in their lakes. Similar beliefs are found in Scotland, where the *each uisge* was a feared creature, with staring eyes, webbed feet and a slimy coat; and in Wales where the *ceffyl dwr* tempted travellers to ride and then galloped away to the sea with them.

Certain periods of the year in Ireland were particularly associated with horses.[4] May Eve, for instance, was a time when the fairies were particularly active, and bunches of flowers were often tied to the horses' bridles to protect them. In County Limerick it was believed that the Great Earl of Desmond, a noted wizard in his day, could be seen on May Morning in full armour, rising from the waters of Loch Gur to gallop about the lake on his silver-shod horse. In County Kerry the hero O'Donoghue of the Glens was said to appear out of the Lakes of Killarney on his milk-white steed, to bestow a blessing on the land. A widespread custom throughout Ireland on the first Sunday of August was to ride or drive horses into water, to guarantee them good health for the coming year. This occasionally involved having races with the horses through a local river or lake, a dangerous activity that frequently led to the loss of life for riders. At Halloween the 'guizers' who went door to door looking for treats in east Cork and Waterford were sometimes accompanied by the *láir bhán* ('white mare'), or hobby horse, a figure wrapped in a white sheet and wearing a carved mare's head. In Dingle in County Kerry the St Stephen's Day revellers called the Wren Boys were also accompanied by the 'white mare', a hobby horse with wooden jaws that could snap at those who did not contribute quickly enough. These customs are similar to the Welsh custom of the *Marie Lwyd*, or 'Grey Mare', where revellers went door to door at Christmas or New Year with a decorated horse's skull, playing music.

MYTHS AND LEGENDS

In Celtic mythology various goddesses were associated with horses.[5] The image of the horse seems to have been regarded as especially appropriate for goddesses who represented the fertility of the land, its sovereignty and its defence in time of war. In Irish legend, the Ulster goddess called Macha was particularly associated with horses. The most famous legend

Horse − Capall − *Equus caballus*

Wolf − Mac Tíre − *Canis lupus*

**Deer** – Fia – *Cervus*

Fox – Sionnach – *Vulpes vulpes*

Stoat – Easóg – *Mustela erminea*

about her, which explains how the royal site Navan Fort in County Armagh got its name (*Emain Macha* – the twins of Macha), makes the connection with horses clear. According to the legend, she appeared one day to a man called Crunniuc whose wife had died. She became his new wife, bringing prosperity to him and his family. One day Crunniuc attended a fair, at which the king's chariot and horses were victorious in the races. The hosts declared that nothing was faster than the king's horses, to which Crunniuc replied: 'My wife is that fast.' Crunniuc was taken to the king at once to explain himself. The king then declared that Macha had to race against his horses, on pain of Crunniuc's death if she refused. Macha pleaded that she was heavy with child, and asked that the race be postponed until after she had given birth, but her words were in vain. Macha declared: 'Well then, the evil you will suffer will be the greater and it will affect the men of Ulster for a long time.' She raced against the king's chariot, even though her labour pains were upon her, and as the chariot reached the end of the field she gave birth in front of it. Macha gave birth to twins, a son and daughter, giving the name *Emain Macha* (anglicised as Navan) to that place ever since. As she gave birth, Macha cursed the warriors of Ulster, declaring that for nine generations they would suffer the pains of childbirth and be as weak as a woman in labour whenever Ulster was most in need. The only warrior unaffected was Cúchulainn, who was left to defend Ulster alone.

In Welsh mythology the goddess Rhiannon is also connected with horses. In the tale *Pwyll, Lord of Dyfed* she first appears dressed in a golden robe and riding slowly on a white horse. No matter how fast Pwyll pursued her on his own horse, she remained just out of reach. At last Pwyll called out to her, and Rhiannon stopped and conversed with him, and eventually they married. She was accused of murdering her son, however, when he was spirited away on May Eve shortly after being born. Rhiannon was then forced as punishment to sit for seven years by the horseblock outside the castle gate, offering to carry visitors into the palace on her back. This rather bizarre punishment derives from the lore linking her to horses. Rhiannon's son Pryderi was restored to her at last by Teyrnon, a vassal of Pwyll who had found Pryderi and reared him, not knowing his true identity. The manner in which Pryderi was found also reinforces the link to horses. Teyrnon had a fine mare which gave birth to a foal every May Eve, but each time it disappeared; eventually, on the same May Eve Pryderi was taken, Teyrnon decided to lie in wait to see what happened. Shortly after the mare gave birth to a sturdy colt, a huge claw came through the window and grabbed it. Teyrnon cut off the claw with his sword and, hearing a terrible scream, rushed out of the stable to confront whatever creature had been there. Instead he found the infant Pryderi wrapped up in a basket. He raised Pryderi as his own son and raised the colt to be the boy's horse. Eventually a striking resemblance between Pryderi and Pwyll is recognised, and it is realised that he is Pwyll's son.

In Gaulish mythology the horse is particularly associated with the goddess Epona, whose name itself derives from the Celtic word for horse. Epona was a popular goddess who was worshipped in the Rhineland and Britain as well as Gaul, and her cult even reached as far as Rome. She is usually depicted either riding side-saddle on a mare, or standing between two horses and carrying a basket of fruit or bread to symbolise the earth's abundance. Her cult was popular among the Gaulish cavalry of the Roman Empire, where she was perceived as a protectress of horsemen and their mounts as they went into battle. In Greek myth the land goddess Demeter assumed the form of a black horse when she mourned for her daughter Persephone, who had been stolen by Pluto, the god of the underworld. This form was taken to represent the darkness and sterility of the land in winter.

The horse is also linked to kingship in Irish legends.[6] Gerald of Wales relates a rather barbaric tale concerning an inauguaration ceremony in northern Ulster, which involved the new king having intercourse with a white mare. After the act, the mare was killed, cut up into pieces and boiled in water. The new king bathed in the resulting broth, and then he and the others present ate the flesh and drank the broth to symbolise the conferral of sovereignty. More palatable is the well-known story of King Labhraidh Loingseach of Leinster who had horse's ears. To keep the secret he had every barber who cut his hair put to death. At last Labhraidh relented from this practice and allowed a young man to stay alive. The man was so burdened by his secret, however, that on the advice of a druid he eventually told it to a willow tree. The young man recovered his health, but the secret emerged when the willow was cut down and made into a harp. Brought into Labhraidh's hall to be played, the only sound it made was to cry out: 'Labhraidh Loingseach has two horse's ears!' The secret was out.

Horses were also frequently described in Irish legends as the companions of warriors. Indeed, their warlike attributes and physical prowess were often described in as much detail as their human counterparts. A good example of this is the description of the two chariot horses of Cúchulainn, the Grey of Macha and the Black of Sanglain.[7] Cúchulainn acquired the two horses by capturing them and breaking them in, the Grey of Macha at a grey lake near Sliabh Fuad, and the Black of Sanglain at the black lake of Sanglain. The fact that the horses seem to have emerged from lakes marks them as otherworldly. The Grey of Macha is also connected by name to the Ulster goddess. The early Irish saga *Táin Bó Cuailnge* describes them both in detail: 'two horses, swift, high springing, big-eared, beautiful, bounding, with flared nostrils, with broad chests, with lively heart, high groined, wide hoofed, slender legged, mighty and violent. In one shaft a grey horse, broad-thighed, small stepping, long-maned. In the other shaft a black horse, flowing maned, swift-coursing, broad-backed.' The Grey of Macha was capable of fighting alongside Cúchulainn, at one point killing an enemy horse. When Cúchulainn later faced his final battle, the Grey of Macha's grief was so great that it refused to be yoked to the chariot, before relenting and shedding great tears of blood at Cúchulainn's feet. Despite this, when Cúchulainn tied himself to the pillar stone and was dying, the Grey of Macha defended him to the last, killing fifty men with its teeth, and another thirty with its sharp hooves.

Horses are described in similarly glowing terms in other early Irish legends.[8] *The Wooing of Étaín*, for example, has Midir and Echu playing chess, and when Echu wins, Midir pays him 'fifty grey horses with dappled, blood-red heads, sharp-eared, broad-chested, wide-nostrilled, slender-footed, strong, keen, tall, swift, steady and yokable'. *Bricriu's Feast* describes one of two chariot horses as 'grey, broad-thighed, fierce, swift, flying, ferocious, war-leaping, long-maned, noisy and thundering, curly-maned, high-headed, broad-chested; there shine the huge clods of earth that it cuts up with its very hard hooves. Its victorious stride overtakes flocks of birds; a dreadful flash its breath, a ball of flaming red fire, and the jaws of its bridle-bitted head shine.' The second horse is 'jet black, hard-headed, compact, narrow-hooved, narrow-chested, strong, swift, arrogant, braided-maned, broad-backed, strong-thighed, high-spirited, fleet, fierce, long-striding, stout-blow-dealing, long-maned, long-tailed, swift at running after fighting'. Folk tales, too, praised the attributes of good horses, including one that described a great stallion with the following qualities: 'three qualities of Finn Mac Cool's slim bay steed – a keen rush against a hill, a swift run on the level, a high running leap; three qualities of the fox – the gait of a fox, gay and proud, a look straight ahead taking in both sides and turning to no side, neat in his tread on the road; three qualities of a bull – a full eye, a thick neck, a bold forehead'. On the other hand, one humorous tale satirises all these marvellous horses in its describtion of the horse of the ragged churl the Giolla Deacair: 'The horse had a broad, surly face; his neck was thick at the throat, and thin toward the body; the beast was scrawny, long-legged, lean, thin-maned, and ugly to look at.' Despite its miserable appearance, this horse is enchanted, and twenty-nine of the Fianna riding on its back are unable to subdue it from kicking and biting everything in sight!

The symbolism linking horses to warfare and hunting can also be found in many Celtic ritual burials throughout Europe.[9] In a Gaulish site at Gournay-sur-Aronde seven horses were buried in a ditch surrounding a sanctuary. The bones of the horses had been grouped according to type, and were buried with numerous weapons, suggesting a ritual connected with war. In another Gaulish burial at Ribemont, a curious kind of bone-house was contructed from 2,000 human long-bones and the bones from thirty horses. No distinction was made between the bones of the two species, and the bone-house was encircled by weapons and shields, suggesting man and horse united in death as warriors. Most ritual burials were at least partly intended as sacrifices, and the horse as a prestigious and expensive animal was a suitable choice. In Britain there was a particular emphasis placed on the burial of horse skulls in ritual pits at locations such as Cadbury and Newstead. Horses were also frequently buried with dogs at locations such as Danebury in Hampshire, probably reflecting an association with hunting. By far the most distinctive symbolic use of a horse, however, is not in a burial, but in the carving on a chalk embankment called the White Horse of Uffington in Oxfordshire. This extraordinary stylistic image of a horse was made by cutting trenches out of the chalk hillside, and the landmark has been maintained by local people ever since. The style of the Uffington horse is Celtic, and archaeological testing has confirmed that its origin is most likely from the pagan Celtic period of about 50 BC, when it was probably carved as the tribal emblem of the local Celtic tribe, the Atrebates.

The swiftness of the horse is another feature to appear regularly in mythology.[10] According to *Lebor Gabála Érenn*, or the *Book of Invasions*, the three horses of the Tuatha Dé Danann were called Attach (blast), Gaeth (wind) and Sidhe (whirlwind). Manannán, the Gaelic god of the sea, had a horse called Aonbharr ('One Maned') that was 'as swift as the naked cold wind of spring, and the sea was the same as dry land to her, and the rider was never killed off her back'. A description of the voyage to the land of Manannán tells of him riding the sea in a horse-drawn chariot, and of the waves as his horses. It is interesting to note that according to Greek mythology, Poseidon, the god of the sea, first created the horse. In Norse mythology, Odin, the father of the gods, rode an eight-legged grey horse called Sleipnir. Sleipnir could outrun any horse in creation and had the power to bear its rider to the land of the dead and back again.

The horse is also associated with the sun in Celtic symbolism, probably due to the idea that it drew the chariot of the sun across the sky.[11] Coins from the Romano-Celtic period frequently showed horses along with chariot wheels and the rayed solar disc. Romano-Celtic statues of the sky god also frequently depicted him riding on a horse and carrying a solar shield, while demonic forces are crushed under the horse's hooves. In Irish myth the sun was sometimes called Echdae, 'the horse of the heavens'. The motif of the horse and sun actually predates the Celts and can be found in other European mythologies. In Norse mythology, Night and Day both travel in horse-drawn chariots. Night leads the way with frosty-maned Hrimfaxi, while Day follows with Skinfaxi, who has a shining mane that lights up sky and earth alike. Greek mythology had the sun god Helios in a chariot drawn by eight horses called Actaeon (effulgence), Aethon (fiery red), Amethea (no loiterer), Bronte (thunderer), Erythreos (red producer), Lampos (lamp-like), Phlegon (burning one) and Purocis (fiery hot).

RELATIONS WITH HUMANS

Horses were first domesticated by early Indo-European peoples living on the Eurasian steppes bordering the Caspian and Black Seas about 4000–3000 BC.[12] The first likely use of the horse was to draw sleighs and packs; the real breakthrough came when people realised that horses could be ridden. This was probably first done as an attempt to manage the semi-wild horse herds more efficiently, but it was quickly seen that the horse increased the mobility and speed of the tribe. Over the next thousand years the horse spread west into Europe, south into Arabia and east into China. It became the swiftest, most efficient form of transport in existence.

A major consequence of these developments was that the horse became essential to warfare, through the invention of the war chariot especially.[13] It is believed that the use of the war chariot enabled the Aryan Indo-Europeans to overrun Persia (modern day Iran) and India and spread throughout Europe. In fact, the old Aryan word for chariot (*ratha*) forms the roots of the English words 'roll' and 'rotate', as well as *roth*, the Irish word for wheel. In a later period, an unrivalled skill in the use of the chariot allowed the Celts to settle over large parts of Europe. The Celtic cavalry was so good, in fact, that the Romans never fully developed a cavalry of their own, preferring instead to recruit regiments of horsemen from Celtic provinces of the empire. The Latin word for workhorse (*caballus*) is almost certainly from a Celtic source, similar to the Irish *capall* or Welsh *ceffyl*. The Latin word for chariot (*carrus*) is also almost certainly from a Celtic source. The Celts were leaders in developing horse-related technology, developing chariots that were particularly light and agile. They were also the first to develop the horseshoe, which was later borrowed from them by the Romans.

Ownership of horses was a major status symbol to the Celts, as well as other early peoples.[14] Horses were (and still are) relatively costly to maintain, and wherever their use became widespread a social division opened up between those who could afford to keep them and those who could not. Indeed, the definition of a nobleman in Celtic society was someone who possessed a horse and arms. The Celtic aristocracy used their horses primarily for warfare, hunting and sport. Prestige was also displayed in the horse gear, which was often richly decorated in bronze. Horses were also dressed in their own armour, with metal or leather head masks. Nor was it unusual for noblemen to be buried with their chariots and horse gear (and occasionally even their horses), in elaborate tombs designed to show their wealth. For example, one Celtic chief from the sixth century BC, who was buried in Hochdorf in Germany with a four-wheeled wagon or cart, was covered entirely in sheet-gold and wore a neck ring decorated with rows of tiny horsemen. Another ritual bronze wagon burial found in Strettweg in Austria depicts naked horsemen wielding oval shields and spears. Although burials as elaborate as these have not been found in Ireland, the many references to chariots and warhorses in early Irish legends show that the horse was held by the Irish in the same high esteem.

Despite their skill with horses, the Celts of pre-Roman Gaul and Britain were reliant on their own indigenous ponies, similar to the modern

Exmoor pony, which were smaller than the horses used in Italy.[15] The Gauls overcame this difficulty by interbreeding their ponies with stallions from Italy to produce larger horses for warfare, but the British remained reliant on their native stock until the last millennium BC, owing to their more isolated island status. The earliest evidence for horses in Ireland dates to about 2000 BC from bones found in Newgrange, County Meath.[16] In early Ireland the Brehon Laws generally make a distinction between two different types of horses: a work-pony or *capall* for farmwork, and a larger, more prestigious horse or *ech* for riding. Generally the work-pony was small and sturdy, similar to the modern Connemara Pony and used as a pack animal for carrying loads such as corn and wheat. Horses were not used for pulling the plough in early Ireland, as this was a task for the heavier ox. Plough-horses did not actually arrive in Ireland until the thirteenth century, when the great plough-horses – originally developed for military purposes – were introduced from continental Europe. The larger type of horse or *ech* was also known as *ech Bretnach* or 'British horse', even though they had originally been introduced by the Romans.

Like the Celts in general, horses in Ireland were closely associated with nobility and warfare.[17] The Brehon Laws state that the lowest grade of lord was expected to own a riding horse with a silver bridle, as well as four other horses with unornamented bridles, while a higher grade of lord was expected to own a bridle of silver and one of gold. Horses were also used to pull the warrior's chariot, and a person who was of chariot-owning rank was of high status. The old Irish sagas commonly portray the Irish warrior as using chariots in warfare, rather than riding horses. The combatants usually came to battle on horse-drawn chariots, but then dismounted and fought on foot. It appears, however, that the use of chariots was abandoned at some stage in Ireland, as they are not mentioned in later descriptions of Gaelic warfare. This would accord with Britain where the last record of their use is in AD 207, when they were used by the Caledonii in northern Scotland against the Romans. Chariots had also ceased to be used in continental Europe some centuries earlier. A ninth-century market cross in Kells, County Meath, showing four horsemen armed with swords and shields, could be an indication that chariots were no longer in use by that stage.

There are several references to horses in the Brehon Laws, though they are not assigned any set value on account of their varying standard.[18] A horse could be worth anything from one cow to as much as five milch cows if it was worthy of a lord. The highest value was as much as ten milch cows if the horse was worthy of a king. Horses also had a special role in the legal procedure for claiming land that was occupied by somebody else. The claimant had first to make formal entry with two horses (cattle or other animals would not do), spend a night on the property, light a fire and tend to his animals. He had to do this three times, with four horses the second time and eight the third time. If the existing occupant failed to react or seek arbitration, the claimant acquired legal ownership. Evidence from the Brehon Laws indicates that horses in early Ireland had a variety of colours similar to modern horses. White or part white was most prestigious, but horses could also be black, grey, brown, yellow, roan and speckled. Horse meat does not seem to have been eaten very much in early Ireland, as horse bones represent barely 2 per cent of all animal bones found in habitation sites. This may reflect the fact that the early Irish church banned the consumption of horse meat, perhaps on the grounds that it had previously been consumed in pagan rituals.

The horse continued to be important to warfare and hunting in Ireland after the Norman invasion.[19] Part of the reason indeed for the success of the Normans in their invasion of Ireland was their more efficient use of horses in war. Unlike the Gaelic Irish, the Normans used saddles and stirrups, which allowed the horseman much greater freedom to use his weapon, whether it was the sword, lance or bow. The Anglo-Norman lords loved their horses as much as any Irish chieftain, and when not using them in battle used them to hunt with hounds. The Grand Juries of Kildare, Kilkenny and Waterford even complained in 1537 about the Earl of Kildare's hounds and huntsmen, 'to the number of forty or three score', ranging the countryside and demanding to be fed at every mansion. The rebellious 'Silken Thomas' Fitzgerald, 10th Earl of Kildare, who rose against Henry VIII, acquired his nickname because his horsemen had their jackets 'gorgeously embroidered with silk'. Hunting continues to this day and there are about seventy packs of foxhounds or harriers (harehounds) operating in Ireland, which are followed on horseback.

Ireland is famous for its horse racing and has many racecourses with an international reputation.[20] In Gaelic Ireland the racecourse was probably the king's own exercise green, but races also took place at fairs and assemblies, particularly at the feast of Lúnasa in early August. The god

Lugh, who gave Lúnasa its name (*Lugh Nasa* – Lugh's fair), is even credited with introducing horse racing to Ireland. So identified with horses were the assemblies that the Old Irish text *Cormac's Glossary* derives the Irish word for assembly (*oenach*) from *aine ech*, which means 'delightfulness of horses'. The oldest and most prominent racecourse is undoubtedly the Curragh in County Kildare, which was presided over by the King of Leinster and has been a place for sports ever since. So synonymous was the Curragh with Irish racing that the word 'curragh' became a generic term for racecourses. The Curragh's modern history begins, however, in 1727, with the first recorded race meeting. It is now most famous for the Irish Derby, which began in 1866 and ranks as Ireland's premier racing event. Another famous racecourse is Punchestown, also in County Kildare, which dates from 1824. Punchestown is one of the premier National Hunt venues in Ireland and Britain, and is most noted for the Irish National Hunt Festival, a five-day event which attracts competitors from all over Europe. Fairyhouse in County Meath, which dates from 1848, is another notable racecourse. It is the home of the Irish Grand National, which has been held on Easter Monday every year since 1870. The best known racecourse in Northern Ireland is probably Down Royal, which was created by Royal Charter by James II in 1685. Ireland is also notable in the lore of horse racing because it is the country where the first steeplechase was performed. The 'steeplechase' (or point to point) gets its name from a famous race in 1752 in Duhallow, County Cork, between Mr Edmund Blake and a Mr Cornelius O'Callaghan, from the steeple of Buttevant Church to the steeple of Doneraile Church – a distance of 4½ miles.

Ireland has also produced many racehorses of world standard.[21] The limestone-rich soil (which builds good bone structure), lush pastures and mild climate mean it can produce some of the best athletic thoroughbreds in the world. The first famous Irish racehorse was probably Harkaway, who won the Goodwood Cup in 1838 and 1839. In the twentieth century, the first prominent racehorse was Golden Miller, who won five consecutive Cheltenham Gold Cups from 1932 to 1936. Arkle, who won the Cheltenham Gold Cup in 1964, 1965 and 1966, was the next superstar. Another famous Irish racehorse was the revered Red Rum (universally known by his nickname 'Rummie'), who won the British Grand National in 1973 and 1974, came second in 1975 and 1976, and won again in 1977. He remains the only horse to have won this race three times. Istabraq, who won three consecutive Champion Hurdles in 1998, 1999 and 2000, is another famous name. Ireland has also become a major player in international showjumping since the Equitation School in the Irish Army was founded in 1926. Irish horses have done very well, including Dundrum, who was International Jumping Champion from 1959 to 1963. Boomerang, ridden by Eddie Macken, came first or second in thirty-two major Grand Prix or Derby showjumping events between 1975 and 1979. Another famous showjumper was Heather Honey, who was part of a team that won the Aga Khan trophy three years in a row from 1977 to 1979, and Kilkenny who was winner of the two team gold medals, two team silver medals and one individual bronze medal and a national championship.

The oldest Irish breed of horse is the Connemara Pony, and a possible clue to its origin lies in the fact that in early Ireland the work-pony or *capall* was also known as the *gerrán*.[22] In Scotland the same name is applied to the mainland type of Highland pony (as opposed to the lighter Western Isles pony) in the form 'Garron'. The old Irish work-pony and the modern Highland pony share the same stocky build and sturdiness, and it is likely they have a common, pre-Celtic origin. There is also an acknowledged link between the Connemara Pony and the Spanish Jennet as both breeds share the same ambling gait or 'easiness'. More modern influences on the Connemara Pony come from the Welsh Cob and the Hackney. Several other Irish breeds of horse exist.[23] The Kerry Bog Pony, another ancient breed also known as the hobby, is similar to the Connemara Pony in appearance. From medieval times until the nineteenth century they were used by the majority of the Irish peasantry, especially for transporting peat. They almost became extinct in the 1990s, but have been brought back from the brink through a breeding programme. The Irish Draught Horse, a more modern breed of horse, has developed locally in different parts of Ireland to allow farmers to work with soils that were not as heavy as those dealt with by other breeds of draught horse abroad. It is a light draught horse that could also be used for pulling a trap or for hunting. Recognised in Ireland as a distinctive breed from the early 1800s, it is now recognised as a breed throughout the world. Ireland's success in the field of international showjumping has also led to the Irish Sport Horse becoming a recognised European breed. Bred in Ireland for showjumping, the horse is an amalgam of the Thoroughbred, Irish Draught, Connemara Pony and Irish riding pony. Interest in all of Ireland's unique horse breeds is growing, with each having its own societies dedicated to continuing the breed's existence. Even if Irish horses are no longer used for transport or farmwork, the Irish horse breeding and horse racing industries are as strong as ever, and Ireland's long love affair with the horse shows no sign of ending.

# Deer – Fia – *Cervus*

---

*The deer was respected for its swiftness, strength and nobility, and the stag with its branching horns was regarded as the symbol of the wildness and fertility of the forest itself. The regular shedding and regrowth of the stag's horns was also linked to the natural cycle of death and regeneration. In Celtic legend the deer or stag was regarded as the Lord of the Forest and of wild animals, and represented the goal of hunting as a noble pursuit.*

### Folk Beliefs and Customs

Surprisingly, Irish folklore about deer appears to be virtually non-existent. The reason is probably due to deer being confined to the last few pockets of woodland in the country, as the Irish forests were cut down over the last few centuries. They were therefore removed from any contact with the vast majority of the population, becoming an exotic creature in the demesnes of the landed gentry. As a result, whatever folklore that may once have existed now appears to have been forgotten.

### Myths and Legends

Deer appear in many stories of the lives of Irish saints, usually through the saint being miraculously able to tame such a wild animal with his holy powers.[1] When St Declan's horse became lame, he commanded one of his men to yoke a stag from a nearby herd of deer instead. The man chose the largest and strongest stag, which surprisingly allowed itself to be yoked to the chariot. Once St Declan reached his destination, he allowed the stag to go free. A similar miracle was performed by St Mochuda. A poor man approached the saint and asked him for a loan of some oxen. Mochuda had none in his monastery, but he asked one of his disciples to go out and bring back a pair of deer to do the job instead. The two deer came in without trouble and stayed with the poor man until the job was done. They were then released by the saint back to the wild. According to another story, when

St Brendan was a child, a hind came down from Sliabh Luachra every day with her fawn to give her milk to the saint. Once the hind had been milked, she would return with her fawn to the mountain. Most miraculous of all is the story of St Kieran, who had a stag that accompanied him everywhere. The stag was so tame that Kieran used to put his prayer book between the stag's horns while it stood there obediently. One day Kieran arose suddenly

when the bell went, and the startled deer ran off with the book in its antlers. The next day, however, the stag reappeared with the book unharmed. Deer also appear in a legend of St Kevin of Glendalough, when the saint gave his foster son and his men the appearance of deer to evade capture by their enemies.

Deer and stags play a central role in the stories of the Fianna, the legendary warrior band of early Ireland.[2] When they were not fighting their enemies, the Fianna were usually hunting, and deer hunts are mentioned frequently in the tales. The amount of deer hunted was often prodigious; on one occasion the Fianna killed a thousand stags in a week. So closely were the Fianna linked to deer that their leader, Fionn Mac Cumhaill, had a son called Oisín, or 'little fawn'. According to legend, Fionn's hunting hounds found a handsome little boy living wild in the forest. The boy said he had been raised by a deer. Nevertheless, from the boy's appearance Fionn realised he was his own son, and so he named him Oisín and reared him. Two different versions of how this situation came about exist in the tradition. One is that his mother, Blaí Dheirg, was an otherworld woman who visited Fionn in the form of a deer, and lured him into the forest to seduce him. She later gave birth to Oisín when in the form of a deer. The other version is that Oisín's mother was called Sadhbh and was Fionn's wife. According to this story, Fionn had been out hunting one day when a beautiful young fawn appeared in front of him. Instead of chasing it, his dogs Bran and Sceolaing went up to it and began licking its neck and face. Fionn was astonished, and when the fawn followed him home to his fort, he was even more astonished to see her become a beautiful young woman. She explained that she had been turned into a deer by a druid called Fear Doirche (Dark Man), in vengeance for her refusing his love. She heard if she received protection from Fionn that the enchantment would have no effect on her, and so she had appeared to him while hunting. Fionn fell in love with her and they married. However, one day when Fionn was away hunting she was abducted by Fear Doirche and spirited away. Also, unknown to Fionn, Sadhbh had been pregnant. For seven years Fionn hunted for Sadhbh without success, until his hounds found Oisín. Oisín was lost and searching for his mother when Fionn found him, and could tell Fionn very little about where he had been or about his childhood. Sadhbh was never found. Oisín, however, grew up to be one of the greatest warriors and poets of the Fianna.

A significant incident in the tales of the Fianna occurs when they are challenged by a prince called Donn of Dubhlinn (Dublin), who had been turned into a stag by enchantment. Donn herded up all the deer of Ireland and declared that Fionn Mac Cumhaill would not dare to challenge him. Unable to ignore this challenge, Fionn and the Fianna went out to seek him. The 'fierce red-brown active stag' was not frightened of their furious shouts and killed a hundred of the men. It was only with the help of Fionn's three hounds, Gaillen, Sceolaing and Bran, that they were at last able to overcome Donn and kill him. The story is significant because Donn of Dubhlinn is obviously a version of the pagan deity Donn. Donn also appears in a friendlier guise as Donn, son of Midhir, who sent a girl in the shape of a fawn to entice the Fianna to his fairy fort to seek their help. Donn was an Irish version of the Celtic god of nature, Cernunnos, who was symbolically linked to the stag. The Fianna's life of hunting was seen as having a pagan aspect, and was often contrasted with the new religion of Christianity. In a poem praising the Fianna, Oisín declared that 'the roar of the stag is sweeter to me / than the music the clerics chant'. Another pagan Irish deity linked to deer was Fliodhais, a goddess of deer and cattle, whose name appears to mean milk.[3] According to legend, during the reign of her son King Nia Seaghamain, cows and does were milked together in Ireland.

Stags feature prominently in the story of *Buile Shuibhne* or Mad Sweeney.[4] Mad Sweeney was a king in early Ireland who later lived as an outcast in the woods. He is portrayed as a tragic figure, moving restlessly from place to place, and so starved and ragged that he is as light as a bird. In his separation from people he feels at one with the nature around him, and with the wild stags in particular. Several times Sweeney speaks of how the sound of their bellowing delights him: 'there is no music on earth in my soul but its sweetness'. Elsewhere he describes riding on a fawn from peak to mountain peak. In the following poem Sweeney praises the many stags he sees around him in the woods, in particular their fine antlers. There is in fact a play on the Irish word *benn* in the poem, which means both a mountain peak and the point of an antler.

*LAOI NA nDAMH*

*Ni charuim an chornaireacht*
*Athchluinim go ten*
*Binni luim ag damhghaireacht*
*Damh dá fhichead benn.*

*Ata adhbhur seisrighe*
*As gach glionn i nglenn*
*Gach damh ina freislighe*
*A mullach na mbenn*

*Cidh iondha dom dhamraidh-si*
*As gach glinn i nglenn*
*Ni minic lámh oiremhan*
*Ag dúnadh a mbenn.*

*Damh Sléibhi aird Eibhlinne*
*Damh Sléibhe Fúaid feigh*
*Damh Ella, damh Orbhraidhe*
*Damh Ionn Locha Léin*

*Damh Seimhne, damh Latharne,*
*Damh Line na lenn*
*Damh Cúailghni, damh Conachla*
*Damh Bairne dá bhenn.*

*A mathair na groidh-si*
*Rolíathadh do lenn,*
*Ni fhuil damh at dheagaidh-si*
*Gan dá fhichead benn.*

*Mí ná adhbhur leinnini*
*Roliathadh dot chenn,*
*Dambenn ar gach meinnine*
*Beinnini ar gach minn.*

LAY OF THE STAGS

No friend to me the horn that blows
With dread I hear its raucous cry
Sweeter to me the stag that lows
With forty pointed antlers wide.

The ploughman could supply his trade
If from glen to glen he'd seek.
For many a stag a home has made
On the point of the mountain peaks.

Though many are the stags I list
In glen to glen where each is found.
Not often does a ploughman's fist
Their pointed antler horns surround.

The stag of Slieve Felim high
The stag of Slieve Fuaid keen
The stag of Ella, the stag of Orrery
The mighty stag of Lough Leane.

The stag of Linna of the streams
The stag of Sevna, the stag of Larne
The stag of Cooley, the stag of Conaghil,
The stag of twin pointed Barran.

Old mother of this mighty horde
Grey your coat and stiff your joints,
Yet there is not a son of yours
With less than forty antler points.

Like a rough cloth for a garment
Grey is your ancestral head
Yet all your fawns have an ornament
Of antlers with a pointy spread.

| | |
|---|---|
| *A dhaimh do gni an fogharán* | O stag who comes a-calling loud |
| *Chugam tar an nglenn* | To me now across the glen |
| *Maith an t-ionadh foradhán* | I'll take a seat to do me proud |
| *I mullach do bhenn.* | On your antler points again. |

The image of Sweeney stitting on the stag's antlers is both sad and slightly ridiculous, but perhaps intentionally so. The mention of a ploughman refers to the use of antlers in tilling soil in early Ireland. Perhaps fittingly, in one version of the story a deer antler is the cause of Sweeney's death. A woman had been leaving milk out for Sweeney to drink (he was too wild and afraid to enter her house to drink it), and her husband became jealous. He placed a deer's antler on the spot where the milk was left so that Sweeney fell onto it and was killed.

Deer appear often in Celtic ritual burials.[5] In Britain they are the most common wild animal to be found in ritual pits, at sites like Winklebury in Hampshire, for example, where a red deer was buried in a pit along with twelve foxes. At Ashill in Norfolk boar tusks and antlers were buried in a well along with more than a hundred pots; a pit at Wasperton in Warwickshire contained two sets of antlers forming a square enclosing a hearth. The Gaulish shrine of Digeon in France contained an assemblage of wild animal remains including deer and fox. Deer also appear in Celtic art and sculpture. At Camonica Valley in Italy the stag was depicted as the companion of the solar god, with antlers curved around to form a circular, rayed sun. Bronze figurines of stags were also common, such as a small stag found near Salzburg in Austria; another, found at a Romano-Celtic shrine at Colchester in Essex, was dedicated to Silvanus Callirius or 'King of the Wood'. The antlers on the figurines are frequently exaggerated and enlarged. In the burial of a nobleman at Stettweg in Austria a model of a wagon was placed among the grave goods. A prominent feature of the wagon is a tableau of figurines, among them two pairs of women holding a large-antlered stag between them. The wagon appears to represent a ritual hunt. On the famous Gundestrup cauldron in Denmark, a decorated ritual cauldron made of silver and dating from the first or second centuries BC, Cernunnos, the Celtic god of nature, appears with tall antlers emerging from his head. Beside him stands a stag with identical antlers, emphasising the link between god and animal.

The ritual burials and artwork reflect the symbolism of the deer in Celtic myth, where the stag with its virility and branching antlers represents wild nature and the forest. Above all else, the stag is associated with Cernunnos (the Horned One). Cernunnos is usually depicted as a man with antlers growing out of his head, as in the Gundestrup cauldron. Other depictions of Cernunnos, especially from the Romano-Celtic period in Gaul, show him sitting cross-legged and feeding groups of animals including stags. Stags were also associated with other Celtic hunter gods, usually in a way that showed mutual respect and dependence between hunter and hunted. For example, at a Gaulish shrine in Vosges an unnamed hunter god is depicted wearing a wolfskin and holding a spear, but his hand rests on the antlers of a stag standing beside him, in a posture of benevolent protection. In the Romano-Celtic period, Celtic hunter goddesses were linked to Diana (or Artemis), the Roman goddess of the moon and hunting, whose sacred animal was the deer. This may account for the incident in the medieval text *The History of the Kings of Britain* in which Brutus, the first king of Britain, seeks guidance from Diana about a land where he might lead his wandering people. After drinking from a vessel of wine mixed with the blood of a white hind, he lay down to sleep upon the skin of a hind before her altar. In his sleep he dreamed that Diana told him of Britain and directed him to go there. In Classical myth deer were also sacred to the goddess of love, Aphrodite, and to the sun god, Apollo.

RELATIONS WITH HUMANS

Deer have been hunted in Ireland from the earliest times, and pins made of antler bones have been found at Neolithic sites in Carrowmore, County Sligo, and Knowth, County Meath.[6] Since the arrival of domesticated animals, however, deer have been hunted in the main for sport and military training rather than food. This is similar to the practice among the Celts of Europe. Indeed, venison is mentioned very little in Gaelic literature, and excavations of Iron Age crannogs in Meath and Westmeath have found that deer bones comprise 1 per cent or less of the total animal remains. This is again similar to the situation in Celtic Europe and Britain, where deer remains make up only a small amount of the animal bones found at sites. Cattle and pigs make up the vast majority of animal bones, a fact that is borne out by the many references to feasts of pork and beef in Celtic legends. However, deer hides may have been used in Ireland to make leather. In the tale *Táin Bó Cuailnge*, Cúchulainn's charioteer Laeg is described as wearing a 'skin-soft tunic of stitched deer's leather, light as a breath'. There do not seem to have been any royal 'deer forests' in Gaelic Ireland, unlike England and Scotland where deer-hunting was also a sport of the nobility. Irish kings did, however, have their own hunters (*selcithi*) and trappers (*cuthguiri*), and deer could be owned under the law by marking them (much as sheep are today). According to the Brehon Laws, there was a fine of one heifer for killing someone else's deer if it was in the owner's field, and a fine equivalent to one eighth of a heifer if it was killed on a mountain or undivided land.

The most common method of hunting deer in Gaelic Ireland was to chase them with hounds; the hunters would then practise their marksmanship by killing the deer with spears or other weapons. There was a strict protocol for dividing up the quarry. The owner of the hounds got the haunch (the most prized part), while the hounds themselves got the legs. The person who actually killed the deer got the neck, while the person who skinned the deer got the shoulder. The landowner got the belly, and the rest of the hunting party had to make do with the intestines or liver. As hunting in this way involved trekking after the deer through woods or mountains, presumably the deer was consumed at a nearby camp rather than being brought home. Another favourite method of hunting involved the hunters lying in wait at a watering hole or deer track, while retainers drove the deer to the site of ambush. The deer could then be killed easily with little risk. Deer were also trapped with nets or by hidden spikes or deer-pits set up in a remote place where the deer were likely to pass. Hunting in Ireland may not have been too difficult, however, as according to Gerald of Wales, writing soon after the Norman invasion of the twelfth century, the stags in Ireland were not able to escape on account of their fatness! Gerald was more impressed by the noble way in which they carried their fine antlers.

Hunting deer with hounds was still practised until recently by the Ward Union Hunt based in Dunshaughlin in County Meath, and by Stag Hounds based in Ballinahinch, County Down. The Ward Union Hunt carried out carted stag-hunting which involves a tame, farmed stag being released from a cart or trailer to be chased by hounds and hunters. The hunt ended with the stag being cornered, recaptured alive and returned to the trailer. This form of deer-hunting has now been made illegal under legislation passed in 2010. In Northern Ireland, the County Down Staghounds have also recently discontinued hunting deer, following public pressure. Deer stalking (that is, hunting deer with a rifle) remains legal under licence in both parts of Ireland.

The only species of deer native to Ireland is the Red deer (*Cervus elaphus*).[7] These almost became extinct in Ireland during the Famine, surviving only in the Killarney region of County Kerry on the game reserve of the Herbert and Kenmare estates (now Killarney National Park). Reintroduced into Irish deer parks from Britain, these deer can now be found in Counties Donegal, Tyrone, Fermanagh, Down, Wicklow, Meath and Kerry. The Donegal deer were introduced from Scotland rather than England, and still show their genetic similarity to Scottish deer. The main threat to the native Red deer is their hybridisation with the Japanese Sika deer, and populations of Killarney Red deer have been established in the Blasket Islands, Connemara, and in Doneraile in County Cork in order to preserve the native stock. Red deer farming has expanded in Ireland recently, and some of the Red deer now seen in the wild are escapees from these farms, especially in the Boyne Valley in County Meath. Precise numbers for Red deer in Ireland are unknown, but the population is believed to be several thousand.

Of the other species of deer living in Ireland, the Fallow deer (*Dama dama*) was introduced by the Normans from Britain in the thirteenth century.[8] Fallow deer, first introduced into Britian by the Romans, were originally native to the eastern Mediterranean, Turkey and Iran. They were very popular with the Normans for their decorative speckled coats, which can vary from almost black to yellowish white. The Normans introduced the Fallow deer to Ireland for the sport of hunting as well as for their decorative qualities, and established many deer parks throughout the country where both Fallow and Red deer were hunted. At one time there were over sixty herds in enclosed deer parks in Ireland, and locations called Deerpark can still be found in at least sixteen counties in Ireland. Escapes from parks led to the establishment of herds in the wild as early as the fifteenth century, and the Fallow deer are now Ireland's most common deer. Like the Red deer, Fallow deer farms have now been established to cater for the venison market, leaving open the possibility that some may escape again into the wild.

The other main species of deer introduced into Ireland is the Japanese Sika deer (*Cervus Nippon*), which was imported into the country for ornamental reasons in 1860 by Lord Powerscourt to his estate near Dublin.[9] Deer from Powerscourt were subsequently released into other parks around Ireland, in Counties Kerry, Fermanagh, Limerick, Down and Monaghan. In the early twentieth century many of these deer parks fell into disrepair, and wild herds became established in the 1930s and 1940s. The result is that Sika deer can now be found in at least twelve counties throughout Ireland. Their population is around 20,000–25,000 and expanding. Sika deer are very similar to Red deer in appearance – except that they are smaller – and are closely related to them. This means that they are able to interbreed with them, and in many parts of the country, especially in Wicklow, a great many deer are Red/Sika hybrids. Ironically, because of a long history of interbreeding in Asia, there are probably no pure breed Sika left in Japan; the only place where they are known to exist is in Killarney, where hybridisation with Reds has not (yet) occurred.

Deer are a protected species under Irish law, but they can be hunted under licence. This is because they can become a major pest in places by causing damage to forestry plantations, eating the young shoots of trees, stripping the bark and scoring it with their antlers. About 500 Red deer are shot each year, although no hunting is allowed in County Kerry to protect the native stock. About 2,000 Fallow, and another 1,000 Sika or Red/Sika hybrids are also culled each year. Despite ongoing hunting and culling, deer numbers are on the rise in Ireland, as increasing afforestation expands the range of habitats available to them. The future of this notable and noble member of our fauna remains secure for the foreseeable future.

# Wolf – Mac Tíre – *Canis lupus*

*The wolf was feared in Ireland as a ruthless predator of livestock, but also admired for its bravery and warlike qualities. In legend this made it a symbol of kings and warriors. The wolf was also presented in stories as an honourable animal that responded with good deeds when treated with respect by saints and kings.*

## Folk Beliefs and Customs

As the wolf has been extinct in Ireland for several centuries, it does not appear in much Irish folklore. However, the wolf does appear in several Irish place names, reflecting the fact that it was once widespread.[1] An old Irish name for wolf is *bréach*, which appears in such names as Ballinabrackey (*Buaile na Bréamhaí* – milling place of the wolf plain), County Meath, Breaghwy (*Bréach Mhaigh* – wolf plain), County Sligo, and Britway (*Bréach Mhaigh* – wolf plain), County Cork. Another old name for wolf is *faol*, which appears in Feltrim (*Faol Droim* – wolf ridge), County Dublin. The modern name *mac tíre* features in Clashavictory (*Clais an Mhic Tíre* – ravine of the wolf), County Tipperary.

## Myths and Legends

Wolves feature regularly in stories of the lives of Irish saints, where the miraculous powers and compassion of the saint combine to tame the wolf's predatory nature.[2] The *Life of St Cainnech* (Canice) tells how he miraculously tamed a wolf that had eaten a calf. The owner of the calf complained to St Cainnech, who told him to return to his cows and clap his hands. When he did this, the wolf returned to the cowshed and stood in the place of the calf. The cows accepted the wolf and licked it as they were all being milked, the wolf returning each morning and evening until the end of the season. In the *Life of St Patrick*, a wolf carried off one of the sheep the boy

Patrick was tending, for which he was rebuked by his foster mother. The next day, however, the wolf returned with the sheep in his mouth and laid it at Patrick's feet unharmed, before running off back to the wood. St Colmán had a covenant with the wolves of his local forest. They would come to him and lick his shoes like domestic dogs, and Colmán would say to them: 'Be here continually, and the day that my name is mentioned

to you in intercession, you must not draw blood on anyone!' The *Life of St Molua* describes how he once took pity on a pack of hungry wolves, and provided them with a cooked calf in the monastic guest house. This became an annual event, and in gratitude the wolf pack began to protect the monastic livestock from other wolves and from robbers. Saints could also use the wolf as a punishment, and St Patrick was said to have turned Vereticus, the King of Wales, into a wolf. Gerald of Wales, in his twelfth-century description of Ireland, includes a story about the people of Ossory, who under the curse of a local saint, the abbot Natalis, had to compel two of their number, a man and a woman, to go into exile for seven years in the form of wolves.

The wolf is linked to kingship, probably on account of its bravery and warlike qualities.[3] The famous Irish king, Cormac Mac Airt, whose reign was a byword for peace and plenty, was reputed to have been stolen from his mother and suckled for a time by a wolf, before a trapper found him and returned him to his mother. Intriguingly, as mother and child were crossing a mountain at night, the wolves of Ireland gathered around them, seeking to take Cormac back. They were only prevented from doing this by a herd of wild horses that protected the pair. The eighth-century tale *Togáil Bruidne Da Derga* describes the peace and prosperity during the rule of King Conaire. So just was his rule that, instead of hunting wolves down as much as possible, the king kept seven of them as hostages by the wall of his house in return for the wolves of Ireland taking only one male calf from each herd during the year. Wolves need not only be associated with kings, however. A poem about the grave of Queen Maedhbh describes her as a 'fair-haired wolf-queen'. Warriors were also associated with wolves. For example, the Ulster warrior Conall Cearnach's name derived from *cuno-valos*, meaning 'strong like a wolf'. Gods could also be linked to wolves.[4] In the *Book of Invasions* the gods of old Ireland, the Tuatha Dé Danann, were said to go about Ireland in the shape of wolves. In the tale *Táin Bó Cuailnge*, or 'The Cattle Raid of Cooley', the warrior-goddess Morrigan attacked the hero Cúchulainn in the form of a 'shaggy russet-coloured she-wolf'.

Wolves were also a symbol of the life of those in early Ireland who lived close to nature.[5] In particular, unlike modern depictions, the howling or crying of the wolf pack was not seen as a malevolent sound. Instead it was stirring and even melodious. Mad Sweeney, in *Suibhne Geilt*, several times mentions that he lived 'in the company of wolves'. On his deathbed he has this to say:

| | |
|---|---|
| *Ba binne liom robhaoi tan* | More melodious to me once |
| *Donálach na gcon alla,* | Was the yelping of the wolves |
| *Ina guth cléirigh astoigh* | Than the voice of a cleric indoors |
| *Ag meiligh is ag meigeallaigh.* | a-baaing and a-bleating. |

Similarly, the hero Fionn Mac Cumhaill, leader of the warrior band the Fianna, was said to love 'the music of wolves far off on a mountain, wolves leaving their lairs'. Another of the Fianna, Caoilte, recalling his life in old age, talked of the music of wolves. The eighth-century text *Cormac's Glossary* defines wolves as creatures 'uplifting great howls'.

There is some evidence that wolves were hunted by the Celts, but wolf remains appear less often in burial remains than other wild species, indicating they were not hunted systematically.[6] Wolf teeth perforated to use as ornaments were found at the Celtic Iron Age site of Choisy-au-Bac in France, while wolf toe-bones were found at the French site of Villeneuve-Saint-Germain. Wolf remains were also found at the ritual sanctuary site of Digeon, also in France. A terracotta trumpet mouth found in Numantia in Spain was in the shape of a snarling wolf's head, indicating the trumpet was probably used in battle. A Romano-Celtic sculpture from the mountain shrine of Le Donon in the Vosges in France shows a hunter dressed in a wolfskin cape, resting his hand on a stag which stands beside him. The Roman writer Diodorus Siculus stated that the Celts used wolfskins for covering house floors. On the famous Gundestrup cauldron from Denmark, a wolf appears in association with the Celtic god of nature Cernunnos. The wolf also appears on some Iron Age coins found in Armorica (present-day Brittany). One coin shows a wolf apparently devouring the sun and moon, while underneath his paws are an eagle and a snake. It has been suggested that this represents a Celtic version of the Norse myth of the end of the world, Ragnarok, when the wolves Skoll and Hoti will swallow up the sun and moon. Another coin shows a wolf perched on top of a horse, perhaps symbolising the dualism of hunter and hunted.

Wolves feature in the mythology of other European cultures.[7] The rapacious and destructive nature of the wolf is emphasised in Norse myth. The great wolf Fenrir had to be bound up by the gods, so alarmed were they by his strength. Tyr, the god of war, lost his hand in the process. Fenrir was also believed to devour the earth itself on the last day, swallowing up Odin, the father god, before being himself killed by Odin's son Vidar in revenge. Vidar achieves this feat by grasping Fenrir's two great jaws and ripping him apart. Classical myths about the wolf are rather gentler. Most famously, the twin sons who founded Rome, Romulus and Remus, are linked in myth to the wolf. The sons of Mars and Rhea, they were left on an exposed hillside to die, because their mother was a vestal virgin who had betrayed her vows. Despite this, the twins survived as they were suckled by a she-wolf. The warlike traits of the wolf came through in adulthood, however, when the twins quarrelled about how to plan their new city and Romulus killed Remus.

An important aspect of the mythology of the wolf is the idea of lycanthropy, namely the change of a person into a wolf through magical means, as punishment for some great offence, or to enable them to gratify a taste for human flesh.[8] There are some examples in Ireland, as described above, of saints turning people into wolves as punishment. In Classical lore there is the tale of Lycaon, the King of Arcadia, who instituted the sacrifice of a child to obtain deliverance from wolves attacking flocks. Jupiter was outraged by this sacrifice of human flesh and turned the king into a wolf, whereupon he raged among the flocks of Arcadia, thirsting for blood and slaughter. The second form of lycanthropy is the better known 'werewolf' (from Anglo-Saxon 'man-wolf'). There is little lore about this in either Britain or Ireland, but plenty from the continent, especially eastern Europe and the Balkans. In France the *loup-garou* was a man who could turn into a wolf at the full moon by plunging into a particular spring or fountain, and go raiding across the countryside, attacking all men or beasts that came his way. When he had finished he could return to the spring and bathe in it to resume his human form. The werewolf was most fully developed as an idea, however, in Greece. In Greek lore a werewolf was someone who could fall into a trance, so that their soul left their body and entered the body of a wolf, which then went ravening for blood, frequenting battlefields to suck the breath from dying soldiers, and entering houses to steal infants. After death the werewolf became a vampire. In the twentieth century these various ideas found their way into books and films to develop into the modern image of the werewolf. It seems, for example, that the idea a werewolf can only be killed by a silver bullet is a modern invention, probably based on the traditional idea that silver is a good metal for repelling evil.

RELATIONS WITH HUMANS

The Old Irish Brehon Laws mainly deal with the wolf in the context of its being a threat to livestock, such as lambs and calves.[9] Wolf-hunting was considered a public duty, one law stating that a client had to carry out a foray against wolves for his landlord once a week. Also, if it was known that a pack of wolves were living in a particular place, it was an offence for a person to drive his neighbour's livestock towards them. The Brehon Laws also discuss the situation where a wolf has been taken from the wild and treated as a pet. In this case, the Laws equate any offences committed by the wolf with those of the domestic dog. It is interesting to note that the Brehon Laws do not appear to regard wolves as a threat to humans, as this possibility is not mentioned anywhere. Indeed, the general consensus among zoologists is that attacks by wolves against humans are rare, usually by old, sick or rabid animals. Nevertheless, the *Annals of Connacht* for the year 1420 record that 'many persons were killed by wolves in that year'. Perhaps this was due to an unusually harsh winter that made the wolves desperate.

The extensive areas of wilderness that continued to exist in Ireland ensured the survival of the wolf until modern times.[10] During the 1500s there was a substantial trade in wolfskins from Ireland into the port of Bristol, with an average of between 100 and 300 skins exported each year. Indeed, as late as 1652 wolves could be found on the outskirts of Dublin, with a public wolf hunt organised for Castleknock. In 1698 an alderman of Cork city wrote of having both wolves and foxes in the district of the city. However, the writing was on the wall for the wolf by that time, as the Cromwellian plantations had put its survival in danger. The new English settlers were horrified to discover that wolves were still common, and in 1653 the Cromwellian government set a bounty of £6 for a wolf bitch, and £5 for a male. As a result of this, and the continuous destruction of Irish woodland, the wolf population rapidly declined throughout the late 1600s and 1700s. By the end of the eighteenth century the Irish wolf was finally extinct. The last authenticated date for a wolf killed in Ireland was 1786 when John Watson of Ballydarton in County Carlow lost a number of sheep to a lone wolf on Mount Leinster. The wolf was hunted down by his wolfhounds and killed. The chances of reintroducing the wolf to Ireland are slim, as there are now insufficient wilderness areas to support a viable population without serious conflict with farmers over livestock, and contact with the public generally. It seems that this fascinating wild creature will have to remain solely a part of the Irish past.

# Fox – Sionnach – *Vulpes vulpes*

*The fox was detested in Ireland as a threat to livestock and poultry, but it was also grudgingly admired for its qualities of cunning and opportunism. As a result, Irish folklore is full of stories of how the wily fox outwitted its enemies, especially man. On the other hand, several legends feature foxes that were friendly to Irish saints.*

### Folk Beliefs and Customs

Stories about the cleverness of the fox abounded in Ireland.[1] For example, one story tells of how a fox once saw a man carrying a load of fish in a horse-cart. The fox immediately lay down on the road in front of the cart, pretending to be dead. The man noticed the fox, and thinking of the value of the fur, threw it onto the cart. Once the man resumed his journey, the wily fox threw the fish out of the cart one by one, and finally jumped off the cart quietly and collected all the fish on the road. The wolf appears in a few

of the tales as the unwitting dupe of the cleverer fox. In one tale, the wolf and fox broke into a cellar at night and began to gorge themselves on food. After a while the fox stopped and walked in and out of the narrow entrance. The wolf jeered him for this apparently bizarre behaviour, but then ate so much that he was too fat to squeeze back out through the entrance. When the humans came after them, the fox who had been watching its size managed to escape, while the greedy wolf was caught.

The fox was also thought to be intelligent enough to use fire to further his ends. In one story from County Kerry, a fox had successfully caught two ducks by swimming out to them using a large leaf as cover. As he returned from the lake with a third duck, he noticed that the first two had gone. Realising they had been taken by an eagle up to its nest high on the mountain, the fox considered how to get his revenge. He noticed a fire smouldering nearby and dragged the remaining duck backwards and forward through the fire. He then left the duck on the shore and hid. Soon the eagle swooped down to take the third duck and carried it up to its nest. However, when the unsuspecting eagle deposited the duck into the nest, the whole nest caught fire immediately and tumbled down the hillside in a blaze. The fox got his ducks back and three dead eaglets into the bargain. Another well-known story tells of how a fox managed to escape when it was caught entering a farmhouse to steal poultry. The fox came through a hole in the door reserved for the use of the household dogs and was immediately seen by the farmer, who began to whistle for the dogs. Quick as a flash, the fox grabbed a burning log from the fire and ran towards the bed next to the fire. Seeing this, the farmer stopped whistling and retreated, and the fox was able to make his escape back through the hole.

Various superstitions about the fox were also held in Ireland.[2] A popular belief was that the fox was originally the dog of the Norsemen, who were supposed to have first brought them to Ireland. The fox was reputed to be able to foresee events, including the weather, and its barking was said to be a sign of approaching rain. The fox was also believed to act like a banshee for certain families, such as the Preston family of Gormanstown in County Meath, whose crest depicts a running fox. If a member of the household was about to die it was said that a group of foxes would assemble near the house and set up a chorus of continuous barking. In Ireland it was thought to be unlucky to meet a woman with red hair or a fox when setting out first thing in the morning, especially for fishermen. Fishermen in the west of Ireland who saw a fox before setting out would return home and not go to sea that day. In England, on the other hand, it was lucky to see a single fox, but unlucky to see a pack of them. Foxes also feature in some rather revolting Irish folk cures. One cure for infertility was for a woman to sprinkle sugar on the testicles of a fox and roast them in an oven. She should then eat the testicles before her main meal for three days in succession. An Irish folk cure for gallstones and kidney stones was to rub the affected area with a fox's blood. The tongue of a fox was also thought to be able to remove a stubborn thorn from the foot, when all else had failed. An Irish proverb about the fox describes its three watchful traits: a light step, a look to the front and a glance to each side of the road.

MYTHS AND LEGENDS

Foxes appear in several stories about Irish saints.[3] St Moling was said to have a pet fox which ate from his own hand. It once ate a hen belonging to another monk, but through a miracle the bird was restored to life. St Kieran had a fox that used to visit him regularly and carry his psalter. At one stage, the fox's natural instinct won through and it gnawed the leather bands around the psalter. The saint's companions began to hunt the fox as a result, but Kieran sheltered the animal under his cowl and forgave it. A story from the life of St Patrick tells of a British tyrant called Cereticus who laughed and mocked Patrick's attempts to convert him. The saint then prayed for God to put an end to his tyranny, and so in the middle of his royal court Cereticus was turned into a fox. A story about St Brigid describes a king of Leinster owning a pet fox which performed many tricks. When one of his subjects killed the fox, thinking it wild, the king sentenced the unfortunate man to death unless he could produce a fox of equal intelligence and skill. At this point, a wild fox came to St Brigid and sheltered under her cloak. She travelled to the royal court and produced the fox, which matched the skill of the dead fox in every way. The king grudgingly allowed the man to be set free. Soon after the man's release, however, the fox reverted to its wild ways and escaped from the court.

Foxes feature, too, in the story of *Suibhne Geilt*, or Mad Sweeney, the king from early Ireland who later lived as an outcast in the woods.[4] Among the animals he mentions in his stories are foxes whose habits he describes with affection:

| | |
|---|---|
| *Gach aonúair ro-linginnsi* | Each and every time I crouch |
| *Co mbinn ar an lár* | To the ground down low |
| *Co fhaicinn an creamhthannán* | So I may see the little fox |
| *Thios ag creim na gcnámh* | Lie chewing on some bones. |
| | |
| *Sionnaigh beca ag bregairecht* | Fox cubs scampering |
| *Chugaim agus úaim,* | Close to me in their play |
| *Mic thíri ara legairecht* | Wolves to the kill scrambling |
| *Teichimsi re a fhúaim.* | Their sound drives me away. |

Some fox remains found at Iron Age Celtic sites suggest a ritual element.[5] For example, a ritual pit in Winklebury in Hampshire contained the strange combination of the bones of a red deer and twelve foxes. Deer and fox also appear together as sacrifices in the shrine at Digeon in northern France. Butchery marks on fox bones from Gaulish sanctuaries such as Mirabeau and Ribemont indicate that the animals were ritually eaten. Fox fur was also used as an armlet or armband for the bog body known as Lindow Man, who was ritually murdered by strangulation and buried in a marshy pool in Cheshire sometime between the fourth century BC and the first century AD. Perhaps this signified his status as a warrior, or it may have been placed on him by his executors to mark him as a treacherous and cunning outlaw who deserved death. Some Celtic personal names were linked to the word for fox.[6] The Gaulish chief Louernius is one example, his name meaning 'Son of the Fox'. The name Louernius also appears several times in Britain.

RELATIONS WITH HUMANS

The fox has always been hunted by man, both on account of its status as a predator of farm animals and for its attractive fur. There is evidence that early Celts hunted the fox, though probably more for its fur.[7] For example, sites in France such as Villeneuve-Saint-Germain contain large deposits of tail and paw bones – indicating skinning – heaped in areas away from sites of food preparation. The deposits are of wolf, bear and badger, as well as fox. In addition, rock art in the Celtic settlement of the Camonica Valley in northern Italy depicts foxes being hunted. In early Ireland, too, there is evidence of fox-hunting. The old Irish tale *Táin Bó Fraích* describes a great hunt organised by the legendary King Ailill and Queen Maedhbh which included foxes among its quarry. The role of the fox as a predator of livestock was also recognised in early Ireland, an early Irish text describing the fox as one of the three most harmful animals found in the country, along with the wolf and the mouse. The skill of the fox was also recognised, one text lauding the animal's ability to steal past sheperds; another refers to the difficulty of tracking a fox in bank, thicket or woodland. The Brehon Laws mention the fox in the context of keeping one as a pet, and equate any offences committed by it with those committed by a domestic dog. They also indirectly refer to the fox when they describe a wandering vagrant as a *sinnach brothlaig*, or 'fox of a cooking pit'.

Foxes have traditionally been regarded as vermin by farmers and gamekeepers, because of their predation of domestic animals and birds.[8] There is little data in Ireland on the impact of foxes as predators, but they can have a major impact locally on henhouses and newly released game birds. However, it is not clear how much of a predator the fox is of newborn lambs, despite the traditional view. All these factors mean that shooting and trapping are carried out on an ongoing basis by farmers, gamekeepers and hunters in a bid to control numbers. An estimated 30,000 foxes are killed per year in Ireland. The effect is minimal as the natural increase in fox population compensates for those killed. The trapping or shooting of foxes for their skins ceased in Ireland only during the 1980s.

Modern fox-hunting with horses and hounds was only developed in the late eighteenth century in Britain, mainly because deer-hunting was becoming too difficult as farmland became more enclosed.[9] Because the countryside in Britain was more open in those days, foxes were actually scarcer than they are today, which meant foxes had to be imported from Europe to keep up the numbers for hunting. Despite fierce opposition from British hunting groups, fox-hunting was banned on animal welfare grounds in Scotland in 2002 and in England and Wales in 2005. It is still legal for farmers and others to kill foxes by humane methods. In Ireland fox-hunting is still legal. Modern Irish fox-hunting developed during the nineteenth century, and there are today about 250 packs of foxhounds and harriers (harehounds) in Ireland, of which about 70 are followed on horseback, with the rest followed on foot. It is not clear how many foxes are killed with hounds in Ireland each year, but the figure is probably fewer than 10,000. Fox-hunters are actually concerned about the conservation of the fox, and the Irish Masters of Foxhounds Association (IMFHA)

Lizard – Earc Luachra – *Lacerta vivipara*

Cow – Bó – *Bos taurus*

Pig – Muc – *Sus scrofa*

Dog − Madra − *Canis familiaris*

Sheep − Caora − *Ovis aries*

Donkey – Asal – *Equus asinus*

played a central role in the 1970s in ending the lucrative trade in fox skins which existed at that time. Irish fox-hunting has, by and large, avoided the controversies experienced in Britain, and there appear to be no serious moves to have it banned in Ireland. However, an increasingly urbanised population and a growing interest in nature have led to a kinder view of the fox, which is now seen by many as simply an attractive part of our native fauna. Whether this leads to British-style clashes over fox-hunting remains to be seen.

Today, despite ongoing persecution, the fox is as much a part of the Irish landscape as ever. Indeed, increased afforestation and the movement of foxes into urban areas means that their numbers are increasing – and now stand at about 150,000–200,000. Whatever the future attitude of humans in Ireland towards the fox, one thing is clear: the wily fox will continue to survive and outwit human efforts to control it, as it always has done.

# Stoat — Easóg — *Mustela erminea*

*The stoat or 'weasel' was regarded in Irish folklore as a highly intelligent, but peevish and bad-tempered animal. However, those who treated the stoat with respect would come to no harm, and to possess a purse of 'weasel' skin brought good fortune, as it meant the owner would never be short of money.*

## Folk Beliefs and Customs

The stoat is often called the weasel in Ireland, but although the weasel (*Mustela nivalis*) is very similar in appearance to the stoat (except a bit smaller), it is not native to Ireland and has never been introduced here.[1] In Ireland the stoat or 'weasel' was regarded as a very intelligent animal, but also vengeful.[2] For example, since they were believed to understand human speech, if a stoat was encountered the correct thing to do was to greet them politely. In County Clare the custom was to raise one's hat in greeting, or even to bow, although some were known to spit and cross themselves for protection. The person who insulted them on the other hand, or pelted them with stones, could expect to lose all their chickens before too long. Deliberately killing a stoat was most unwise, since it caused all the deceased animal's relations to descend on the house of the killer and attack with great savagery. The only way to avoid this fate was to kill one of your own hens as compensation. In addition, the spit of the stoat was (wrongly) believed to be poisonous, because they had an affinity with serpents, and anyone who came in contact with it was believed to get blood poisoning. However, a popular story involving the stoat's poison also shows a more forgiving side. According to the story, a group of men mowing a field were approaching close to where a stoat had its nest. The stoat was worried that its young would be killed, so it spat poison into the workmen's tea-can. When the workmen came upon the nest, however, one of them gently put it to one side so that it would be unharmed. The men then stopped for their break and headed towards the tea-can. As they approached the can, the stoat ran towards it and knocked it over so that they would not be poisoned.

Various other superstitions surrounded the stoat.[3] In Ireland the habit of the stoat or 'weasel' to form packs occasionally may be the origin of the widespread belief that it held funerals for its dead, in much the same way as humans. Two of the chief mourners were said to go in front, each holding one end of the body of the deceased between their teeth, while a respectful procession of mourners followed behind. Another widespread belief was that a purse made of the skin of a 'weasel' would bring its owner

great good fortune, as it would never be empty of money. However, the purse should be found by accident, because it would be extremely bad luck to deliberately kill a weasel for this purpose. Another common notion in folklore was that the stoat or 'weasel' was the cat of the Norsemen, who had brought them into Ireland as pets. It was also thought to be a bad omen to see a stoat when setting out on a journey. In County Donegal a stoat eating grass meant that rain was coming; while to hear a stoat screeching was a sign of mist.

The stoat features in some Irish folk cures. The skin of the stoat was thought to be a cure for rat bites, while the testicles of a male stoat were used for contraception. This involved the woman castrating the unfortunate 'weasel' while still alive, and then stitching the testicles into a piece of skin from a gander. This was then hung around her neck at all times, especially during intercourse (perhaps the thought of it alone was supposed to do the trick!). In Ulster the stoat was often called the *whutret* or *whitrick*, a name believed to come from 'white rat'. The Irish name for the stoat (*easóg*) refers to its eel-like sinewy shape (*eas* being the Irish for eel). The stoat does not appear in many Irish place names, though one example is Drumaness (*Drom an easa* – ridge of the stoat), County Down.[4]

## MYTHS AND LEGENDS

The stoat appears little in Irish mythology.[5] However, a story about a hero of the Fianna called Gaoine recounts how he proved his worth as an infant by killing a stoat. As the stoat ran across his mouth several times looking for food, the infant Gaoine seized it in his hands, grasping it so firmly that it was later difficult to loosen his grip. The eighth-century text *Cormac's Glossary* derived the stoat's Irish name from *ni fhois*, or 'unquiet', a reference to its constant restless movement.

## RELATIONS WITH HUMANS

There is some evidence that the Celts occasionally hunted the stoat for its pelt, as small amounts of stoat remains have been found at Gaulish Iron Age sites. The only reference to the stoat in the early Irish Brehon Laws concerns what legal penalties might apply for offences committed by one kept as a pet. In this unusual scenario, the stoat would be classed with the domestic cat. The Latin name for the stoat, *Mustela ermine*, is derived from the Old French for stoat, *hermine*. The white winter pelts, known as ermine, were used to trim ceremonial robes in medieval Europe. The native Irish stoat is a distinct subspecies, *Mustela erminea hibernica*, which only very occasionally turns white in winter due to our milder climate. The stoat was traditionally considered by gamekeepers and farmers to be vermin as it can cause damage to poultry or game bird pens. It is now, however, a completely protected species in all parts of Ireland.[6]

# Lizard – Earc Luachra – *Lacerta vivipara*

*T*he lizard was regarded with some fear in Irish folklore, owing to the mistaken belief that it was a kind of worm that could live as a parasite inside a person. However, the lizard was also believed to have the power to cure burns, scalds and bruises.

## FOLK BELIEFS AND CUSTOMS

In Ireland lizards, newts and large caterpillars were often grouped together under the term 'worm'.[1] They were supposed to be dangerous to men and cattle. The reason is clear from another popular name for the lizard or newt, namely the Mankeeper or Mancreeper, which derived from the belief that the lizard would creep down the throat of anyone who fell asleep in the open air. The lizard or 'worm' was then believed to live as a parasite inside the stomach, and be the cause of abnormal hunger to the afflicted person. The only cure was to tie the sufferer's feet to the rafters and place some sweet-smelling dish below his mouth to coax the lizard out. Failing this, eating or drinking some disgusting concoction would force out the creature. Another strange folk belief was that menstruating women should not walk in long grass, because their condition would attract lizards that might run up their legs and attack. Needless to say, none of these folk beliefs have any basis in fact. The same negative beliefs about lizards do not appear to have been shared in England where they were considered lucky. Indeed, if a snake was approaching a person sleeping outdoors, lizards were thought to protect the sleeper by promptly waking them.[2]

More positively, the lizard was involved in some Irish folk cures.[3] A common belief was that licking a lizard endowed the tongue with the cure for burns, scalds and bruises. For some reason, this was especially effective if done on Shrove Tuesday and by a young person. For best results, the lizard should be licked all over – head, feet, belly, legs and tail. The cure was then carried out by applying the spit of the licker to the affected area.

A cure for heartburn was for the sufferer themselves to lick the back of a lizard. The lizard's Irish name, *Earc luachra* (Rushy lizard), survived into Hiberno-English in various forms, such as Arklooker, Athlukard and Dark Looker.[4]

MYTHS AND LEGENDS

The belief that a lizard had the power to cure burns and scalds probably derived from the Classical myth of the salamander.[5] The salamander was said to be a lizard-like monster that could live in fire, which it was able to quench with the chill of its body. King Francis I of France adopted the lizard in flames as his badge, along with the motto *Nutrisco et extinguo* – 'I nourish and extinguish'. The name salamander was subsequently given in zoology to a group of newt-like amphibians called the Caudate, probably because many of them are coloured bright red or yellow.

RELATIONS WITH HUMANS

The Viviparous lizard is the only lizard native to Ireland.[6] It gets its name from the fact that it produces its young live from the mother, instead of laying eggs. This helps it survive Ireland's cooler climate. The lizard is not important enough to be mentioned in the Brehon Laws. Nevertheless, both Gerald of Wales and O'Sullivan Beare, writing in 1185 and 1625 respectively, mention the lizard as a native species.

SIMILAR SPECIES

Common Newt – *Earc sléibhe* – *Triturus vulgaris*
There is only one species of newt living in Ireland, the common newt, which is generally regarded to be native. The newt's Irish name, *Earc sléibhe*, means 'Mountain lizard', indicating that the Irish did not really distinguish between the lizard and the newt. This meant that the folk beliefs attached to the lizard applied equally to the newt. The newt was not considered significant enough to get a mention in the Brehon Laws. Gerald of Wales does not refer to it either, but this may be because he also assumed it to be the same animal as the lizard.

*Earthy Animals*

# Cow – Bó – *Bos taurus*

*Cattle were revered in Irish tradition as a major source of sustenance, providing milk, butter, cheese and meat to the entire population. They also provided clothing from their leather. Not surprisingly, cattle were regarded as a primary source of wealth in early Ireland, and were a symbol of the fertility and goodness of the land. The cow was particularly revered for its life-giving and nourishing milk, while the bull was held in high esteem for its great strength and virility, and as a symbol of power and vigour.*

## Folk Beliefs and Customs

The cow was the most precious animal on the Irish farm, and much of Irish folklore about the cow concerned methods of keeping it safe from the fairies and other harmful influences.[1] A favourite and simple method was to hang a St Brigid's cross in the cowhouse, as Brigid was regarded as the patron saint of livestock. (The rushes left over from making the famous crosses on St Brigid's Day, 1 February, were also added to bedding for the livestock to protect them.) Many customs also existed about how best to protect the cattle around May Day, when the fairies were always particularly active. Milk or butter should not be given to anyone in case the luck of the dairy for that year went with it, and no fire should be given away either. Despite this prohibition, it was considered prudent on May Eve to spill milk on the threshold to prevent fairies from gaining entry. The rowan tree (or mountain ash) was also used widely around May Day, as it was traditionally considered a powerful charm against the fairies. Sprigs of mountain ash were tied around the milk churn, and crosses of the wood tied to the tails of cattle. Another method of protection was to follow the cattle on their way to the field and take up the clay that their feet touched. Posies of yellow flowers, such as primroses, buttercups and marigolds were also tied to their horns or tails. In some parts of Ireland cattle were driven between bonfires to protect them, a custom which appears to have ancient roots. According to the old Irish text *Cormac's Glossary*, the custom in ancient Ireland on May Day, or *Belteine*, was to light two fires in the name of the god Bel (*Bel-teine* – Bel's fire) and drive the cattle between them. These fires were made by druids with great incantations, and believed to protect the cattle against disease.

Despite the prominence of May Day, traditions concerning cows also existed for other times of the year.[2] A well-known story in Ireland was that of the Borrowed Days, which told of how the first three days of April always brought bad weather. According to this story, *An tSean Bhó Riabhach*, or the Old Brindled Cow, boasted on the last day of March that the rigours of that month had not killed her. Hearing these words, March borrowed the first three days of April, and brought such appalling weather that the poor old cow was killed and skinned. Another name for these days was thus the Skinning Days. The tale was even more elaborate in parts of the north of Ireland, consisting of the first nine days of April – three for the blackbird, three for the stonechat and three for the grey cow. St John's Eve (23 June) was another time when cattle needed to be protected. This usually involved large midsummer bonfires, with the cattle either driven through the smoke of the bonfires or over the embers, or else driven between two fires. Alternatively the cows could be touched with a smouldering torch, have their hair singed, or have the ashes of the fire strewn over them. On the first Sunday in August a widespread custom was to drive cattle into lakes or rivers to swim, as it was thought that drenching the cattle at this time protected them for the rest of the year. The folk belief that the cows and donkeys gained the power of human speech on Christmas Eve, in view of their role in the birth of Christ, made this another time to treat them well, giving them a generous feed and decorating their stable with evergreens.

Various beliefs also surrounded the process of milking and making butter or cheese.[3] In some parts of Ireland it was thought unlucky to spill as much as a drop of milk when milking, while in other areas it was held that the first 'spring' of milk should be allowed to fall on the ground for the 'good people' or fairies. Alternatively, the first drop was squirted onto the finger, and the sign of the cross made on the cow's flank while saying 'God Bless the Cow'. Any visitor to the stable was offered a small drop of milk in a cup, after which he would also say 'God Bless the Cow' to avert any fairy influence. The process of making butter by churning the milk took a lot of effort, and it was thought that various things could upset the process. If any visitor came to the house while churning was in process, they were required to take a hand at the churning, if only for a few moments. Similarly any visitor lighting their pipe from the fire while churning was in process could upset the procedure, or even be guilty of stealing the 'goodness' from the milk. If a black dog with no white hairs on its body entered a dairy, no butter would be had from the milk.

It was also considered lucky to use a willow or sally rod to drive the cattle, as this would increase the yield of milk. However, letting a cow

spend too much time in the shade of a whitethorn tree was unlucky, as it was liable to be milked by unseen hands. Neighbours, especially old women living on their own, were suspected of trying to steal the goodness of the milk by various magical means, particularly on May Day. A favourite method for the local witch was to suck the milk from the cows, while in the form of a hare. Another was to take the first water from the farmer's well on May Day morning, or to collect dew on the land where the cattle grazed. In Donegal it was believed that putting dung into the mouth of a newborn calf ensured that its milk would never be stolen by the fairies. However, the fairies could sometimes bring goodness to the milk as well as steal it.

An Irish folk tale tells of a man called Maurice Griffen who received the gift of herbal knowledge from the fairies. This happened because his cow ate a white piece of foam that floated down from the sky in front of her. The cow then gave four extraordinarily foamy pitchers of milk. Maurice drank three of them, and thus gained the herbal knowledge. The Gaelic poet Cearbhall Ó Dálaigh was also said to have received his poetic powers from drinking the milk of a fairy cow.

It was believed in Ireland that the fairies were more likely to take a white cow than one of any other colour.[4] For this reason it was considered unlucky to have a white cow on a farm. On the other hand, if a snow-white heifer appeared in a farmer's herd it brought very good luck for the following year. A very popular tale about a white fairy cow relates how the first black cow came to Ireland. According to the tale, the fairies liked to herd their white fairy cows by the borders of an Irish lake. One day one of the white cows strayed from the fairy herd and was caught by an old farmer. He was very taken with the cow's silver-white colour, as at that time in Ireland there were only red and white cows. The cow produced very good milk and many calves, and the farmer was very pleased. Despite this, the foolish old farmer decided that he would butcher the cow for its meat. The butcher arrived, but before he could carry out his task a voice was heard on a nearby hill saying: 'Arise and come here.' Immediately the white cow and her calves rose up in the air and vanished. However, one of the calves did not hear the fairy voice, and when the farmer looked at her she had turned jet black. From that calf all the native Kerry cows were said to be descended. There are also numerous Irish folk tales of the fairies taking cows and their milk, although sometimes they could be generous in return. One such tale from County Donegal tells of a man called Pádraig who had a white cow that was forever heading toward a particular furze bush at the bottom of a field. One day Pádraig tried to rouse the cow out of the bush with the intention of selling it. However, a voice spoke to him saying: 'Don't do that until our own cow has calved, and you will be rewarded.' After that the cow gave great milk, and in gratitude for not selling her, the fairies carried Pádraig to New York the following Halloween to help him collect some money owed to him, returning him safely home afterwards.

Another popular folk tale was that of the fairy cow that appears from a nearby lake.[5] In a version from County Donegal a very fine yellow hornless cow appeared outside the house of a man called Rory O'Boyle. The cow gave the best of milk and over time produced eight fine calves. One day, however, Rory had trouble keeping all nine cattle out of his potato pits and began to curse the day they arrived. A being arose from a nearby lake and called out: *Teich, teich, ón mhaol mhór go dtí an maol bheag; agus ón mhaol beag go dtí an gamhain!* – 'Come, come, from big moiley (hornless cow) to small moiley, from small moiley to the calf!' The cow and her calves walked into the lake and were never seen again. Similar motifs are found in other countries. In Scotland the *tarbh-uisge* or 'water-bull' dwelt in lochs and was generally friendly to man. It emerged from the waters occasionally to mate with ordinary cows, and could be identified by the fact that it had no ears.

Some superstitions surrounded the birth of cows.[6] In Ireland the afterbirth of a cow was sometimes hung in rafters to bring good luck to the other cattle. It was also the custom to light a blessed candle under a cow that had given birth, and make the sign of the cross over her. Occasionally a calf might be born with a little bit of flesh in its mouth. This piece of flesh was thought to be very lucky, and if it was found it should be hung on the cowhouse wall. If a cow had twin calves it was thought in Ireland that it would bring misfortune to the house for that year, especially if they were bull calves. Several folk cures also involved cows.[7] In Ireland a good cure for burns was to put cow dung on it, because the cow was believed to eat the best of herbs and grasses. In England it was believed that cow dung was also good when made into a poultice for ailments such as pneumonia. In Ireland it was believed that a good cure for freckles was to anoint the face in bull's blood.

## MYTHS AND LEGENDS

Cattle are frequently associated with Irish saints, nurturing the saints' blessed qualities through their milk, or deriving special milk-yielding abilities through the saints' power.[8] St Brigid in particular is portrayed as having an affinity with cattle, and was regarded as their patron and protector. According to tradition, Brigid was reared on the milk of a white, red-eared cow, which was given only to her. Even as an adult, Brigid retained her special link with milk and cows. On one occasion she performed a miracle by blessing a pail of water so that it turned into milk, in order that a sick member of her household could be cured. On another occasion Brigid was visited unexpectedly in Kildare by seven bishops. She milked the cows for the third time that day, and even though they should not have been able to produce any more, all the cows gave so much milk that they could have filled all the vessels of Leinster. Other saints are also depicted as having an affinity to cattle. In an echo of the *Life of St Brigid*, the *Life of St Kevin* recounts how a white cow came to his parents' house and fed the infant saint with her milk. Later, when the saint was living as a hermit in Glendalough, a cow belonging to a local herdsman would wander to the hollow where Kevin lived and lick his garments. Soon the cow was giving a prodigious amount of milk, and when the herdsman looked for the cause he discovered St Kevin's retreat and disclosed it to others, thus ending the saint's isolation. In a similar vein, a popular legend about St Colmcille tells how, after the saint's death, his body was put in a stone coffin on the seashore in Scotland; the coffin miraculously floated across the sea to come ashore in Colmcille's beloved Derry. One of the cows of a local farmer began to eat the seaweed that grew on the coffin, and to lick the stone coffin itself, and soon after was giving as much milk as four cows. When the herdsman investigated, St Colmcille's coffin was discovered and he was buried beside SS Patrick and Brigid. According to the legend, their two graves moved apart, leaving a space for Colmcille in between.

The *Life of St Patrick* relates how a cow in his foster mother's byre went mad and killed five other cows before escaping. The young Patrick miraculously brought the cows back to life, and blessed the mad cow so that it was gentle as a sheep thereafter. A very well known folk tale concerns how Patrick later used a bull to best the pagan chieftain Crom Dubh. The story goes that Patrick set about building a church, either at Croagh Patrick in County Mayo or Downpatrick in County Antrim. He went to the local chieftain, Crom Dubh, and asked him to provide some food for the workmen. Crom Dubh had a fiery bull that killed all who approached it, and he gave this to Patrick in the hope that the saint would be killed. Instead the bull submitted quietly and gently to being taken and slaughtered. Crom Dubh was enraged by this and demanded that Patrick give him back the bull. The saint gathered the bones and hide together, blessed them, and the bull came back to life. Crom Dubh was so impressed that he was converted to Christianity; less forgiving versions have him killed by the bull. When St Patrick died, his body was put in a cart pulled by two untrained oxen, and it was decided to bury him wherever they stopped. The two oxen stopped in Downpatrick, and so there he was duly buried. St Kieran of Clonmacnoise was reputed to own a dun-coloured cow famous for yielding twelve measures of milk at every milking – one for each of the twelve apostles. The hide of the cow was treated as a holy relic, and it was believed that anyone who died on it was assured of going to heaven. The *Annals of Inisfallen* record that Tadg Mac Conchubair, the King of Connaught, died lying on the hide in AD 900. According to tradition the hide was later used in the making of *Leabhar na hUidhre*, 'the Book of the Dun Cow', an important Irish manuscript which still survives.

Various mythical cows appear in Irish legends.[9] One of the best known is the *Glas Goibhneann* or *Gaibhleann*, the Grey Cow of Goibhniu, the ancient Celtic smith god. According to legend, she could provide an inexhaustible supply of milk and fill any vessel put under her. However, a jealous woman claimed that she had a vessel that the *Glas* could not fill. The treacherous woman then brought out a sieve and began to milk the cow. The *Glas* yielded enough milk to fill a lake but it all ran through the sieve. Eventually the *Glas Goibhneann* became exhausted by her efforts and died. The *Glas Gaibhleann* is particularly associated with County Donegal, where she appears in the legend of 'Balor of the Evil Eye'. Balor, a famous warrior who lived on Tory Island, had an eye that could kill with one look due to its poisonous beams. He coveted the miraculous *Glas Gaibhleann*, which was owned by a local farmer called Mac Kinelly, and so he stole her and brought her over to Tory Island. She was eventually recovered after Balor had been killed by his own grandson. Many folk traditions surround the *Glas Gaibhleann*. For example, it was said that she would often appear on May Day, bringing good fortune to the farmer among whose herd she was seen. She was also believed to make especially fertile any grass she lay down on. In County Clare it was said that the hoofprints of the *Glas Gaibhleann* could be seen on rocks all over the eastern Burren. Another mythical cow was the goddess of the River Boyne, whose Irish name *Bóand* derives from *Bo-vinda* or 'white cow'. The Celtic word *vind* also meant 'wise or illuminated', and the name derives from an image of the sacred River Boyne as milk issuing from the mystical cow goddess. In early Ireland it was said that anyone drinking from the River Boyne in June would acquire the power of poetry. Similarly, in modern Irish, the Milky Way is called *Bóthar na Bó Finne* – 'the Road of the White Cow'.

A regular feature of Irish legends is white cattle with red ears, which appear to be particularly prized as the tribute for kings and poets.[10] For example, among the tributes paid to King Tuathal Techtmhar by the men of Leinster were thirty red-eared cattle and calves with bronze halters and spancels (hobbles) and bosses of gold. In the tale *The Wooing of Étaín* Midir and Echu play chess for a stake which includes fifty white, red-eared cattle and fifty white, red-eared calves, each with a bronze halter. The collection of early Irish poems called the *Metrical Dindshenchus* mentions how the poet Aithirne the Cruel took a tribute of 700 pure white, red-eared cattle from the Leinstermen. White, red-eared cattle appear in other contexts, too. In the tale *Táin Bó Cuailnge*, the war goddess Morrigan challenged Cúchulainn while in the form of a white heifer with red ears. It may be that the breed of cow is purely mythical, but there is in fact a breed of white cattle with red ears in existence, which may have been regarded as a rare and prestigious breed in early Ireland. On the other hand, white, red-eared dogs from the otherworld also appear in Irish and Welsh legends, and there is no evidence of the existence of such a breed of dog.

Bulls often appear in Celtic mythology as symbols of strength and virility.[11] The most famous in Irish legend are the Brown Bull of Cooley or *Donn Cuailnge* from the tale *The Cattle Raid of Cooley* or *Táin Bó Cuailnge*, and his rival, the Fair-horned or *Finnbheannach* of Connaught. The Brown Bull of Cooley was the prize bull of Ulster, who had no match in size or comeliness of form among the bulls of Ireland. His virtues are evocatively described in the *Táin*: 'He would bull fifty heifers every day, fifty youths used to play games every evening on his back, he could protect a hundred warriors from heat and cold in his shadow and shelter. No spectre or sprite or spirit of the glen dared to come into the same canton as he. Each evening as he came to his byre, his musical lowing was enough melody and delight for all the men of Cuailnge.' The story of the *Táin* begins with Queen Maedhbh and King Ailill of Connaught comparing their possessions. The only difference is that Maedhbh had no bull to compare with Ailill's famous white-horned bull, the *Finnbheannach*. Hearing of the famous Brown Bull of Cooley, Maedhbh resolved to have it. Her requests to buy the bull came to nothing, and so she decided to invade Ulster and take the bull by force. Ulster is defended almost single-handedly by the hero Cúchulainn, and after much fighting the men of Ulster prevail. The tale climaxes as the two prize bulls of each province face each other: 'Each of the bulls caught sight of the other and pawed the ground and cast the earth over them. Their eyes blazed in their heads like distended balls of fire, their cheeks and nostrils swelled like a smith's bellows in the forge, and each collided with the other with a crashing noise. Each began to gore and to pierce and to slay and to slaughter the other.' The two bulls traversed the whole of Ireland in their fight, but the next morning the *Donn Cuailnge* appeared with the *Finbheannach* a tangled mass upon his horns. After casting bits of the *Finnbheannach* around Ireland (his loin at Athlone, his ribcage in Dublin, and his thigh in Waterford), the *Donn* in his frenzy attacked the women and children of Cooley, slaughtering many of them. Then the great Brown Bull 'turned his back to a hill and his heart broke like a nut in his chest and he died'.

Bulls also appear frequently in Celtic symbolism.[12] On the continent bulls were associated with Cernunnos, the horned god of animals, appearing in Gaulish shrines in Burgundy, Rheims and Saintes. Bulls were also associated with Gaulish healing shrines such as Fontes Sequanae and Beire-le-Châtel. An unusual and widespread image was the triple-horned bull which was depicted throughout Romano-Celtic Europe, usually in the form of a bronze figurine. As well as appearing at the healing shrines just mentioned, the figurines have been found at locations such as a child's grave in Colchester in England, and at a shrine dedicated to the Roman Emperor at Auxy in Gaul. The number three was a powerful religious symbol to the Celts, and the addition of a third horn must have reflected the idea of the natural potency and aggression of the bull being multiplied for greater effect. The bull was also regarded by the Celts as a symbol of good health and strength, and a bringer of good fortune.

The sacrifice of bulls was a feature of Celtic beliefs.[13] In the early Irish tale *The Destruction of Da Derga's Hostel*, a rite called *tarbhfheis* or 'bull feast' determined who would be king. In the rite a bull was killed and one man ate his fill of the beef and drank a broth made from the meat. The man then went to sleep, and an incantation of truth was chanted over him. Whoever the man saw in his dream would be the future king – and if he lied he would die. The Roman writer Pliny describes the mistletoe rite of Gaulish druids in his *Natural History*, whereby mistletoe that grew on an oak tree was collected with great ceremony. After the mistletoe had been cut from the trees with a golden sickle, two white bulls were sacrificed to give thanks for the gift of the all-healing plant. Its perceived healing and fertility properties meant mistletoe continued to be connected with cattle in folk customs. For example, in the north of England and in Wales it was believed that to ensure that the dairy thrived, a bunch of mistletoe should be given to the first cow that calved after New Year's Day.

Cattle also appear in ritual Celtic interments in Britain and on the continent, usually as part of a feast where they were offered to the gods as symbols of wealth and prestige. For example, at the sanctuary of Gournay-sur-Aronde in France a large number of cattle were sacrificed and left to rot in a large pit before their bones were piled at the entrance to the sanctuary. It is believed that the purpose was to offer the flesh of the cattle as 'food' to the gods of the earth to replenish it. Ox or cow burials are also present at a number of Romano-British sanctuary sites such as Brigstock, Caerwent, Muntham Court in Sussex, and Verulamium in Hertfordshire. Sometimes it appears to be the case that the cattle are offered as food for the dead. In Dorset in England, Iron Age Celtic burials were often accompanied by a joint of beef placed at the head of the deceased. Cattle may also have been included in burials as a sign of the prestige and wealth of the deceased. In a burial of a Celtic nobleman at Soissons in France, two oxen were included, along with two horses and their chariot, two goats, three sheep, four pigs and a dog.

Oxen (or castrated bulls) also feature in Irish legends, generally with an agricultural theme as befits their status as draught animals.[14] According to *Lebor Gabála Érenn* or the *Book of Invasions* the first cattle in Ireland were four oxen brought over by Parthalán, who was said to have come from Greece to found the first colony in Ireland. Their names were Leic, Lecad, Imair and Eitridi, and they ploughed the land of Ireland for the first time. The *Book of Invasions* also recounts that the goddess Brigid (as opposed to the saint) possessed two faithful oxen called Fea and Femen, who gave their names to two plains, *Magh Fea*, the plain of the River Barrow in County Carlow, and *Magh Feimhin* in County Tipperary. The oxen were said to cry out if rapine had been committed in Ireland. Also reflecting agricultural lore, the tale *The Wooing of Étaín* relates how Echu, the King of Tara, learned from the people of the *sidhe* (or otherworld) that the correct way to yoke oxen was across the shoulders, instead of across the forehead, which had been the Irish custom until then.

Relations with Humans

The ancestor of the modern domestic cow is believed to be the wild ox or aurochs (*Bos primigenius*) which was originally found across Europe and northern Asia.[15] The aurochs is now believed to be extinct, with the last recorded specimen killed in Poland in 1627. It appears that the aurochs were first domesticated about 6000 BC in the Middle East. One consequence of domestication was a considerable reduction in size to a small, short-horned cow called *Bos longifrons* or *Bos brachycerus*. These cows of Neolithic farmers in Europe, Britain and Ireland were similar in size to the small, hardy breeds found in mountainous parts of Europe today. Domestic cows did not reach Ireland until about 3500 BC, and although a direct identification with Neolithic breeds cannot be assumed, the consensus among archaeologists is that cattle in early Ireland were generally similar in size and build to modern Kerry cattle. Another similarity with Kerry cattle is the fact that black was a common colour for early Irish cattle. For example, an eighth-century text speaks of milch cows 'as black as a blackbird'. Cattle could also be other colours, namely crimson red, flame red, brown, dun and, most rarely, white. It seems that black cows were considered the hardiest and white cows the most delicate. Despite this, white cattle were highly esteemed, especially for their milk, which is probably an association based on their colour. Cows could also be more than one colour, as there are references to brindled or speckled cows (*riabhach*); later sources mention white-backed cows (*droimfhionn*) with red, grey or black bodies. Cows of this colour called 'drimmons' are still found in County Kerry today.

In general, however, differences in colour did not imply that there were cattle of different breeds in the modern sense in early Ireland. An exception may be the white, red-eared cow which was often mentioned as a distinct breed in early Irish texts. As it appears mostly in myths and legends, it might be thought that the cow was a purely magical breed, but there is some evidence that it may have existed in Ireland. In fact, an old British breed of white, red-eared cattle does exist and is still found at Chillingham in Northumberland, as well as other places in Britain. White, red-eared cattle also appear in Welsh law texts, which contain no magical material. One thirteenth-century text states that the fine for dishonouring the Lord of Dinefwr must be paid in white, red-eared cattle, while another thirteenth-century text states that the fine for a similar offence against the King of

Aberffraw should include a white bull with red ears. These references are very similar to an instance in an Irish law text where seven white cows with red ears were part of a fine for satirising Cernodon, a legendary king of Ulster. These examples suggest that white, red-eared cattle might have been a rare and precious breed associated with nobility.

So important were cattle to the economy of early Ireland that one of their most important functions was to serve as currency.[16] In Gaelic society the primary means of measuring wealth was in how many cattle a person owned, and it became the main method of payment for goods and services, and for the levying of fines. In this respect Ireland was like other Celtic societies. The Roman author Tacitus stated that for the Celts, the number of cattle they possessed was the key to their status, and that cattle were the most highly prized possessions they had. This statement holds true for early Ireland. Given that cattle were so valuable, it is not surprising that large-scale theft occurred in the form of cattle raids. The subject of many Irish tales, most famously the *Táin Bó Cuailnge*, the cattle raid usually took place across political boundaries, and was therefore difficult to prosecute under the law. The Catholic Church in Ireland was strongly opposed to cattle-raiding – not least because it had extensive farmland of its own to protect. One law text emphasises this by stating that stealing cows was strenuously forbidden by none other than St Patrick himself.

In ancient Ireland cattle were reared according to a system known as 'booleying' (from the Irish *buaile* for 'cattle-enclosure'). Cows were kept near the farm during the spring to consume the fresh grass growth, and then driven off to the hills or other rough ground to graze during the summer.[17] This is an ancient practice found among cattle herders throughout the world, and it reflects the natural tendency of cattle to migrate seasonally in search of pastures. Sometimes this could involve moving the cattle quite a distance. In the *Life of St Kevin* there is a reference to a Meath farmer bringing his cattle to a valley near Glendalough in County Wicklow. The cows would naturally be accompanied by a cowherd and a herd-dog to guard against wolves and robbers. Once autumn arrived the cattle were generally driven back to the same ground where they had been in the spring, to graze during the winter on the grass that had regrown during their absence. This would be supplemented by allowing the cattle to graze on the stubble of cereal crops after they had been harvested, and by cutting winter fodder such as branches of holly and ivy. Ireland was unusual in that prior to the coming of the Normans there was hardly any tradition of cutting and drying grass to make hay as winter fodder. The eighth-century English historian Bede, commenting on this, believed the reason was the mildness of the Irish climate which made cutting hay unnecessary. This is the most likely explanation, as there was probably sufficient grass growth during the winter to sustain the cattle. Another factor is that the wetness of Irish summers discouraged hay-making. Even today there is no special word in Irish for hay – the word *féir* or grass is used instead. In fact, Ireland was so famous for its mild climate that one Roman writer stated, 'It is so rich in foliage, not only lush but sweet, that in a small part of the day the cattle fill themselves so that unless they were kept away from foliage they would burst if fed any longer'.

The main purpose of keeping cattle was naturally for their milk and meat.[18] The vast majority of milk consumed in Gaelic Ireland came from cows, and the wide variety of dairy products derived from milk comprised a major part of the Irish diet. As well as milk, cheese, cream, butter and buttermilk, several other products were consumed that are not so familiar today. These include fresh milk diluted with water to form a drink called *englas*; and milk mixed with rennet to form a thickened coagulated milk known as *bainne clabair*, or 'bonnyclabber' as it became known in Hiberno-English. Several types of drink were produced from whey, which is the rather sour liquid produced as a side product of making cheese. It could be diluted with water to make a drink for those who were fasting, or made from boiled milk and buttermilk to create a more palatable version called *treabhander*. Butter was regarded as a luxury food in Gaelic Ireland, and law texts specify that butter must be given to high-ranking visitors; commoners were entitled only to milk and cheese. Butter was valued for its ability to keep fresh for long periods when kept cool, and storing butter in bogs was a frequent practice. Such butter has been found in Irish bogs, still recognisable after thousands of years. For example, a five-stone lump of bog butter was found in 1999 in Poll na gCapaill bog in County Galway. The butter was thought to be over 3,000 years old and, although not edible, it retained its buttery smell and texture. Many different types of cheese were also manufactured, from soft cheeses to one called *mulchán* or 'mullahawn', which was so hard a hatchet was required to cut it!

Most cattle were slaughtered before they were three years old, when their meat became old and tough.[19] Male cattle were castrated long before slaughter, as bull flesh is very red and strongly flavoured and generally regarded as unpleasant tasting (the only reference to eating bull flesh in Irish texts is during the ritual *tarbhfheis* or 'bull feast' described earlier). Slaughter took place throughout the year, as the meat was generally consumed fresh and roasted on a spit or boiled. The flesh could be boiled in a large cauldron over a fire, or in a *fulacht* or cooking pit. This was essentially a large hole in the ground which was filled with water and then brought to the boil by putting hot stones into it. This is a very ancient method used in many parts of the world, and Irish archaeologists have found a large number of these cooking pits. Accounts from Irish legends indicate that there was often a protocol, whereby the choicest cuts of meat (such as the haunch) went to those of highest rank and prestige.

Cattle were also used for their hides, bones, horns and tallow (or fat). Cowhide performed many functions, including coverings for beds, vellum for manuscripts, and surfaces for laying out corn to be flailed. Turned into leather by being tanned with oak bark, cowhide was used for shoes, bags, halters and muzzles, as well as the covering for boats and currachs. Naturally it was also made into clothing. For example, the hero Cúchulainn is described as wearing 'a heroic deep battle-belt of stiff, tough tanned leather from the choicest parts of the hides of seven yearlings … and a dark apron of well-softened black leather from the choicest parts of the hides of four yearlings'. Cow bones were used to make pins, needles, spindles and combs, while horns were turned into drinking goblets. However, because of the small size of the horns of early Irish cattle, wild ox horns were frequently imported from the continent instead. Tallow was used to make candles by dipping a stripped rush into it, and the early Irish Brehon Laws stipulated that a landlord was due three handfuls of candles from his client every year.

Those cattle not slaughtered for meat when young fulfilled other necessary functions.[20] Most obviously, the female cows were kept to provide milk, and the small proportion of males that were not castrated were used as breeding bulls. Most farmers, even small ones, had at least one bull, generally for every seven to ten cows. However, another important function of cattle was the use of some of the castrated males, known as oxen, as draught animals. A properly trained ox was highly prized for pulling the plough and heavy farm cart, and it remained the main draught animal until the Normans introduced the plough-horse. Another valuable function of the ox was when it was used as a *dam conchaid* or 'wolf-fighting ox'. This meant an ox that was brought along with a herd of cows to the summer pastures to defend against attack by wolves.

There are several breeds of cattle still in existence in Ireland today that are considered distinctively Irish.[21] The most famous is the Kerry Cow, a small, black breed of cow that closely resembles the first cattle brought into Ireland by Neolithic farmers. It is regarded as one of the oldest breeds of cattle in Europe, and is related to the Heren, a small, black mountain breed in the Alps, and to the fierce black bulls of the Camargue. The Kerry Cow has the distinction of being the first breed developed primarily as a milk producer, rather than for draught and meat, and is known for being extremely hardy and able to thrive under low-feeding conditions. Kerry cattle were the dominant breed in Ireland up to the seventeenth century, when larger European breeds began to be imported. The Kerry Cattle Society was founded in 1917 to preserve and promote the breed, and the Irish government has funded various grant schemes to conserve them over the years. In recent years the Irish Cattle Breeding Federation has been tasked with the co-ordination of conservation efforts, through a mating advisory service and semen and embryo cryoconservation. A survey carried out in 1998 by the Kerry Cattle Society found a total of 781 females in Ireland, and it would seem the future of the breed is secure. Another native breed of cattle is the Dexter, which was bred in the 1750s by a Lord Hawarden on his farm in County Tipperary. Lord Hawarden produced the Dexter breed by selecting the best mountain cattle of the area, and so the Dexter is closely related to the Kerry Cow. Like the Kerry Cow, it is renowned for being hardy and economical, and is now well established in Britain, where it is regarded as the smallest breed of British cattle.

Another distinct breed of Irish cattle is the hornless cow or Moiled (from the Irish *maol* – 'bald, hornless'). It is sometimes claimed that the Moiled was brought to Ireland by Norse settlers, but hornless cow skulls have been found at early Christian sites. There are also references to hornless cattle in pre-Norse texts. For example, Fliodhais, the Irish goddess of deer and cattle, had a hornless cow which could provide milk for 300 men and their families at one milking. Also, according to myth, a king of the Tuatha Dé Danann called Bres put a tax on every household in Ireland of the milk of a hornless dun cow. Hornless cows arise naturally in bovine populations and various other hornless breeds have been developed, such as the Aberdeen

Angus, the Galloway and the Red Poll. The main advantage of breeding hornless cattle is that there is less danger of injury to farm workers or other cattle. The Irish Moiled is predominantly red with white markings, and is noted for its placid temperament. It is now Ireland's rarest breed of native cattle, with about forty breeding animals throughout Britain and Ireland. Like the Kerry Cow and Dexter, it is renowned for producing good beef and milk from poorer quality grazing. The vast majority of Irish cattle today are foreign breeds, with the Friesian, Charolais, Hereford and Angus predominating. Nevertheless, the beef and dairy industries continue to play the major role in Irish farming, and remain an extremely important part of the Irish economy.

# Pig – Muc – *Sus scrofa*

*The pig was always highly prized by the Irish for its succulent meat, and in legend it was the favourite meat of gods and heroes at their feasts in the otherworld. The pig was also respected by hunters for its bravery and ferocity in defending itself against attack, and so was seen as a symbol of the warrior spirit.*

## FOLK BELIEFS AND CUSTOMS

As the wild boar has been extinct in Ireland for several centuries, Irish folklore about the pig concerns the domestic animal.[1] In some parts of Ireland it was considered good luck to drive a pig into the house on May Morning, so as to ensure good luck for the coming summer. Pigs were believed to be able to see the wind, and thus forecast the weather. It was also thought that pigs had such acute hearing that they could hear the grass growing. In England it was believed that it was bad luck for a bride to meet a pig on the way to her wedding – fortunately a rather rare occurance nowadays! In Irish folklore it was believed that the mating of pigs was linked to the cycles of the moon. If the sow came into heat for the boar when the moon was full she would have a full litter. If she came into heat when the moon was in its last quarter, then the litter would be small. In Britain it was similarly believed that animals, especially pigs, should not be slaughtered when the moon was waning, or the meat would shrink too much when boiled. They should be slaughtered instead when the moon was waxing. It was also believed in Ireland to be unlucky to slaughter a pig on a Monday. The favourite time for slaughtering animals, especially pigs, was the feast of St Martin on 11 November, in order to provide for the winter's meat supply, and traditionally some of the meat was given to the poor. According to legend St Patrick decreed that every nun and monk should also have a pig killed for them in honour of St Martin, as it was St Martin who had conferred the monks' tonsures on them. It was also a common practice to sprinkle some of the blood on the doors and in the four corners of the house to ward off evil. In Scotland many people would

not eat pork at all, probably because of the Old Testament prohibition in Deuteronomy about pork being an unclean meat. For some Scottish people this prohibition was so strong that it was considered unlucky to even say the words 'pig' or 'swine'; misfortune could only be avoided by touching 'cauld iron' afterwards.

Ominous spirits were often said to appear in the form of a black pig, and it was widely thought the pig was the worst of all forms for fairy folk to take. However, harm could usually be avoided by ignoring the apparition completely and blessing oneself as one passed. If that failed, a hazel stick was a good implement for warding off the spirit. Making for the nearest bridge on the road was another good idea, as it was well-known that the creatures could not pass running water. Halloween, when the barriers between this world and the otherworld were weakest, was a favourite time for the Black Pig to be abroad, so the wise did not travel alone on this night. A folk tale often told in Ireland concerned a rich woman who turned away with contempt a poor woman who had come to seek alms, comparing her and her children to a sow with a litter of bonhams. When the rich woman gave birth herself soon after, the child was born with a pig's head. Along the southern border of Ulster, from Leitrim to Armagh, is a series of bank and ditch earthworks known in folklore as the Black Pig's Dyke. According to legend these were formed when an ill-tempered schoolteacher was transformed into a black pig by one of his pupils who had got hold of a book of magic spells. In his rage the transformed teacher ran through the countryside carving out a trench with his tusks, and throwing up the earthworks beside it. The earthworks were in fact probably constructed in Iron Age times to prevent cattle raiding.

The pig features in some Irish folk cures.[2] A cure for a child with mumps was to take it to the pigsty and rub its head on the pig's back in the hope that the illness might transfer to the animal. A prayer should be said while this was being done, or else the following words repeated: *Muc, muc, seo chugat an leicneach* – 'Pig, pig, here's the mumps for you.' In County Cork it was believed that a cure for toothache was for the sufferer to put their head to the ground in the place where a pig had been scratching its behind, and make the sign of the cross with their mouth. If this was done it was said they would never suffer from toothache again. A rather disgusting cure for jaundice involved swallowing up to a dozen live lice from a pig. Some Irish proverbs also concern the pig.[3] These include: *Tá cluasa fada ar mhuca beaga* – 'Little pigs have big ears'; 'The quiet pig eats the cabbage'; and 'The priest's pig gets the most porridge.' The best known of all is to describe a lucky person as being 'on the pig's back', or more poetically to be 'lying in lavender like Paddy's pig'.

MYTHS AND LEGENDS

Pig-hunting appears in many early Irish tales, especially of the Fianna.[4] The pigs could often be prodigious in size and ferocious. For example, one pig that the Fianna hunted near Loch Léin in County Kerry was described as huge, with rough, sharp tusks, a gloomy black jowl and a red mane. When the pig was finally killed after a long hunt, she had killed thirty-nine men and seven score hounds. Another pig, of the breed of Balor's swine, was of 'grisly shape and power' and provided a week's eating for the Fianna. In one poem Fionn Mac Cumhaill, the leader of the Fianna, lists the thirty fierce boars that his hound Bran had successfully hunted all across Ireland, including 'the boar of Druim an Eoin, swiftly you brought him down in his despite, the boar of Magh Gluin of mighty tramp, the boar of Fionnabhair, the boar of Fionnchairn'. The amount of pigs hunted by the Fianna could also be prodigious. At one point, they are said to have killed a thousand pigs after one week's hunting. Inevitably, some of the pigs they pursue turn out to be enchanted. For example, in one tale the Fianna hunted a great wild pig on the mountain of Bearnas Mór, and Fionn's hound Bran got the better of it. When the pig began to scream a tall man came out of a nearby *sidhe* or fairy fort and asked Fionn to let it go. When Fionn agreed, the man struck the pig with a druid rod and it turned into a beautiful young woman called Scáthach (shadowy one). The tall man invited the Fianna into the fairy fort for a feast, and Fionn became so enamoured of the young woman that he asked the man (her father) for her hand in marriage. The man agreed, and Scáthach began to play the harp for the guests. She played the harp so beautifully that Fionn and all the Fianna fell asleep. When they awoke they were outside on the mountain of Bearnas Mór, and Scáthach and her father were nowhere to be seen. In another tale, Aongus Óg of the Tuatha Dé Danann challenged the Fianna that they and their hounds could not kill any of the pigs that he owned. The Fianna took up the challenge, but when they arrived at the appointed place they were confronted with 'a terrible herd of great pigs, every one of them the height of a deer'. A long battle ensued and many of the pigs were killed, but also many of the men and hounds of the Fianna. The Fianna then marched in anger on Brú na Bóinne (Newgrange), seeking vengeance on Aongus. Aongus explained that the hurt he had suffered was equal to that of the Fianna, as the pigs were in fact the sons of kings allied to him, in enchanted form, including his own foster son, who had been among those killed. The Fianna made peace with Aongus, and each side paid the other the fines that were due under the Brehon Laws.

Probably the best known story of an enchanted pig is that of the Boar of Ben Gulban in County Sligo, a boar whose life was bound up with that of the hero Diarmaid.[5] This came about when the son of the Head Steward of Aongus Óg was killed by Diarmaid's father, Donn, who was jealous that the child was receiving greater attention than Diarmaid. Donn killed the boy during a moment of confusion in Aongus' house, by squeezing the child to death when he ran between his legs. The Head Steward discovered by magic that Donn had killed the child, and was within his rights to decide the fate of Donn's son. But the Head Steward did not kill Diarmaid. Instead he took a magic rod and struck his own dead son with it, turning him into a great boar without bristle, ear or tail. He then said to the boar: 'I put you under bonds to bring Diarmaid, grandson of Duibhne to his death; and your own life will be no longer than his life.' With that the boar rose up and ran out the door, and went to ground on Ben Gulban.

Many years later Fionn Mac Cumhaill, who had become an enemy of Diarmaid's because of their rivalry over the beautiful woman Gráinne, hunted the boar at Ben Gulban while Diarmaid was nearby. He warned Diarmaid not to pursue the boar, telling him that his life was bound up with it, but hoped secretly that Diarmaid would be enticed. Fionn got his wish when Diarmaid declared that he was not afraid and pursued the boar anyway. The boar was famous for being fierce and none of the Fianna proved able to overcome it. Diarmaid, however, grabbed hold of the boar when it charged him, and held on as the boar leaped over streams and heights. The boar eventually freed himself at the top of the mountain and made another rush at Diarmaid, ripping him open so that his bowels fell about his feet. Nevertheless, Diarmaid managed to strike the boar with his sword and dashed its brains out. As Diarmaid lay dying Fionn approached, and Diarmaid reminded him that he had the gift of healing someone if he gave them a drink of water from the palms of his hands. Fionn was reluctant, but Diarmaid and the other Fianna present reminded him of all that he owed to Diarmaid. Fionn went to a nearby well, but remembering Gráinne let the water slip from his fingers. He did this a second time, but was rebuked by the Fianna into complying. He then carried the water in his palms to Diarmaid a third time. Before he could reach him, however, Diarmaid had died. The story is similar to the Greek myth of Adonis, the beautiful youth who was killed by a boar while hunting, because of the jealousy of his rival Ares.

Pigs are noted for their habit of turning up the land in search for roots and any other food they can find. In the days when they roamed free this could cause great destruction to agriculture.[6] A story reflecting this from the *Metrical Dindshenchus* (or lore of place names) recounts how a plain in Connaught called *Magh Mucrímhe* ('the plain of pig counting') near Athenry in County Galway got its name. The story recounts how a plague of magical pigs infested the kingdom of Connaught, destroying land and crops, and forcing Queen Maedhbh and her consort Ailill into action. The pigs derived a magical power from the fact that they could not be counted accurately. It seems that the only way to accurately count the pigs, and so break their power, was by hunting and killing them, as the following poem relates:

## MAGH MUCRÍMHE

From Cruachan's Cave, their dwelling place
A black, enchanted herd did race,
Aroused by a demon the skinny throng
To Maedhbh and Ailill's land did come.

These pigs a wondrous power did wield
A hundred counting them in the same field
Could add them up until the Last Day
But never could number them the same.

Crops and ground alike they spoiled
In Connaught of the bardic voice
Leaving upheaval and upset
In every district where they went.

Ailill and Maedhbh at last did go
To hunt them and so number them true
And found the pigs on clear, bright sands
Resting in the open on Magh Fraích.

On that day all here and there
The wild pigs were counted in Magh Fraích
And the twist in the tale it seems
That plain was henceforth called Magh Mucrímhe.

The habit of pigs digging in the earth did not always have negative consequences. According to the *Life of St Patrick* the saint was able to buy his freedom from his owner, Miliuc, when a boar dug up a mass of gold. Patrick gave the gold to Miliuc, but when he had gone the gold turned back into earth.

The pig is associated with feasting in many Irish legends, and pork was considered the tastiest of meats.[7] A ninth-century triad includes the death of a fat pig among the 'three deaths which are better than life'. Another triad refers to the boar 'which removes dishonour at every season', or, in other words, provides a feast for high-ranking visitors whenever they visit.

Goat – Gabhar – *Capra hircus*

Badger – Broc – *Meles meles*

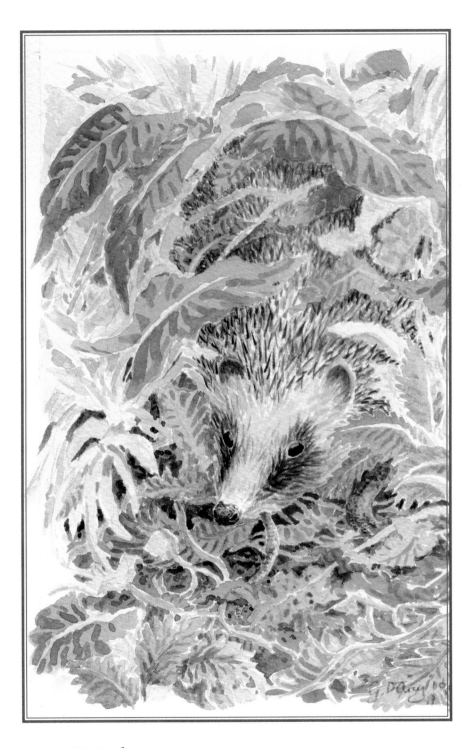

Hedgehog – Gráinneog – *Erinaceus europaeus*

Rabbit – Coinín – *Oryctolagus cuniculus*

*The Tale of Macc Da Thó's Pig* tells of a dispute between the warriors of Ulster and Connaught over who should have the choice of carving the pig at Macc Da Thó's feast. The pig was monstrously fat, having been fed for seven years on the milk of sixty cows, until seven inches of fat lay on its snout. The pig was so large that forty oxen could lie across it, and its tail had to be carried on a cart pulled by nine men. Conall Cernach of the Ulstermen was finally chosen to carve, but he took all the pig, leaving nothing for the warriors of Connaught except the front trotters. A fight immediately erupted with great slaughter on both sides. In myth, Manannán, the Irish god of the sea, was in charge of the otherworld feast of the gods, and provided his own magical swine as food. Though killed and eaten one day, these swine would be magically brought back to life the next, ready to be eaten again. In the *Book of Invasions* Lugh asked for the pigs of Easal, King of the Golden Pillar, which 'though they are killed every night, they are found alive again the next day, and there will be no disease or sickness on any person that eats a share of them'.

There is archaeological evidence that pigs were a favourite food of the Celts for ritual funeral feasts, both for the deceased and for the mourners.[8] It seems that vast quantities of succulent piglets and lambs were consumed at the banquet, and the bones then tossed into the grave. Pigs were also commonly included in burials as provision for the dead person for their otherworld feast. At La Gorge Meillet in France a fourth-century BC chariot burial of a young warrior included eggs, a fowl, joints of pork, and a knife with which to eat them. A superbly crafted flagon also accompanied him to hold his wine. Similarly, a burial at Soissons, also in France, included two horses for the chariot, two oxen, two goats, three sheep, four pigs and a dog. In Dorset in England several late Iron Age burials feature joints of pork placed near the heads of the deceased, while a woman in Yorkshire was buried clasping part of a pig in her arms. Pigs were also buried as ritual offerings at a Romano-Celtic site in Chelmsford in England, while at Sopron in Hungary a ritual deposit contained a complete boar packed into a stone-lined grave. Boar tusks have also been found buried in a ritual well shaft in Norfolk.

The wild pig or boar was a favourite image of fierceness and courage in Celtic art and decoration, usually depicted with its dorsal ridge of stiff hairs erect in challenge to attackers.[9] Boars appear on the famous Gundestrup cauldron, the decorated ritual cauldron made of silver found in Denmark.

Leabharlanna Poibli Chathair Bhaile Átha Cliath
Dublin City Public Libraries

Boar figurines were common, either as statuettes or as helmet crests. Images of boars also appear on coins and sword stamps. Several images on other objects depict boars being hunted, such as a third- or fourth-century BC flagon from Bavaria that shows boars and stags being pursued by a hunting dog; a bronze cult wagon from Mérida in Spain shows a boar hunted by a man on horseback. Most striking of all are the bronze carnyxes or Celtic trumpets, whose mouth was usually made in the form of a boar. One such first-century AD trumpet found in Grampian in Scotland had a snarling open mouth containing a pig's palate and an articulated wooden tongue. When blown the wooden tongue would vibrate, giving off a ghastly braying shriek to add to the terror of the battlefield.

Pigs are often also associated with the fertility and well-being of the land itself.[10] When the Milesians first arrived at Ireland's shore, the Tuatha Dé Danann cast a spell so that the land was covered in cloud, giving it the appearance of a pig in shape. The *Book of Invasions* recounts that the goddess Brigid, daughter of the Dagda (as opposed to the saint) possessed a pig called Torc Triath, who was king of the boars in Ireland. He gave his name to a plain called Treithirne in southeast County Tipperary, and was said to cry out if rapine had been committed in Ireland. *Cormac's Glossary* states that the word *triath* for a boar comes from the fact that it 'turned up' (*sodathar*) the land in search of food. The same text derives *muc*, the Irish word for pig, from *mucna* or truculent. Brigid's boar, the Torc Triath, apparently appears in Welsh form as the Twrch Trwyth in the tale *How Culhwch won Olwen*. In the tale King Arthur came to Ireland to pursue the Twrch Trwyth, seeking the magical razor, shears and comb that lay between its ears. The boar destroyed a fifth of Ireland in his long fight against Arthur. Eventually the great boar was so angry that he set out for Wales in order to destroy it also. After wreaking havoc in south Wales, the Twrch crossed the River Severn and ran down into Cornwall, pursued by Arthur and his men. After much effort the magical treasures are obtained, and the Twrch Tryth driven into the sea off Cornwall. It is also mentioned in the tale that the boar was once a king who had been turned into a boar on account of his sins. Another Welsh pig is Henwen ('old white') who appears to be linked to agriculture. According to legend she travelled across south Wales, dropping a wheat grain and a bee in Gwent and a barley grain and a bee in Dyfed, so that that those two places became the best for producing wheat and barley respectively. She was not so generous to north Wales, however, where she dropped a wolf-cub, an eaglet, and a kitten that became the monstrous Palug's cat.

Gods and goddesses linked to the pig were also worshipped by the Celts.[11] Cocidius, the British god of war, was generally shown on stone carvings with spears and boars. In Belgium a goddess called Arduinna was worshipped by the Celtic people of the Ardennes. She is usually depicted as a huntress armed with a knife and riding on a wild boar. This symbolises her dual role as both hunter and protector/companion of the creatures of the forest. Similarly, another Romano-Celtic god called Mercury Moccus (compare Irish *muc*) was worshipped in Burgundy in France. A striking image of another boar-god from Euffigneix in northern France shows the god in the form of a man lying down while a great boar with bristling dorsal ridge strides along his torso. The pig also appeared in the mythology of other European cultures. Freyr, the Norse god of fertility, had a magical boar called Gullinbursti, which could run over earth, air and sea alike. It was always surrounded by brilliant light, even in the gloomy underworld, because of its shining bristles. In Classical myth, the pig was sacred to Ceres, the Roman goddess of agriculture, because it taught mankind to turn up the earth.

RELATIONS WITH HUMANS

The domestic pig originates from the wild pig (*Sus scrofa*), and was domesticated about 7000 BC by Neolithic farmers in both Europe and the Middle East.[12] The pig was famous for converting all types of household leftovers – including grass, roots, acorns and even carrion – into succulent meat. The Celts of continental Europe were famous for their huge herds of livestock, including pigs. The Greek geographer Strabo wrote that: 'They have such enormous … herds of swine that they afford a plenteous supply of salt meat, not only to Rome, but to most parts of Italy.' Pork was later a favourite food of the Roman army. Wild pig bones, however, as opposed to those of the smaller domestic pig, are rare among the food remains at Celtic settlements in Europe, and they seem to have been hunted mainly for sport by the nobility and not food. The domestic pig was introduced into Ireland by Neolithic farmers several thousand years ago, and bones have been found at Neolithic sites such as Ringneill Quay, County Down, and Tankardstown South, County Limerick. It is assumed that the wild pig also existed in Ireland as a native species, but it cannot be definitively proven as the early domestic breeds were practically indistinguishable from the wild variety. In particular, the skull of the Long-Faced or Greyhound Irish pig, a now extinct domestic variety, is very similar to the wild kind, making identification difficult. The early Irish domestic pig was much smaller, narrower and hairier than modern breeds, which have been interbred with fatter Asian varieties.

It was standard practice in early Ireland to bring domestic pigs to forage in oak woods to fatten up on acorns and roots, supervised by a swineherd camping out for long periods. This blurred the distinction between wild and domestic further, as it must have been very easy for pigs to escape from human control and become feral. The tale *The Cattle Raid of Cooley* refers to this practice when the King and Queen of Connaught, Ailill and Maedhbh, set about counting up all their livestock to see who had the most. Their great herds of swine 'were brought from woods and sloping glens and solitary places' to be counted.

Of particular importance was the acorn crop which came in September and October and served to fatten up the pigs for winter, either for slaughtering for their meat, or for having reserves to survive the winter. An early Irish phrase *mucc remi-thuit mess* or 'a pig that dies before the acorn crop' was even used to describe a lost opportunity. One legal text claimed that a single oak could provide enough acorns to fatten one pig in a good year. Acorn crops are uncertain and can fail completely in some years. However, the *Annals of Clonmacnoise* record that the acorn crop in AD 1038 was so abundant that even the runts of the litters were fattened. Another favourite food of pigs seems to have been the root of the dandelion, which was called in early Irish *serbán mucc* or 'the bitter one of pigs'. Apart from their meat, the hide of pigs was sometimes used to make clothes, as several Irish tales speak of pigskin jackets worn by charioteers.

Early Irish pigs appear to have come in different colours, and one source lists the different kinds of pigs as white, grey, black, reddish brown and blue-black. In the old Irish Brehon Laws pigs generally had the same value as a sheep. A piglet was worth one penny, and gained in value as it got older until it was worth nine pence when fully grown. The rent which a lord received from his clients commonly included a flitch of bacon. The Brehon Laws also deal with the various issues arising from pig-rearing. For example, the runt of the litter was generally taken from the sow and hand-reared on milk, usually by the farmer's wife, who was therefore entitled to two thirds of its meat. The hand-reared pig could become a pet in the process, which had the potential for trouble as it followed everyone around looking to be fed. The Laws mention the offences and trespasses of such a pig, and it was a common enough problem to lead to the Irish proverb: *Na trí peataí is measa – peata sagairt, peata bacaigh, peata muice – 'The three worst pets – a pet priest, a pet beggar, a pet pig.'* The Laws also deal with the damage caused by trespassing pigs, which could be extensive given their habit of digging up the soil with their snouts in search of roots. The Laws state that the pig's owner must provide alternative grazing land until the damaged land has recovered. The land is judged to have recovered when two horses yoked together can graze on it without any earth adhering to their teeth as they graze. Injuries caused by pigs were also covered in the Brehon Laws, as pigs can be very aggressive towards humans, and cause serious injury or even death with their very sharp teeth. Wild (or feral) pigs were hunted regularly in early Ireland as numerous tales testify, but unlike elsewhere the emphasis appears to have been more on meat than on sport. Generally pigs were hunted with dogs, but they could also be caught by trapping, or shot with an arrow.

Writing just after the Norman Conquest of the twelfth century, Gerald of Wales in his account of Ireland stated that the wild pigs of Ireland were 'small, badly formed, and inclined to run away. They are equally inferior in their want of boldness and courage as in their physical make up.'[13] Whatever the truth of Gerald's comments, the archaeological evidence indicates that wild pigs did not long survive the Norman invasion, probably due to over-hunting and the destruction of the oak woods on which they depended. Despite this, various contemporary accounts insist that 'wild' pigs existed in Ireland up until the seventeenth century, even if the suspicion must be that they were really feral. Moreover, writing in 1625, O'Sullivan Beare in his work *The Natural History of Ireland*, stated that: 'wild woodland pigs are reported *to have been* very fat here' (my italics). The use of the past tense seems to imply that such pigs no longer existed in Ireland. In folk tradition the last boar in Ireland is said to have been killed in Kanturk (*Ceann Toirc* – the boar's headland) in County Cork sometime in the early seventeenth century, but there are no records to confirm the story, or indeed any records about when the Irish wild pig died out.

The only distinct breed of Irish pig that existed historically was the so-called 'Greyhound pig', which was domesticated in Ireland in Neolithic times, and was a direct descendant of the wild European pig.[14] It got its strange name from its physical features, as it had long legs, a high narrow back and a long head. The Greyhound pig was similar to other native European breeds, so this account of German pigs would apply to the Irish variety, and helps to give a clearer picture of the animal: 'They really appeared to have no hams at all; their bodies were as flat as if they had been squeezed in a vice; and when they turned sideways their long sharp noses and tucked up bellies gave to their profile the appearance of starved greyhounds.' The Greyhound pig was also white or grey in colour, adding to the similarity. It was also claimed that the Greyhound pig was sometimes used instead of dogs by hunters in the nineteenth century to retrieve game, but this seems unrealistic. The main value of the Greyhound pig was its ability to survive on scraps, so that even the poorest farmers could afford to keep them. The meat it yielded, however, was thought to be inferior to that of today's pigs. The Greyhound's days were numbered when pig breeders in Britain began to cross their own native breeds with exotic breeds from Asia in the eighteenth century. The Asian breeds were smaller but fattened up more easily, and breeders were soon producing pigs that combined the European size with the Asian ability to put on meat. Irish breeders began to do the same, and the Greyhound pig declined in numbers until it became extinct in the early twentieth century. The legacy of the Greyhound pig is not entirely lost, however, as one of the rare British breeds, the Tamworth pig, is a cross between the greyhound pig and the native British variety. It was first bred on his Tamworth estate in England by Sir Robert Peel in 1809, and survives as a rare breed today, valued for its hardiness and ability to withstand harsh conditions.

Another distinctive Irish breed, the Large White Ulster, was bred in the early twentieth century from a mixture of Greyhound pigs and imported hybrid pigs like the Berkshire. Although it was popular in the early decades of the century, the Large White Ulster fell out of fashion because its meat was too fatty. The continuing preference for lean meat meant that the Large White Ulster became extinct in the 1960s. Today, the Irish pig industry relies upon breeds of mixed European and Asian origins such as the Landrace, and does not appear to feel the loss of the native breeds. Pork is still popular in Irish and European diets, and the Irish pig industry remains very important to Irish farming, being second only to the beef and dairy industries.

# Dog – Madra – *Canis familiaris*

*The dog has always been seen as the loyal and faithful companion of man, guarding his home and livestock and following its master wherever he has gone. The dog was also valued for its skill in helping with the hunt and in war, and its saliva was believed to have healing properties. This meant that it was regarded in Celtic legends as the guardian animal of gods and heroes, linked with stories of hunting and with healing shrines.*

FOLK BELIEFS AND CUSTOMS

A general belief about dogs in Britain and Ireland was that they were able to see ghosts, and were themselves capable of becoming ghosts after their death.[1] In Ireland dogs were also believed to howl rather than bark in the presence of fairies and spirits. So effective were dogs as guardians against fairies that in a poem from County Donegal a fairy woman laments how dogs disrupt her going about her business (indeed anyone walking in the countryside will sympathise):

| | |
|---|---|
| *Madaidh ar thús na dtor* | Dogs in front of the bushes |
| *Madaidh ar deireadh na gcró* | Dogs behind the folds |
| *Madaidh ag cur mí-roinn ar mo mhéis* | Dogs who upset my dish |
| *Madaidh i mo dhiaidh nach rabh beo!* | Dogs who hunt me, may they die |

The baying hound or *gaidhrín caointeach* occasionally took the place of the banshee, and was heard before a death in certain families, such as the O'Keeffes of west Cork. Even for an ordinary dog to howl near a sickroom was a very bad sign, as it meant that the patient had little hope of recovering. In County Cork it was believed that when a person was dying, any morsel of bread should be thrown out, to entice away the death hounds that would be watching the soul. Tales of ghostly black dogs were common in Irish folklore, usually large and vicious animals seen by those who stayed out too late at night. In County Clare a spectral dog, the spirit of a well-known

95

local called 'Robin of Ross', was said to haunt the road between Carrigaholt and Ross. Another well-known ghostly dog was the 'Black Dog of Cratloe'. It was a good omen if it ran alongside the carriage, but a bad omen if it leaped at the carriage. On one occasion the dog leaped at the mail coach; the driver was soon after thrown off and killed at the same spot. On the other hand, it was said in Ireland that a black dog was the best kind of dog to fight off the fairies. A well-known folk tale about a demon dog explains why one should never say 'God Bless it' about a dog. According to the story, a priest was making his way to the home of a dying man, when he heard a sweet voice singing the old tune *Cailín Deas Crúite na mBó* ('The Lovely Milkmaid'). The priest was intrigued, as it was the most mellifluous and beautiful rendition of the song he had ever heard, and he lingered to listen. The priest was known for his love of music and, curious to find out who it was with such a lovely singing voice, clambered into the adjoining field. To his horror, he saw that the voice came from a demon dog singing to its heart content. Only then did the priest remember the urgency of his mission to the dying man, and he hurried off to the man's house to administer the last rites. Alas when he reached the house the man had already died, as the priest had been lingering captivated by the song much longer than he realised. Full of remorse, the priest declared that no one should ever say 'God Bless it' of a dog again.

Various other beliefs existed in Ireland about the dog.[2] It was thought that one should never ask a question of a dog because it had the capacity to answer, and if it chose to do so the one who posed the question would die in the near future. A popular Irish folk tale tells of how the cat and the dog argued about which of them should be allowed to live inside the house. They agreed that the matter should be settled by having a race, with the winner being the one who reached the house first. The dog was winning the race, but stopped to attack a poor beggarman that he did not recognise. The cat shot past the distracted dog and reached the house first. In County Cork it was believed that it was possible to tell from the position of the 'seven starlets' in the sky that all guard dogs had gone asleep, and it was therefore possible to go and steal. Perhaps it is just as well that the exact constellation of seven stars is not described! In County Clare it was believed that to dream of a dog foretold a friend. An Irish cure for chapped skin, bunions or burns was to get a dog to lick the affected part. In Scotland it was thought to be bad luck to drive a dog from the door on New Year's

Eve, as it would carry the luck of the year with it.

There are quite a few Irish proverbs about dogs.[3] Examples include: 'Every dog is valiant at his own door' or the similar 'Every hound is brave on his own dunghill'; 'Often the hound that was made fun of killed the deer'; 'Hold onto the bone and the dog will follow you'; 'Little dogs start the hare but great dogs catch her'; and 'A great barker seldom bites'. Some proverbs concern the 'old dog', for example: 'It's hard to teach an old dog how to dance'; 'An old dog sleeps close to the fire, but he'll not burn himself'; and, of course, 'It's the old dog for the hard road, and the pup for the boreen.' The simplicity of dogs is captured in the proverb: 'A dog owns nothing, yet is seldom dissatisfied.'

MYTHS AND LEGENDS

Probably the most famous dog in Irish legend is the fierce hound in the tale of how the great Ulster warrior Cúchulainn got his name.[4] According to the story, when Cúchulainn was only six, Conchubar, the King of Ulster, saw him playing hurling against 150 other boys and beating them all. So

97

impressed was Conchubar that he invited the boy, then called Setanta, to feast with him at the house of the smith Culainn. Setanta replied that he would follow the king when he had finished playing. Some time after, Conchubar arrived in Culainn's house and forgot to tell the smith that the boy was following. Culainn, thinking that no one else was due to arrive, locked up the gates of his house and released his fierce hound. So vicious was this dog that it took three chains with a man holding each one to restrain it. Following the tracks of Conchubar's horse, Setanta arrived at Culainn's house some time later. The hound saw the boy and ran at him. Having no other means of defence, Setanta took his hurley and made a cast of the ball at the hound. So great was its speed that the ball went through the gaping mouth of the hound and carried all its entrails out its behind. Setanta then took the dog by its legs and dashed it to pieces against a nearby standing stone. Hearing the commotion, Conchubar remembered Setanta with horror, and the entire household ran out to see if the boy could be rescued. They were all astonished and relieved to see that he was safe. However, Culainn was also rather put out that his finest hound had been killed. He pointed out that he had now no means of protecting his livestock and household. Hearing this, Setanta offered to stand in as a guard until a pup could be reared to replace the hound. One of the Ulster warriors then remarked that he would be known as the 'Hound of Culainn' or *Cú Chulainn*. Bold as ever, the boy replied: 'I prefer my own name'. Nevertheless, Cúchulainn was his name from that moment on.

Cúchulainn's link with dogs contributed to his death, too, as it meant it was taboo for him to eat dog meat. This was normally not difficult to abide by, but it was also taboo for Cúchulainn to refuse an invitation to a meal. This meant he was tricked into breaking one or other of the taboos by three enemy witches who met him while he was on his way to battle. They were roasting a dog on a spit and invited him to join them in their meal. Whatever Cúchulainn did would bring him misfortune, but he chose to accept the meat with his left hand and eat a small piece of it. A large part of his strength left him immediately, and when he was attacked soon after he was unable to defend himself properly, and was mortally wounded.

Also famous in Irish legend is Bran, the favourite hound of the hero Fionn Mac Cumhaill.[5] Bran's mother was Queen Uirne Aithbhéil, who was turned into the shape of a dog by an enchantress. In that shape she gave birth to both Bran and Sceolaing, another famous hound of the Fianna. Bran was said to have great sense and knowledge, which he used to warn Fionn of danger or to help him. *The Lays of Finn* includes a poem telling the story of Bran, and in the following extract Fionn praises his virtues.

*BRAN*

BRAN

*Rí na gcon do bíodh am laim*
*Os leicnibh Sléibhe Colláin*
*Is ni raibhe ar bith go mbáigh*
*Cú ar a mbeith a túaruscbáil.*

The king of hounds I used to hold
On the slopes of Slieve Callan,
There was not boast in all the world
Of any hound of his reknown.

*Da taobh geala do bhi ag Bran*
*Earball nua corcra gléghlan*
*Ceatramha corcra go roinn*
*Ótha earball go hiardruim.*

Two bright flanks there were on Bran
A glossy, scarlet tail so fine.
Scarlet haunches comely formed
From start of tail to top of spine.

*Ceithre cosa gorma faoí*
*Re himteacht oidhche agus laoí*
*Cruibh úaine nár teachtsat báigh*
*Ingne ettrochtra iucháin.*

Four feet of blue-ish grey below
For going every day and night
With grass-stained paws that never slowed
And pale-red claws so gleaming bright.

*Rocs dreagain ina ceann cóir*
*Ris nir fedadh iomarbháidh*
*Aluinn agus caoimh a clú*
*Mo is gasta na gach míolchú.*

A dragon's eye in his shapely head,
To quarrel with him no one would dare.
Lovely and noble was his fame
Quickest of hounds to hunt the hare.

*In cú ba hairde sa Féin*
*Thigead gan cromadh fo a bléin*
*Is a ceann ba gasta in roinn*
*Ba comard é rem ghúalainn.*

The tallest hounds need not stoop
When passing underneath his breast.
His lively head that never drooped
Would reach as high as my own chest.

*Ceithre míl do leiginn uaim*
*Míol budhdheas is míol budhthuaidh*
*Míol siar agus míol soir*
*Do bidís uile a mbél Bhrain.*

Four hares at once would I release
A hare to the north, a hare to the south.
A hare due west, a hare due east,
Bran would catch each in his mouth.

The poem has a sad ending as it goes on to tell of Bran's death. This occurred when Fionn struck Bran to urge him on in the hunt, and the metal chain of Bran's leash hit him painfully on the head. So hurt was Bran by this injustice that the tears streamed down his face. He then broke free from Fionn's hold and raced to a nearby mountain lake and plunged into it to drown. The poem ends with Fionn's anguish and remorse over his careless cruelty. Although Bran was Fionn's favourite, he did have other hounds, among them Sceolaing, Lomaire, Brod and Lomluath.

The baying of dogs appears several times in myth as a portent of doom.[6] In the early Irish tale *The Destruction of Da Derga's Hostel* the death of King Conaire was foretold by a youth who dreamt of various omens of misfortune, among them the cries of Ossar the hound. In the tale *The Fate of the Children of Uisneach* Princess Deirdre has a premonition of the death of the sons of Uisneach in a dream where she hears the howling of dogs. A widespread tradition in England and Wales is that of the 'Yell Hounds' or 'Hell Hounds', or in Welsh *Cwn Annwn*. These hounds of the underworld are said to travel the skies in search of the souls of the dead, filling the air with their terrible baying on stormy nights. It has been suggested that the story originates from the sound of migrating geese calling to each other. The baying of hounds was not always a bad sign. In his famous dialogue with Saint Patrick, the warrior Oisín described how the twelve hounds of Fionn would set up a tuneful chanting when they were set loose, which was more magical to him than the chanting of any Christian.

As well as fierce hunting or guard dogs, several stories appear in Irish legends about smaller pet dogs or 'lapdogs'.[7] According to the *Book of Invasions*, the first jealousy in Ireland occurred when the settler Parthalán killed his wife's lapdog in a fit of wrath, after learning of her adultery with an attendant. Also, the lore of place names called the *Metrical Dindshenchus* tells of how two rocky crags off the coast of Meath got their name from the lapdog of Boann, the goddess of the River Boyne. Swept out to sea the lapdog Dabilla was torn into two bits, which became the crags called *Cnoc Dabilla* or 'Hill of Dabilla'. Finally, the eighth-century text *Cormac's Glossary* recounts how the mother of all Ireland's existing lapdogs was brought there from Britain through a trick of the Irishman Cairbre Musc. When staying with a British friend Cairbre saw the lapdog, and desiring it for himself, he devised a plan to gain ownership of it. He rubbed grease and fatty meat into the handle of a precious knife he owned and set it beside the lapdog at night. The next morning the dog had chewed the handle of the knife and, feigning outrage, Cairbre was able to claim the lapdog as compensation. The dog's name was Mug-Éime, and was a bitch expecting young. Mug-Éime gave birth to three pups, from which all the lapdogs of Ireland were descended. *Cormac's Glossary* also gives an amusingly accurate definition of the Irish word for pup (*cuilen*), deriving it from *cú lén* or 'dog that follows'. In addition it gives an interesting origin for the Irish word *cáinte* or 'satire' from the Latin *canis* or dog – 'for the satirist has a dog's head in barking'. This seems to echo the Greek word 'cynic', which derived from 'dog-like' and meant flattery or impudence.

In the same way as cows, white, red-eared dogs appear in legends as special or otherworldly.[8] In his trip to the Land of Youth, the hero Oisín sees a white, red-eared dog chasing a hornless deer; in Welsh myth, the hounds of Arawn, a king of the underworld, are a dazzling, shining white with red ears. It is probable that these hounds are purely mythical rather than based on a real breed of dog, but they may be inspired by the more common white, red-eared cattle of various stories. These cattle may in turn be based on a real breed which existed in Celtic times, and which was considered prestigious.

Dogs appear in Celtic ritual burials in Britain and on the continent.[9] For reasons that are not entirely clear, ritual burial of dogs in pits or wells was widespread. For example, the Romano-British site at Staines had a well in which sixteen dogs were deposited, and in Caerwent in Wales the skeletons of five dogs were found at the bottom of a well. The same pattern appears at Gaulish sites such as Saint Bernard, Bordeaux and Saintes in Aquitaine, where entire dog skeletons were deposited in deep shafts. It seems that dogs in Celtic myth were seen as underworld creatures, perhaps the guardians of hidden sources of wealth and fertility. Easier to understand are recurring instances of dogs being ritually buried with horses, such as at Danebury in Hampshire and in Cambridge. The likelihood is that the association is based on both animals' importance in hunting. There are also instances where a dog has clearly been buried with its master, such as the Gaulish burial at Tartigny where a man was buried with a hare, the jaw of a horse and a young dog. This probably reflected a love of hunting. More disconcerting for the modern mind is the evidence that dogs were regularly eaten in Celtic Europe, in places such as the Gaulish sites of Ribemont and Gournay, where dog bones were among the animal remains of ritual feasting.

Dogs were linked in Celtic myth to gods of hunting and healing.[10] The association of dogs with healing comes from the ancient belief that its saliva had curative powers. In Britain the shrine of the god Nodens in Lydney in Gloucestershire, overlooking the River Severn, was an important sanctuary where people came in search of cures, especially for eye complaints. Nine different representations of dogs were found there, indicating it was an animal sacred to Nodens. The Gaulish hammer god of Burgundy was often represented in engravings with a dog seated at its feet, gazing up at it. The hammer god was a local version of Mars and Silvanus, the gods of war and hunting, who were also gods of healing. The role of dogs as guardians was also reflected in Celtic myth. The goddess Nehalennia was worshipped by Celtic tribes in what is now the Netherlands. She was the protecter of sailors, merchants and travellers, and every depiction of her includes a large hound lying at her feet in a pose suggestive of a watchdog. In Classical myth the dog accompanied Hermes or Mercury, the messenger of the gods, and was connected with Asclepius, the great physician and healer. Dogs also accompanied goddesses associated with hunting, such as Artemis and Diana.

## RELATIONS WITH HUMANS

All modern dogs descend from wolves that were domesticated and bred in South Asia and Europe from about 15000–10000 BC.[11] The first dogs to be domesticated were probably orphaned wolf pups scavenging around camp fires who developed a friendship with humans. Over time, the friendlier and more biddable animals were bred with each other to produce dogs that were comfortable with humans and could be trained. The process was aided by the natural instinct of the wolf to obey a pack leader, and this meant a young wolf cub could be trained to obey its human master and thus tamed. Dogs were originally domesticated to help with hunting, as their keen sense of smell and great speed and agility made them useful. Dogs also proved useful for guard duty at human encampments and for killing vermin. During Neolithic times, about 8,000 years ago, humans learned to grow crops and domesticate other animals such as goats, sheep and cattle, and so dogs began to fulfil their other important role of herding. As certain dogs proved better at different tasks, the process of breeding different types began. For example, greyhounds are depicted in Egyptian frescoes from around 5,000 years ago. At least five different types of dogs were known to the Romans: small dogs like today's dachshund; fast, hunting dogs like greyhounds; large, heavy guard dogs like the mastiff; and dogs that resembled today's pugs and borzoi. Celtic hounds, the forerunners of the Irish wolfhound and Scottish deerhound, were established in Britain before the Roman invasion. In fact the first evidence of the domestic dog in Britain dates from as early as 5500 BC, at Starr Carr in Yorkshire. Their skeletons show they were about the size of a terrier and resembled the Australian dingo.

The Celts in general were noted for their hunting dogs, especially in Britain and Gaul.[12] The Roman writer Strabo referred to the export of British hunting dogs to Rome, describing them as small, rough-haired, strong, swift and keen-scented. Another Roman writer, Claudian, described British dogs as strong enough to break the necks of great bulls. Gaulish hunting dogs were mentioned by the Roman writer Aurian, who stated that they were called *vertragi*, a name derived from the Celtic word for speed. He described them as being muscular, with lean flanks, broad chests, long necks, big ears and long muzzles. There is also physical evidence of what were probably Celtic hunting dogs. The Iron Age site of Danebury in Hampshire produced remains that were large enough to be a dog capable of hunting big prey; while a bronze sculpture from the third century AD found at the shrine of the Celtic god Nodens in Gloucestershire depicts a hunting dog similar in appearance to the modern Scottish deerhound.

In early Gaelic Ireland the most prestigious dog was the *árchú* or 'slaughter-hound', a large, fierce guard dog, bred and trained to kill, which protected the homes and farm buildings of nobles and other powerful men.[13] The best known example is the hound famously killed by Cúchulainn. In the Brehon Laws anyone who illegally killed an *árchú* had to pay the owner ten cows in compensation and replace the dog with another of similar breed. Another function of the slaughter-hound was to track down and seize offenders of serious crimes. This *árchú* usually belonged to a local champion and had to be a 'dog of three accomplishments': to be able to track a trail of blood, to seize the quarry, and to protect a man under attack from two warrior bands at the same time. This '*árchú* of a champion' was actually considered to have the same worth as a man under the Brehon Laws. An early reference to Irish hounds that sound like the fierce *árchú* is made by the Roman writer Symmachus. In the fourth century AD he reported that seven Irish hounds of great size were exhibited at the circus in Rome, where their strength and fierceness excited much admiration. According to Symmachus, the hounds were considered so dangerous that they were only exhibited in cages.

The next most valuable kind of dog was the *mílchú* or 'animal hound' used for hunting, and bred for speed and ability to detect prey rather than size and aggression.[14] Again this was a hound usually owned by the nobility, for the sport of hunting deer, wild pigs and hares. The hunting dog was considered of less value than the guard dog, and was worth about one milch cow. There is some evidence that two different breeds of dog were involved in hunting: the *gadar*, whose role was to track down the scent of the game, and the *mílchú* proper, whose job it was to attack the game once found. Also important in early Gaelic Ireland was the herd dog. In the Brehon Laws the herd dog actually had a greater value than the hunting dog, as the fine for killing one was five cows and a replacement of similar breed. Irish herd dogs were considered highly enough to be exported to Scandinavia, and one Norse saga praises the skill of an Irish dog which was able to divide a mixed herd of cattle in two based on their markings. Also existing in Gaelic Ireland was the *oirce* or *messán*, or pet dog.[15] According to the Brehon Laws, it was usually kept by physicians, harpists, queens and hospitallers, and had the same value as a hunting dog. This list of owners reflects its main purpose of amusement, and the pet dog was listed in an Old Irish poem as one of the three entertainments of a gathering. Pet dogs seem to have been owned not just by queens, but by any woman of high rank. As a consequence, the pet dog was expected to perform the peculiar role of protecting a woman from the harmful actions of fairies while she was giving birth. This role was taken seriously enough for the Brehon Laws to lay down that a person who killed a pet dog while its mistress was in labour not only had to pay a fine, but also had to provide a priest to protect her by reading from scripture day and night for as long as the labour lasted.

The Brehon Laws lay down penalties for various offences committed by dogs.[16] For example, a severe line is taken towards dog owners who allow their dogs to defecate on other people's land. The dog owner is required to remove the contaminated soil and give the landowner its equivalent in butter, curds and dough, and even soil affected by the smell of the faeces must be removed (one law that perhaps could be usefully revived!). Penalties also apply to dogs which attack people or animals. The penalty for a first offence of a dog attack varied. Either the owner of the dog was responsible for the medical expenses of the person who was attacked and had to pay a fine, or else the dog concerned became the property of the victim. It was then his decision either to have the dog killed or to keep it as his own. In general, dogs known to be aggressive were required to have a bell or rattle around their neck, and be chained up or on a leash in daytime.

The long history of hunting with hounds continues in Ireland, especially in the south of the country.[17] The most famous modern Irish hounds are probably the Scarteen Hounds of Tipperary and Limerick. Known as the 'Black and Tans' the 59 cm pure-bred Kerry Beagles are unique and have been in the possession of the Ryan family for over 300 years. The Muskerry and Duhallow Foxhounds in County Cork are the oldest surviving hunt packs in the country. Muskerry was founded by the Rye family of Ryecourt in 1742, and Duhallow was founded by the Wrixon family of Ballygiblin in 1745. At present there are about 250 packs of foxhounds or harriers (harehounds) in Ireland. They hunt foxes, hares and, increasingly, mink. About seventy of these packs are followed on horseback; the rest are followed on foot. Greyhounds are also involved in hare coursing, which is organised by the Irish Coursing Club.[18] This was established in 1916, although the sport goes back a century or more in Ireland. About thirty to forty coursing licences are issued each year in the Republic. At the time of writing, hare coursing remains suspended in Northern Ireland, pending review on conservation grounds. Greyhound racing is now also a very popular sport in Ireland, beginning in 1927 when Celtic Park in Belfast and Shelbourne Park in Dublin were both opened. Today there are seventeen greyhound tracks in the Republic of Ireland and three in Northern Ireland. Greyhound racing began in 1876 in England with the first use of artificial hares on the track as a more humane alternative to hare coursing.

The only truly ancient Irish breed of dog is the Irish wolfhound.[19] As their name suggests, Irish wolfhounds were supposedly bred to hunt wolves, and the Brehon Laws state that it is a public duty to hunt regularly for wolves in order to keep livestock safe. However, neither the Brehon Laws nor any other early Irish source mentions any breed of dog specifically kept for hunting wolves, so it is unclear what breed exactly was used for the purpose. Certainly, the placid temperament of the modern breed of wolfhound does not seem compatible with the fierce *árchú* or 'slaughter-hound' (although it is claimed that the Irish wolfhound is fearsome when eventually roused). The modern Irish wolfhound is in fact a kind of Celtic hunting dog, dating back to the Celtic Iron Age at least, and with similar origins to the Scottish deerhound and the greyhound. The Irish wolfhound was actually regularly described as a greyhound up until modern times. This is not as strange as it may seem, as earlier breeds of greyhound were much larger and hairier than the modern kind. The last use of the Irish wolfhound for its original purpose of hunting wolves was during the Cromwellian settlement of Ireland in the seventeenth century, when the new settlers decided that the wolf had to be exterminated. Oliver Cromwell himself banned the export of 'wolfe dogges' from Ireland for this purpose. When the wolf became extinct in Ireland in the eighteenth century, the Irish wolfhound almost followed it into oblivion as its services were no longer required. The breed was rescued in the nineteenth century by Captain G. A. Graham, an officer in the British army, who gathered together all the remaining dogs he could find and revived the breed with an infusion of Scottish deerhound, Borzoi and Great Dane blood. The Irish wolfhound is purported to be the largest breed of dog in the world, matched only by the Great Dane.

The other Irish breeds of dog are just a few centuries old, specially bred from dogs originating on the continent.[20] The Irish Red Setter and Red and White Setters were bred as game dogs from spaniels in the seventeenth century, and were considered one breed at that time. It was only later that attempts were made to breed all-red dogs on account of their fine coats. The Kerry Blue Terrier dates from about 1800 and originates in mountainous areas of Kerry, although its exact origins are unclear. One belief is that it is related to Irish wolfhounds, who also have blue-grey coats, while some link the Kerry Blue to the Bull Terrier. A more fanciful story has it that a small spaniel of blue-grey colour jumped off one of the ships of the Spanish Armada and swam ashore. The dog interbred with a female belonging to the Lord of Kenmare, and the result was the Kerry Blue. Kerry Blues are noted for their bravery, and it was traditionally said that a Kerry was not worth its salt unless it could draw a badger from its den and destroy it.

By far the greatest numbers of dogs in Ireland today are simply domestic pets, rather than hunting or guard dogs. However, alongside the love and respect most Irish dog owners have for their pets, there is also a sad story of neglect. According to the ISPCA, despite its much smaller population, Ireland has five times more stray dogs than the UK, and the chances of a dog ending up a stray and being put down are twenty times greater in Ireland than in the UK.[21] A lack of neutering means there is a dog overpopulation crisis in Ireland, and 25,000–30,000 dogs are put down in Ireland as a result each year. Unfortunately the careless attitude of a minority of Irish owners to their dogs means that things have quite a way to go before Ireland could be called a nation of dog lovers.

# Donkey – Asal – *Equus asinus*

---

*The donkey or ass was seen in Irish folk belief as a blessed animal from the cross on its back, and its association with Jesus Christ. Probably for this reason it was believed to have the power to cure many ailments. The donkey was also a much loved and valuable beast of burden on the traditional Irish farm.*

## Folk Beliefs and Customs

The donkey was regarded in Ireland as a blessed animal associated with the Holy Family.[1] It was the animal that carried Christ into Jerusalem, and as a reward was given the distinctive cross on its back. The donkey was also associated with the Holy Family and the story of Christmas, and the Virgin and Child travelled on a donkey's back during the flight into Egypt. According to Irish folk belief, at midnight on Christmas Eve the cows and donkeys knelt in adoration of the Christ Child, and for that moment they gained the power of human speech. In recognition of this, the animals should be shown every kindness and given a generous feed around Christmas, and the stable decorated with evergreens. In Ireland mothers in childbirth would wear a strip of skin and a piece of hoof from a donkey around their neck as a talisman against harm, in memory of Our Lady in the stable in Bethlehem. In County Mayo tradition held that there was always a black spot on a donkey's leg that was put there by Our Lady's thumb. Some Irish proverbs concerned the donkey or ass.[2] Of a light-fingered person it was said they 'would steal the cross off a donkey's back'. The donkey was also widely considered to be lazy, and a work-shy person would be described as 'lazy as an ass'. On the other hand, the donkey was considered dependable, as another popular saying made clear: 'Better the ass that carries you than the fine horse that throws you.'

The donkey was also associated with a large number of Irish folk cures.[3] If two parents had shared the same surname before marriage, they could cure their child's jaundice by putting a donkey's halter on the child and leading it to a well. The child was then made to drink three times from the well. Giving a donkey some cake to eat could also work, with the crumbs gathered up afterwards and given to the patient to eat. Whooping cough or mumps could be cured by putting a donkey's halter on the child and leading it three times around a pigsty. After praying, the parents called on the unfortunate pigs to take the malady. Another cure for whooping cough was to pass the suffering child under the belly of a donkey's foal three times. Epilepsy could similarly be cured by passing the patient under a donkey nine times. Scarlet fever could be cured by taking a hair of the affected person and putting it down the throat of an ass, thus transferring it to the animal. The donkey was also supposed to be the only animal that could kill the 'conach worm', or caterpillar of the hawk moth. This 'worm' was believed to be responsible for a variety of ailments in livestock, such as murrain (redwater fever). A hair from the cross on the donkey's back was placed on the affected animal's sore or wound, and any moth or worm coming near it would be killed.

## MYTHS AND LEGENDS

The mythology of the donkey or ass contrasts sharply with its image in folklore as a blessed animal.[4] In Egyptian mythology the wild ass or donkey was sacred to the god Set or Seth, the god of chaos, persecutor of the goddess Isis and murderer of her husband, Osiris. To the Egyptians, therefore, the ass typified wildness, cruelty and animal passions. This image of the ass led to it being associated in Roman mythology with the winter festival of Saturnalia, a time of debauchery when the natural order was overturned, and masters changed places with their slaves and served them at table. The festivities were presided over by a Carnival King, chosen by lot from among slaves and criminals, who wore an ass-eared cap as a symbol of his status as Lord of Misrule. Similar customs carried on into medieval Europe when Christmas replaced the pagan Saturnalia. Asses were covered with ceremonial robes and brought into churches to have the services performed before them, accompanied by excessive amounts of eating and drinking. These customs were responsible for establishing the popular association of asses with foolishness. The ass also appears in the Greek legend of King Midas. Famed for his ability to turn anything he touched into gold, his ears were changed into those of an ass as a sign of his ignorance and stupidity. Midas tried to keep this a secret on pain of death, but one of his servants

who saw them was unable to keep from telling someone. In desperation he dug a hole into the earth, whispered his information into it, and covered up the hole again. However, reeds later grew up on the spot and, when blown by the wind, whispered the secret that had been buried with them.

RELATIONS WITH HUMANS

The most likely origin of the donkey or domestic ass is the African Wild Ass (*Equus asinus taeniopus*), which is native to Nubia, Ethiopia and other places east of the Nile. This species was probably domesticated in Egypt by about 3500 BC.[5] It shares many of the characteristics of the donkey, such as the dorsal strip along the ridge of the back, the cross stripe over the shoulder, and the mouse-grey colour. However, there has probably been interbreeding over the years with the Asiatic Wild Ass (*Equus onager*). Asses were first domesticated by African and Middle Eastern traders as useful beasts of burden, both to carry baggage on their backs and to pull small loads and carts.

Despite its status as an iconic image of Irish rural life, the donkey appears to have been little used in Ireland before the eighteenth century.[6] There is no native Irish word for donkey, and the Irish *asal* comes from Latin *assellus* ('little ass'). The earliest certain reference to a donkey or ass is in a medieval Irish legal manuscript that recounts the journey to Ireland of a cardinal from Rome. The cardinal was sent to instruct local clerics during the reign of Domnall Mór Ua Briain, King of Munster, who died in 1194. However, the clerics concerned appear to have rewarded the cardinal for his efforts by stealing his horses, mules and asses! Perhaps one reason for the absence of donkeys in Ireland is that they were also very scarce in Britain, despite having been introduced there before Norman times. As late as the reign of Elizabeth I in the seventeenth century, asses were very scarce and valuable in Britain. It is not clear when donkeys were finally widely introduced into Ireland. However, one of the earliest modern Irish references comes from 1642, when the captors of Maynooth Castle registered their complaint that they got the benefit of only one ass in their loot. An Irish Act of Parliament of 1743 held out the threat of death to anyone killing a mule (among other livestock) for its flesh, skin or carcase; a later 1783 Act imposed a 20-shilling tax on any person travelling with a horse, ass, mule or any other beast of burden.

The main usefulness of the donkey in Ireland was to the small farmer, for transporting seaweed, turf, milk churns and groceries. Donkeys were also sometimes used in pairs for ploughing and for piling hay for haystacks. Throughout the nineteenth and early twentieth centuries the donkey was invaluable in Ireland for these reasons, and it is during this time that it became an iconic symbol of the Irish countryside. The donkey was immortalised in countless paintings and postcards, usually in some romantic scene from the west of Ireland, accompanied by a curly red-haired child with freckles. It may come as a surprise to the modern reader to learn that another major reason why the ass was valued was for its milk. In 1772 John Rutty wrote in 'An Essay towards the Natural History of the County of Dublin' that 'the female ass is of no small use for its milk in populous and distempered cities, though better supplied from places at a distance, where their food is less succulent'. It was widely believed that donkey's milk was a good cure for tuberculosis (or 'consumption' as it was called), whooping cough, gout and the complexion of the skin. The skin of the donkey was also used to make leather for drums, sieves and shoes. The skin of the wild ass was called 'shagreen'. Donkey numbers have plummeted in Ireland in modern times, with the mechanisation of agriculture and the motor car making them redundant. Today the only donkeys likely to be encountered in the Irish countryside are essentially pets, regarded with affection by their owners for their charming appearance and (usually) docile behaviour.

# Goat – Gabhar – *Capra hircus*

*The goat was seen in Irish folklore as an independent-minded and often contrary animal. Nevertheless, the goat was highly valued in poorer areas, as it could thrive and provide meat and milk in conditions where cattle could not. In Classical myths the goat was seen as a symbol of fertility and of the wild spirits of the pastures and forests, such as Pan.*

## FOLK BELIEFS AND CUSTOMS

The most famous use of the goat in Irish folk customs is the crowning of a billy goat as King Puck for the Puck Fair in Killorglin, County Kerry.[1] The three-day fair is held from 10 to 12 August each year and dates back to at least 1613, while there is evidence of a goat being crowned at the fair as far back as the 1700s. A later development from 1841 is that of King Puck being hoisted onto a 'throne' (a high stage) to hold court over the proceedings for the duration of the fair. Various popular stories exist to explain how the fair came about. One story was that English soldiers were plundering the area long ago, but a billy goat collected up all the farm animals and rescued them by leading them away to a mountain for safety. Another explanation was that when the fair was first set up, no animals were brought there except for a solitary billy goat led by an old man. The townspeople were so grateful that they made the goat the symbol of the fair. While it is sometimes suggested that the custom is a survival of ancient paganism, the fair itself dates only from Norman times. The true explanation is that King Puck is probably a medieval custom, used to highlight what is still an important livestock fair. Similar customs existed in other parts of the country. As late as 1940, a Puck Fair was held in Mullinavat, County Kilkenny, on either 2 September or 3 October. Male goats were brought to the fair, decorated with ribbons, and the best one was set up on a cart and paraded through the fair. In Greencastle in County Down a ram was enthroned to preside over an important sheep fair in the town.

Various beliefs existed about the goat in Irish and British folklore.[2] In Ireland it was considered lucky to keep a goat with a herd of cattle to ensure the cows' fertility and to prevent them from calving too early. It was similarly held in England that the stink of a billy goat was good for keeping diseases away from the other animals. In Ireland the goat was widely believed to be able to see the wind and to know when bad weather was coming, making its way to shelter as soon as possible. In the Scottish Highlands the connection of goats with the wind was brought further, in the custom of the Western Isles of hanging a he-goat from a boat's mast to secure a favourable wind. In the Burren in County Clare the goat is known as 'the poor man's cow', not in an insulting way, but as a recognition that the hardy goat could provide meat and milk to poor farming families when all else failed. In County Clare also it was believed that the fairy known as the pooka could sometimes appear to people in the form of a hideous black puck-goat with fiery eyes. Indeed, in some parts of Ireland it was believed that the goat was first introduced into Ireland by the devil.

The goat was involved in some Irish folk cures.[3] A cure for baldness was to fill the bladder of a goat with human urine, and dry it out over the fire. The bladder was then ground down and rubbed into the scalp along with raw onions. Goat milk was thought to give resistance against tuberculosis and to be effective against skin diseases such as eczema. Some proverbs involving the goat include: 'There's no point going to the goat shed if you looking for wool' and 'You can put silk on a goat, and it's still a goat.' The goat was generally believed to be the most mischievous and troublemaking animal of all. This is reflected in the proverb: 'When a goat enters a church, he goes straight up to the altar.' The goat appears in some Irish place names, especially in remote highland areas, indicating that feral goats are probably involved.[4] Examples include Carnagore (*Carn na Gabhar* – cairn of the goats), County Donegal, Carricknagower (*Carraig na Gabhar* – the goat's rock), County Westmeath, and Dromgower (*Droim Gabhair* – goat ridge), County Kerry.

MYTHS AND LEGENDS

Goats appear several times in legends of St Patrick.[5] The *Life of St Patrick* includes a story about three men in County Monaghan who stole one of Patrick's goats. When they went to swear a false oath to the saint denying their guilt, the goat bleated from the gullet of the third man. Patrick replied: 'The goat himself declares the place in which he was eaten.' He then told the man that goats would follow him and his kin wherever they went. A similar story is told about the inhabitants of Skerries in north County Dublin. According to the story, Saint Patrick arrived at the small island off Skerries which still bears his name, accompanied by a goat which provided milk. From this island Patrick would go to the mainland to convert the people, but during one trip the people of Skerries stole his goat and ate it. When Patrick got back to the island and found the goat missing, he flew into a rage and returned to the mainland in two giant strides. He confronted the people of Skerries at Red Island. When they tried to deny having seen the goat, they found they could only bleat. It was only after they confessed their crime that their voices returned.

The goat sometimes appears in Celtic rituals and artwork as a symbol of fertility.[6] Bronze goat figurines with exaggerated horns have been found at Romano-British sites in Dumbartonshire in Scotland and Gwent in Wales. There is also a depiction of a female goat in the *Book of Kells*. Goats have also featured in ritual burials in Iron Age Celtic sites, such as Danebury in Hampshire, where a goat was buried at the bottom of a grain storage pit. At Soissons in France goats were sacrificed along with other domestic animals as part of an elaborate funeral 'cortège' to accompany the dead men, who were obviously of some importance. At West Uley in Gloucester goats and fowl were sacrificed at a Romano-British shrine to Mercury, who is associated with both creatures. In Norse myth, goats drew the chariot of the god Thor. He would skin and eat them each night, but they would come alive again the next morning.

In Classical myth the goat was sacred to Artemis and other hunting goddesses.[7] It was also sacred to Dionysus or Bacchus, the god of wine, who took the form of a goat when fleeing the giant Typhon. In Greek myth Amalthea was a she-goat or nymph who suckled the infant god Zeus. Her horn became the Cornucopia or Horn of Plenty, and her skin became the cover for Zeus' shield, the Aegis (hence the expression 'to be under the aegis' of something). The spirits of the woods called Satyrs were half-man, half-goat, with goat's horns and beards. The most important of these was Pan, the god of pastures, forests, flocks and herds. Pan was seen as lustful and licentious, and was therefore a symbol of fertility. This link between the lustful Pan and goats developed into the Christian image of the devil, as a man with horns and cloven hooves. The goat also became linked with the devil through rabbinical scholars, who called him a goat because goats were considered to be unclean animals.

## Relations with Humans

The goat was first domesticated for its meat, milk and hide around 8000 BC in the Middle East, probably from the bezoar goat (*Capra aegagrus*) that is native to the region.[8] Goats probably reached Britain and Ireland about 3,000–4,000 years ago with the first Neolithic farmers. Goat bones are difficult to distinguish from those of sheep, so it is not possible to say exactly how widely they were kept, but the indications are that goats were not particularly common or important in early Ireland. Neolithic, Bronze Age and Iron Age farmers maintained small numbers, mainly for milk. One reason for this may be that goats are less hardy than sheep in the cold and damp of northern Europe, being much more at home in the hotter, drier Mediterranean. The old Irish Brehon Laws do not have much to say about goats, and give them a value of only two thirds that of a sheep. It seemed to be only the female goat that had any value, on account of its flesh, milk and the kids it produced. The value of the male buck-goat is not mentioned at all. However, two law texts do state that a lord may give both the female goat and the buck-goat to his client in return for services. In return for a female, the client had to supply to the lord with a twelve-inch tub of sweet cheese one year, and a similar tub of butter the next year. In return for a buck-goat, the client had to supply three days' labour at road clearing for the lord. The goat was also valued in early Ireland for its skin, mainly for making shoes. In Celtic Britain goats may have been kept for their horns, as skulls of goats have been found at various British sites with the horns chopped off. The horns would then be boiled in water to remove the bony core, and made into drinking horns and spoons.

Traditionally the goat has been used for a wide variety of products in addition to meat and milk.[9] The hair has been used to make items as diverse as wool, ropes, paint brushes and judges' wigs. In Asia, Cashmere and Angora goats were bred purposely for their fine hair, in order to make the valuable woollen clothing of the same names. Goat fat was used for candles and the horns could be fashioned into musical instruments, handles and bows. The skin was used for containers, parchment, and in Ireland for making bodhráns. In later years in Ireland goat keeping became more widespread, so much so that by the mid-eighteenth century over 200,000 goats were bred for export to Britain. Numbers have reduced a lot since then, but goats are still widely kept as domestic animals in Ireland, mainly for their milk. In the Burren in County Clare young goats or kids were traditionally kept in a small stone hut or *cró* and reared in confinement and darkness, only being let out at night to suckle their mothers. The result of this was that the 'milk kids' had a soft, sweet meat and were a popular Easter dish.

Escaped goats quickly revert to a feral state, and the original populations of wild goats in Ireland date back to the Stone Age.[10] There are around 3,000–5,000 wild or feral goats living in Ireland, scattered into about thirty herds, mainly in the Burren, County Clare, Glendalough and Bray Head in County Wicklow, Fair Head, County Antrim and Killarney, County Kerry. Herds of goats are also found on offshore islands such as Rathlin, County Antrim, and the Great Blasket and Valencia islands in County Kerry. Although most feral goat herds are a mixture of origins, the traditional Old Irish Goat, dating back to the Stone Age, still exists. Generally the Old Irish Goat is black or dark grey and white in colour, with a long coat of harsh hair. It is characterised by its small size, long body, long and dished face (even in males), and small, pricked ears. The horns are set close together and sweep backwards like scimitars. The Old Irish Goat can be described as a 'landrace' breed, meaning that it is especially adapted to local conditions, and is an example of the Northern Breed Group of goats of northwest Europe. The other examples of this Breed Group are very much endangered, making the preservation of the Old Irish Goat of great importance. Efforts are now being made to establish a breeding stock to ensure its survival into the future.

Goats can have both positive and negative effects on the landscape. On the one hand, they can be a pest in commercial forests, browsing on young trees and stripping their bark. On the other hand, exactly the same habits make them valuable in places such as the Burren, where they prevent the spread of hazel and willow scrub from taking over the sensitive grassland areas. Consideration is being given to encouraging local farmers to use wild goats for this purpose, with the dual benefit of maintaining biodiversity in an important ecosystem, and of preserving an important part of our fauna. On the whole, wild goats are considered to be a positive part of the Irish landscape and worthy of conservation.

# Sheep – Caora – *Ovis aries*

*T*he sheep was valued in Ireland for its meat and especially for its wool, which could be used for clothing, blankets, bedding and other materials. In Celtic myth the ram was a symbol of strength and virility; while in Christian symbolism the lamb represented Christ in his role of saviour and shepherd.

## Folk Beliefs and Customs

In Ireland various folk beliefs existed about sheep.[1] It was considered bad luck to meet a flock of sheep coming towards you early in the morning, but good luck to see a flock some distance behind on the road in the evening. It was also believed that if the first lamb of the season was black, the people of the house would be wearing mourning clothes that year. On the other hand, it was very lucky to meet a white lamb first thing in the morning, especially if the sun was shining on its face. Along the west coast of Ireland it was believed that the best knitting was done after dark, because then the sheep were asleep. When an Irish shepherd died, the custom among his next of

kin was to place a fistful of sheep's wool in his coffin. This was to excuse him for all the times he missed Sunday Mass on the days he was minding his flock. A ram was the centre of a large fair held in Greencastle in County Down until the end of the nineteenth century, in a similar manner to the present-day Puck Fair in Killorglin, County Kerry. Known as the Ram Fair, it was held annually from the 12–14 August from 1611. The chosen ram – the 'King of the Bens' – was enthroned high on the walls of the old castle to preside over the gathering.

The sheep was also involved in some Irish folk cures.[2] Acquiring the blade bone of a sheep was supposed to give its owner the power to heal. This was done by going out at night, killing and dressing the sheep, and then picking the right shoulder bone as clean as possible. The person then slept with the bone under their pillow, which was supposed to talk to them while they slept, giving them the knowledge of any cure. The blade bone of a sheep was also used in love divination in Ireland. This involved finding a weather-bleached bone and keeping it until the next full moon. At midnight the bone was then stabbed with a knife, while saying: 'It is not this bone meant to stick, but my true love's heart I mean to prick, wishing him neither rest nor sleep, until he comes to me to speak.' In Ireland and Britain it was believed that the smell of sheep would cure consumption (tuberculosis) and fever. In Ireland it was also thought that a house whose occupants had died from fever could be reoccupied safely if a certain number of sheep were driven in there to sleep for three nights.

MYTHS AND LEGENDS

Sheep appear in some stories of the lives of Irish saints.[3] A legend about the feast of Michaelmas on 29 September relates how St Patrick prayed to Michael the Archangel to restore the life of the son of Laoghaire, the King of Ireland in the fifth century. When Patrick's prayers were successful, his mother decreed that a sheep should be killed and given to the poor on the feast of Michael in gratitude. In fact, the custom of killing an animal and giving portions of meat to the poor at Michaelmas remained a widespread custom in Ireland until modern times. When St Brendan was baptised, three purple wethers (castrated rams) miraculously leapt out of a nearby well as the fee. When St Kevin was a boy minding a flock of sheep, some poor men came to him looking for alms. Kevin was touched by their poverty

Cat – Cat – *Felis domesticus*

Pine Marten – Cat Crainn – *Martes martes*

Hare – Giorria – *Lepus*

Rat – Francach – *Rattus*

Bat – Ialtóg – *Chiroptera*

Mouse – Luch – *Mus*/*Apodemus*

and gave them four sheep in the name of God. However, when evening came and Kevin's flock was counted, it was discovered that the number had miraculously not decreased.

Sheep are also mentioned in various Irish legends.[4] According to the early Irish text the *Book of Invasions*, the first sheep were brought to Ireland by Cessair, the daughter of Noah. The goddess Brigid owned a great wether called Cirba, which was king of all the Irish wethers. The Irish god of the sea, Manannán, had seven sheep in his home in the Land of Promise that could produce enough wool to clothe all the men of the world; in one story, Caoilte, a hero of the Fianna, received a present of a crimson cloak made from their wool. In another tale, a bald warrior of the Fianna called Conan was stripped of the skin on his back while escaping from a seat where he had been held by magic. However, he was healed of his wounds by having a sheepskin fitted onto his back. The sheepskin remained on his back for the rest of his life, and grew wool every year. This is more than could be said of Conan's head, which remained as bald as ever!

Sheep feature in a curious legend about Lochrea (Loch Riach) in County Galway.[5] The *Rennes Dinnshenchus* (a manuscript on the lore of place names) tells how the lake there was famous for its ability to turn scarlet every seven years, the reason being that it had been the site of a great battle between different fairy forces. So great was the slaughter that the lake erupted out of the ground to quell the bloodshed, returning to its original scarlet colour every seventh year. Another manuscript on place names, the *Metrical Dindshenchus*, also features the tale, and recounts how it became the custom to dye scarlet the wool of Ireland's sheep in the lake as a result:

LOCH RIACH

Each sheep in Erin was dipped in the water
Every seven years by ancient decree
Entering it, no sheep were whiter
Leaving it, all with a scarlet fleece.

So the Sheep's Thorn standing near
Marking the spot with colour bright
And the Fair Ford of the Sheep
From this custom are named alike.

There is some evidence from Celtic Europe that sheep were buried along with other domestic animals as a ritual sacrifice to accompany the remains of a prominent person.[6] In Soissons in France two elaborate burials have the dead men, obviously prestigious Celtic noblemen or warriors, accompanied by a chariot and horses, and also cattle, pigs, sheep and other livestock. The overall evidence nevertheless is that sheep were of lesser significance in Celtic ritual burials than other animals, despite (or perhaps because) of their economic importance. However, there is evidence from remains found at Celtic sites that succulent lambs, along with young pigs, were a favourite food for the ritual feast at funerals.

Sheep feature in an extraordinary symbol favoured by the Celts, namely the ram-horned serpent, or snake with the head and horns of a ram.[7] The idea appears to have been to create a powerful image from the combination of the snake, a symbol of regeneration and the earth, with the force and virility of the horned ram. The ram-horned serpent usually appears along with Cernunnos, the antlered god who represents nature, fertility and abundance. The horned snake appears three times along with Cernunnos and other animals on the famous Gundestrup cauldron from Denmark. At Sommerécourt in France a stone sculpture depicts Cernunnos encircled by a pair of horned snakes that feed from a bowl of food on his lap. At a site in Gloucester in England the horned snakes appear to merge with Cernunnos' own body as they reach up to feed from fruit or corn around his ears. The ram-horned serpent occasionally also appears alongside the Celtic Mars and the Celtic Mercury, probably in their role as promoters of healing and fertility.

In Classical myth the ram was sacred to Zeus as a symbol of its virility, and to Dionysus, the god of wine, for its regenerative powers.[8] In Greek myth the Golden Fleece hung on an oak tree in a grove sacred to Ares, the god of war, and was guarded by a dragon. It was captured by the hero Jason and his band of sailors, the Argonauts, after many adventures. In Christian symbolism the lamb represented Christ himself, the 'Lamb of God', on account of its innocence and unblemished nature. Also at the Jewish feast of Passover the Paschal lamb was sacrificed, and this became a symbol of Christ dying for the world, and of his role as the Good Shepherd.

Relations with Humans

Sheep were first domesticated in the Middle East about 8000 BC, probably from the Asiatic Mouflon (*Ovis orientalis*).[9] Sheep were first kept for their flesh until breeds were created that could produce wool, adding enormously to their value. Neolithic farmers brought sheep to Britain and Ireland about 3,000–4,000 years ago, and the first sheep to arrive here probably resembled the rugged Soay sheep found today on St Kilda in the Outer Hebrides. These sheep looked more like goats than modern sheep, being brown with white underparts, slender and agile, and with both sexes having horns. Similar sheep were kept by Iron Age Celts across Europe, and in fact the Celts were noted for their skill at raising livestock. The Greek geographer Strabo wrote that: 'They have such enormous flocks of sheep … that they afford a plenteous supply of *sagi* [woollen coats], not only to Rome, but to most parts of Italy.' Apart from the thick coats, 'which they call *laenae*', Strabo also commented on the fame of Gaulish and British woollen blankets, so much so that a heavy tax was placed by Rome on the *birrus britannicus*, a kind of duffel coat. The Celts kept sheep primarily for their wool, and only slaughtered the older animals for meat towards the end of their life. In early Ireland a similar situation existed, as the Brehon Laws make clear that sheep were valued far more for their wool and skins than for their meat. Most Irish sheep at this stage were black or dun coloured, and sheep with white fleeces appear to have been relatively uncommon. Gerald of Wales, writing after the Norman Conquest, still described Irish sheep as dark coloured. Because of their more attractive appearance and suitability of wool for dyeing, white sheep are recorded in the Laws as being two or three times more valuable than their darker counterparts. Another valued trait of wool was that it should be long and straight rather than tufted or curly, and so easier to shear.

Apart from providing wool from which to weave garments, the sheep had other uses in early Ireland, most of which are still familiar today. Sheepskins with the wool left on could be made into warm outer clothing, rugs and bed covers. Sheep milk could be used to make cheese, although it was regarded as inferior to goat's milk. Nevertheless, sheep milk was important enough to give its name to the Irish festival of Imbolc, on 1 February, which celebrated the spring lactation of ewes. Mutton was also consumed at times, especially for wedding feasts when it was the custom to kill wethers. A more unusual custom was to use rams' horns for making combs. The horn was straightened after being boiled or heated over the fire, and then cut into shape by the comb-maker. It is possible that four-horned breeds of sheep, such as the Manx Loaghtyn were bred especially to provide greater amounts of horn for this purpose.

The evidence from Brehon Law texts is that sheep farming in early Ireland was different from today, with sheep kept mainly on greens and plains rather than on high ground and mountains.[10] It seems as well that the job of the shepherd was to lead the flock and not drive the flock as is done today. In addition, the main role of dogs in those days was to protect the sheep from wolves and other predators, rather than to round them up. An important additional role for sheep in early Ireland was that they were used as currency. In the same way as cattle, but for smaller amounts, sheep were used for fines and other payments. For example, the fine due to a noble for a small facial wound was a milking cow, while a small landowner was only entitled to one sheep in prime condition. At the lowest social ranking, the apprentice with a master was owed two fleeces for the same offence, while the apprentice with no master was owed just one. In general, female sheep, or ewes, were considered more valuable than male sheep (rams or wethers), usually by about one third. This was because of the ewe's ability to provide milk and lambs. The role of women in processing wool and cloth also meant that the Brehon Laws regarded sheep as more closely associated with women than men. If a woman wanted to claim a legal right to land, she had to enter the land accompanied by ewes, whereas a man in the same situation had to be accompanied by horses.

In modern times, the only native breed of sheep is the Galway sheep, a long-wool breed, which was first recognised in 1922, when the Galway Sheep Breeders Society was formed.[11] From a figure of 350,000 breeding ewes in 1962, the numbers of Galway sheep declined enormously, until by 1992 just 300 breeding ewes remained. The situation has improved somewhat since, with a flock being managed on the Aran Islands, but the future of the breed remains critical. The most common breeds of sheep in Ireland today are the Blackface, Suffolk, Texel, Île de France, Rouge de l'Ouest and Charollais. The main value of keeping sheep in Ireland today is for their meat, as the Irish wool industry has been in steep decline. This is due to the collapse of the Irish textile industry, with cheaper foreign clothing from developing countries and wool from New Zealand. However, the outlook may not be totally bleak, as Irish wool may find a new role as an insulating material for houses. As sheep farming is so integral a part of the Irish countryside, it seems likely to find some way to adapt to changing market conditions and so survive into the future.

# Badger – Broc – *Meles meles*

*The badger has an ambiguous status in Irish folklore, as it is regarded as a clever and industrious animal, but is also disliked for spreading tuberculosis in cattle. In early Ireland the badger was considered valuable enough to be hunted for its skin and meat.*

## Folk Beliefs and Customs

The badger was considered a clever and hard-working animal in Irish folklore.[1] Indeed, it was believed to be able to save hay for farmers overnight if it chose to do so. The badger was also said to be clever enough never to take poison, and to relish eating the roots of the wild plant tormentil (*Potentilla erecta*). Another widely held belief was that badgers were the descendants of pigs that the Vikings had brought to Ireland. Badgers were also regularly eaten by poorer people in Ireland. The flesh of the 'pig badger' was said to be particularly flavoursome if eaten with cabbage. It was thought to be especially good for women who had recently given birth, and who needed to restore their strength.

Some curious examples of 'folk zoology' have gathered around the badger.[2] A common belief was that there were two kinds of badger: dog badgers and pig badgers. Dog badgers were carnivores, eating carrion and even digging into graves. Pig badgers were strictly vegetarian, and so were safe for humans to eat. For some reason the badger was also thought not to have a backbone. Another widespread belief was that the badger had a special method of travelling fast if it was in a hurry. It did this by tucking its snout into a special pocket under its tail, curling up into a ball, and rolling down hills or slopes. Gerald of Wales, writing about Ireland in the twelfth century, reported that badgers had a curious method of removing the dirt from their setts. One badger was said to lie on its back, pile the loosened soil onto its belly, and then hold a length of wood in its mouth. Other badgers then gripped the piece of wood and pulled it backwards, dragging the first badger and all the earth out of the hole. Unfortunately, none of these colourful stories has any basis in fact.

A curious folk tale from County Clare concerns a child born out of wedlock to cowherds, and then raised by a badger.[3] According to the tale, the parents left the child in a badger burrow, hoping the badgers would eat him. Instead one of the badgers adopted the child as her own, and brought him to her den where she suckled him. The child stayed there until he was a few years old and found by a local man. The child acquired the nickname *Gárlach Coileánach* ('the foundling whelp') and grew up to be very glib-tongued and crabby.

## Myths and Legends

Badgers feature in some stories about Irish saints, for example, appearing in a helpful role in a story about St Kieran.[4] According to the story, the saint lived happily in the woods surrounded by the wild animals. One day, however, a fox stole one of his sandals. But before the fox had gone too far, a badger raced after him, grabbed the thief by the ear, and obliged him to return to face Kieran. A considerably less pleasant badger features in a story concerning St MacCreahy of Clare. According to the story, a *broc sidh* or 'demon badger' living in a cave near Inchiquin was terrorising the area, killing both men and cattle. It had resisted the prayers of six local saints, but MacCreahy was able to chain up the creature and throw it into a local lake.

The badger also features in some early Irish tales.[5] The exiled king *Suibhne Geilt*, or Mad Sweeney, who lived as an outcast in the woods, described the sweet sound of badgers squealing as a delight. The eighth-century text *Cormac's Glossary* relates a story concerning badgers and the Munster king Tadhg Mac Céin. The story explains the term *gaileng*, meaning 'paltry valour' or 'dung valour', by relating how Tadhg's son Cormac prepared a feast for his father of every kind of animal. As he did not have any badger meat, Cormac went to a badger sett and persuaded the badgers to come out on the word of his father's honour. However, when the badgers emerged from their sett, he killed a hundred of them and displayed them at the feast. On hearing of his son's ignoble deed, Tadhg flew into a rage and banished him, naming him *gaileng*. The name Tadhg itself means 'badger' and the king appears to have had a special relationship with badgers, including it being taboo for him to eat their flesh.

## Relations with Humans

Badgers were often used by the Celts for their skins, as evidenced in the burial in Hochdorf in Germany of a Celtic chieftain on a bronze couch covered with a bed of horsehair, wool and badgerskin. Badger bones have also been found among the remains of animals skinned for their fur at Celtic sites in Villeneuve-Saint-Germain in France and Danebury in England. There is evidence, too, that the badger was hunted and eaten in early Ireland. One legal text refers to badger as one of the three game animals, along with deer and wild pig, and an early Irish poem refers to *sail bruicc a Bérre* – 'the salted badger meat (or fat) from Bérre'. In one tale of the Fianna, the hero Caoilte refers to hunting 'heavy-sided, low-bellied badgers'. The *Book of Leinster* states that badger bacon is fit for the table of kings. In the tale *The Exile of the Sons of Uisneach* Deirdre mentions eating badgers at her home in Scotland: 'fish and venison and badger fat / this was my fare in Gleann Laoidh'. The early Irish Brehon Laws also refer to badgers in the unlikely event of one being kept as a pet, where it is classed with the pig in terms of the legal penalties. The habit of the badger in rooting and digging into the soil in search of food is probably the reason for this stance, as the Brehon Laws deal with the penalties that apply for damage caused by rooting pigs.

The badger is native to Ireland and a protected species, but it can be culled under licence to remove the threat of tuberculosis (TB) spreading to cattle. It is estimated that about 20–25 per cent of badgers in Ireland are infected with TB, and that somewhere between 10–20 per cent of cases of TB in cattle come from cross-infection from badgers. A future vaccination programme for badgers, similar to the European vaccination programme for rabies in foxes, represents a more effective long-term strategy than culling. It can also be said that badgers are actually beneficial to farmers, as they eat many farming pests, such as slugs, snails, beetles, leatherjackets, rats, mice and young rabbits. Another threat that badgers face is that, despite their protected status, there is evidence that the illegal and cruel practice of badger baiting still takes place in Ireland. A nationwide survey of badger setts found that between 15–22 per cent showed evidence of either digging or blocked entrances, indicating badger baiting. Therefore, although the status of the badger in Ireland is secure, these issues mean that its relationship with man will continue to face difficulties for the foreseeable future.[6]

# Hedgehog – Gráinneog – *Erinaceus europaeus*

*The hedgehog is a distinctive sight in the Irish countryside, with its coat of spines and long sensitive snout. It was often persecuted out of a false belief that it sucked the milk out of cows' udders, but is in fact a useful animal for farmers, as it eats many agricultural pests.*

## FOLK BELIEFS AND CUSTOMS

Various beliefs existed about the hedgehog in Irish folklore.[1] One that was widespread was that hedgehogs sucked the milk from cows as they lay down in the field at night, especially on May Eve, so that many hedgehogs were often cruelly killed. Hedgehogs were also wrongly thought to suck the contents of hens' eggs in the nest. Another trait of the hedgehog was to predict the weather in springtime, when it emerged from hibernation. If bad weather was set to continue, it returned to its hiding place to sleep, but if it stayed out it meant that better weather was coming. It was taken as a particularly good sign if a hedgehog was seen around St Brigid's Day on 1 February, as this meant milder spring weather was on the way. Later in the year, hedgehogs were thought to enter orchards to steal the apples lying on the ground, by sticking them onto their spikes and making off. The hedgehog was also believed to have helped Christ after his forty-day fast by rolling on the ground and collecting apples for him.

The hedgehog is part of a curious Irish folk cure for aches and pains, which involved frying an unfortunate specimen and rubbing its grease onto the affected area. This was probably an example of sympathetic magic, where an animal with prickly spines was thought to be effective at combating the pricks of pain from arthritis and similar complaints. An Irish proverb to describe something that cannot be found or does not exist was *cnuasach na gráineoige* – 'the hedgehog's store'. The hedgehog appears in a few place names in Ireland, such as Inchagreenoge (*Inis na Gráineoige* – water meadow of the hedgehog), County Limerick, Garrynagranoge (*Garraí na Gráineoige* – garden of the hedgehog), County Cork, and Meenagranoge (*Mín na Gráineoige* – level field of the hedgehog), County Donegal.[2]

130

## MYTHS AND LEGENDS

Classical writers held some ideas about hedgehogs that have clearly influenced later folk beliefs.[3] The Roman writer Plutarch said that hedgehogs collected fruit, particularly grapes, by rolling on them and taking them home on their spines. The hedgehog was also said to be able to survive a fall from a great height by absorbing the shock in its spines. The Roman naturalist Pliny said that hedgehogs could foretell a change of wind, and shift the entrance to their nests to face away from it. This last notion is still a part of folk belief in England today.

## RELATIONS WITH HUMANS

There are no early fossil records for hedgehogs in Ireland, and Gerald of Wales, writing in the twelfth century, declared that there were no hedgehogs in Ireland at that time.[4] It has since been assumed that they were introduced into Ireland by the Normans for food. This explanation has problems on several counts. The first is that the hedgehog has its own native name in Irish – *gráinneog* ('ugly little one'). If the Normans had introduced the hedgehog to Ireland, the Irish name would most likely have been borrowed from the French *hérisson* or Latin *Erinaceus* – just as the Irish name for rabbit *coinín* derives from the Latin *cuniculus*, reflecting the rabbit's Norman origins. Could the hedgehog have been brought in by the Vikings a bit earlier? Again the Danish *pindsvin* or Norwegian *pinsvin* ('pinswine') are very different from the Irish word. Closer to home, however, the Welsh word *draenog* ('thorny little one') has an obvious similarity. Incorporated into Irish and following its rules of pronunciation, '*an dhraenog*' could easily have been changed to the more understandable '*an ghráinneog*'. This makes a Welsh origin more plausible. There were known historical links between Ireland and Wales in the early medieval period. The south Welsh kingdom of Dyfed (modern-day Pembrokeshire) was settled by the Irish in the early centuries AD, and retained its Irish character until the tenth century. It would therefore have been easy for the hedgehog to be brought over to Ireland from south Wales in pre-Normans times.

The second problem is the motive for introducing the hedgehog. The hedgehog has only ever been eaten as food by those on the margins of society, such as gypsies or the very poor, as there is a lot of effort involved in cooking a hedgehog for little reward. The most usual way of cooking hedgehog was to encase the dead animal in clay and roast it in the fire. The spines stuck to the hardened clay coating, which could then be removed before eating the flesh. It is hard to see the Normans (or indeed the Vikings) bothering much with such a procedure. In modern times the only people in Ireland said to eat hedgehogs this way were Travellers. A more compelling reason for regarding hedgehogs as useful animals is pest control. Hedgehogs are avid eaters of slugs, snails and various garden pests. They are also effective in controlling rats and mice in barns and outbuildings, seeking out their nests and happily consuming the young inside. Throughout Europe hedgehogs have traditionally been regarded as useful animals by farmers, and there is evidence that hedgehogs were introduced into many parts of

Europe for this purpose. This process continued in modern times with their introduction into the Hebrides in the 1970s (with disastrous consequences for the local birdlife, as hedgehogs are also fond of eggs). Even today, advocates of wildlife gardening recommend making gardens attractive to hedgehogs for their help in keeping pests down. A much more plausible explanation, therefore, is that the hedgehog was brought to Ireland from Wales by farmers and gardeners as a form of pest control. Given that most gardening at that time was done in the *lubgort*, or enclosed herb and vegetable garden attached to a monastery, it is probable that the hedgehog was brought to Ireland from Wales by an early Irish monk anxious to keep the slugs off his cabbages.

It may also be possible to reconcile this account with the statement by Gerald of Wales that Ireland had no hedgehogs. It could be that the hedgehog remained confined to the southeast of the country for a century or two before it spread throughout Ireland, so it is possible that Gerald's source was not aware of its arrival. This is not so far-fetched when it is considered that the faster and more agile grey squirrel has still not colonised all of Ireland, although it arrived here a century ago. The theory of an introduction into the southeast of Ireland from south Wales shortly before the Norman arrival is consistent with the fact that the earliest record of a hedgehog in Ireland is in Waterford City in the thirteenth century. But whatever way the hedgehog arrived in Ireland, and for whatever reason, it is a now a much loved and integral part of the Irish fauna.

# Rabbit – Coinín – *Oryctolagus cuniculus*

*The rabbit was valued in Ireland in earlier centuries as an important source of food and fur. In modern times, however, it has fallen out of favour as a pest of agriculture and forestry. In folklore the rabbit was regarded as a fairy animal, and sometimes the souls of the dead were believed to appear in fairy form as rabbits.*

## FOLK BELIEFS AND CUSTOMS

In Ireland various superstitions surrounded the rabbit.[1] It was believed that the souls of the dead often appeared in the form of a rabbit, particularly white ones. In County Donegal it was also thought that the fairies went about in the form of rabbits, and those trapping them would make sure to have their pipes lit or 'reddened' as a protection. A fairy woman called Clíona was often said to appear in the form of a white rabbit around a large rock associated with her near Mallow in County Cork. It was also held to be unlucky if a fisherman saw a lone rabbit while on the way to his fishing. Similar beliefs were held in Scotland where it was considered unlucky to have rabbit or hare skin anywhere in the boat. In England it was a widespread custom for people to say 'rabbits, rabbits' when they met someone on the first day of the month. The probable origin of this custom, which was thought to bring good luck, is in a corruption of the Latin *orabitus* or 'let us pray', a religious phrase widely used in England before the Reformation. The well-known custom of keeping a rabbit or hare's foot as a lucky charm, and as a cure for various ills, is one that goes back to Roman times.

An Irish proverb about the rabbit highlights its skill at finding food: 'The rabbit gets fat on what the hare misses.' Rabbits appear in many place names in Ireland, reflecting the widespread existence of rabbit warrens.[2] Examples include Kylenagonneney (*Coill na coiníní* – wood of the rabbits), County Limerick, Warrenpoint, County Down, Coneyburrow, County Kildare and Coniker (*Coinicéir* – warren), County Laois.

### RELATIONS WITH HUMANS

Rabbits were probably first domesticated in Spain about 2000 BC, and when the Phoenicians reached Spain a thousand years later they called it *shofan* (meaning hyrax – a marmot-like animal from North Africa).[3] *Shofan* is the origin of the word 'coney' (the Irish word *coinín* derives from Middle English *cunin* or *conyng*). Coney was in fact the original word for rabbit, while 'rabbit' only referred to the young. The Romans kept rabbits in walled gardens, along with hares and dormice, for food and fur. Inevitably the rabbits escaped to populate the surrounding countryside throughout Europe. Later the Normans introduced the rabbit to Britain, using a similar system of rabbit gardens called 'coney garths', 'coneyries' or warrens. The purpose of this system was to keep predators out and be able to supply the rabbits with extra food. The 'coney garth' consisted of a small enclosed field surrounded by a deep ditch, and a high turf mound planted with gorse and blackberry to keep the rabbits in. Escape was easy, however, and the rabbit soon became free game for yeoman and serfs, even though it was illegal. In England the surnames Warren and Warrener originate from those who were employed to keep the rabbits.

When the Normans reached Ireland they also introduced rabbits, and kept them in a similar way for food and fur. The earliest references to rabbits in Britain or Ireland are to warrens on Lambey Island in County Dublin in 1191 and in Connaught in 1204. There are also Norman records of 'coney-warrens' in Ballysax, County Kildare, in 1282 and around the same period in Ardmayle, County Tipperary, and Rosslare, County Wexford. In 1333 the rental of the Manor of Lisronagh valued the rabbit warrens on the estate at ten shillings. The warrens were expected to provide an annual crop of twenty-four rabbits at one penny each. Islands were a favourite location to establish warrens, and today offshore islands with rabbit populations include the Blaskets, the Saltees, Aran, Inishboffin, Inishturk, Clare Island and Rathlin Island. As in Britain, rabbits became established in the Irish countryside soon after their introduction and became locally numerous over the next 200 years.

Rabbits were only properly domesticated by medieval French monks due to the belief that newborn litters of rabbits were allowed as food during Lent. This led to selective breeding and the emergence of tame varieties of rabbits which could be kept as pets. This breeding also led to the appearance of black, white and piebald rabbits by the sixteenth century. The earliest picture of a white rabbit dates from 1530 and hangs in the Louvre in Paris – the 'Madonna with a Rabbit' by Titian. By the seventeenth century in England domestic rabbit breeding was in full swing, and the silver-grey colour pelt was particularly prized for lining cloaks, hoods and bed covers. Elizabeth I decreed that no one whose income was less than £100 a year could wear the fur of 'conies'. All parts of the rabbit were used for various purposes, and gardeners today still use rabbit tails fixed to canes to pollinate plants, while the glue from rabbit skins was used to fix book bindings, tapestry and embroidery pictures, and to mend violins. Rabbits' feet are also sometimes used to apply cosmetics, and rabbits' paws were widely sold as charms. In Lincoln in England the fur of angora rabbits was used in the hat-making industry to make felt hats. Domestic and wild rabbits became an important export industry in Ireland in the seventeenth and eighteenth centuries, with over two million skins processed annually. In addition, rabbit meat was also exported, and in the 1870s most of the rabbit meat in the Manchester market came from Ireland. The use of rabbits for food greatly declined in Britain and Ireland thereafter, and by the second half of the twentieth century appeared to have died out. Perhaps this was thanks to improved standards of living, leading to a better diet and a perception of rabbit as a 'poor man's food'.

The Romans bred their rabbits to have high reproductive rates, and this has led to rabbits generally being considered a pest in the countries to which they have since spread.[4] Rabbits can indeed become invasive and over-abundant in a particular area, and can cause considerable damage to crops and young forest plantations wherever they spread. In more recent times rabbit populations throughout Europe and Ireland have been devastated by the introduction of the disease myxomatosis. This virus, which originated in South Africa and is spread by the rabbit flea, was released illegally by farmers to control rabbits in Ireland in the early 1950s – the earliest case being recorded in County Carlow in 1954. When it first arrived it killed 99 per cent of all rabbits, but since then the co-evolution of the rabbit with the virus has led to less virulent strains of the virus and to more resistant rabbits. Another viral disease, rabbit viral haemorrhagic disease, has also spread through Europe in more recent times, with a similarly devastating effect on wild rabbit populations. It was first detected in domestic rabbits in Ireland in 1996 and may be expected to reach Irish wild rabbit populations in the near future. Despite these challenges, and the numerous predators it faces, there is little danger that the rabbit will become scarce in the Irish countryside.

*Airy Animals*

# Cat — Cat — *Felis domesticus*

---

*T*he cat has always had an ambiguous reputation in myth and folklore. On the one hand it is the playful and useful companion of man, and so widely thought of with affection and respect; but on the other hand its cool, independent nature, ruthless skill at hunting, and links to night time and the dark have often caused it to be regarded with suspicion, and even persecuted as an animal of witchcraft and magic.

## FOLK BELIEFS AND CUSTOMS

The cat is surrounded by many superstitions in Ireland.[1] A traditional Irish greeting on entering a house was 'God save all here, except the cat', on account of its association with the devil. Despite this it was also believed to be lucky for a stray cat to come into the house. Many of the superstitions concern the cat's supposed 'sixth sense'. In County Clare it was thought that to be looked at fixedly by a cat after it had washed its face was a sign of approaching marriage. On the other hand, to be looked at fixedly by a cat for no apparent reason was an omen of sickness or death. To dream of a cat foretold an enemy; to dream of a dog, a friend. In Ireland generally a purring cat or a cat with its back to the fire was a sign of rain, while in County Donegal it was believed that a cat washing its face by the fire foretold bad weather. Another Irish belief was that it was an omen of bad luck if a cat caught a mouse and allowed it to escape for no reason. In County Cork it was considered bad luck to bring the cat along when moving house, but if the cat found its own way to the new house that was fine. In Limerick it was thought that putting a cat under a pot brought bad weather, and it was apparently a common practice among sailors' wives in order to keep their men at home!

Black cats are considered the most powerful in terms of magic and superstition.[2] They are lucky in Britain, especially for a bride on the way to her wedding. In the United States, Belgium and Spain, on the other hand, it is considered unlucky to meet a black cat. In Ireland it was considered lucky to have a black cat cross your path on New Year's Eve; and if a black cat came into the house on Christmas night the inhabitants would have great luck for the coming year. In Ireland black cats were also believed to provide cures for some ailments, but this usually meant the unfortunate cat being harmed in the process. For example, it was believed that blood from a black cat was a cure for the skin disease called erysipelas or 'wildfire'. Also, a cure for burns was to rub the affected area with the singed fur of a black cat. Most unfortunate of all, however, was a black cat with white paws. The powdered liver of such a cat was believed to be effective as a love potion when administered to the intended person. Less fatally, nine hairs of a black cat chopped up, soaked in water and then swallowed could relieve whooping cough. In Cornwall it was believed that a stye in the eye could be cured by stroking it nine times with the tip of a black cat's tail.

The Irish also held a number of curious beliefs about the nature of cats.[3] Perhaps the strangest is that cats were believed to have once been serpents. They were thought to still have a serpent's tooth, which could poison a person if they were scratched or bitten by a cat. It may be that this belief gave rise to the appearance in Irish folk tales of cats guarding gold and fairy treasure, in a similar way to serpents in European folkore. There was also a widespread belief among country people in Ireland in the existence of 'wildcats'. There are no genuine wildcats (*Felis silvestris*) in Ireland, at least since historic times, so it appears that feral domestic cats or pine martens are what were meant. Wildcats were nevertheless thought to be different from ordinary cats, not least because of the venomous claw supposedly at the end of their tails. One story from Connemara tells of a man collecting seaweed who was attacked by a wildcat. The man's two dogs killed the wildcat, but when he inspected the huge cat he saw that it had a large, bright, crook-like claw in its tail. It was also believed that 'wildcats' gathered at night to discuss their affairs, and to plot various schemes which they would use against humans.

Many folk tales about cats emphasise that they have a wild, untrustworthy nature, even the seemingly fully domesticated pets.[4] A very popular story concerns the death of the king of the cats. The story goes that a man out travelling met a huge cat which attacked him, and which with difficulty he managed to slay. As it lay dying, the cat told him that it was the king of the cats. On his return home, the man told his wife how he had killed the king of the cats. Hearing this, the couple's domestic cat, which had been sleeping by the fire, leaped up and attacked the man, sinking his claws into his throat and killing him (although in some versions the man manages to fight the cat off). In another story from County Donegal, a woman was sitting one night by herself by the fire when a crowd of cats entered the house. She could tell from their appearance that one was the king, one the queen, and the rest of them their kittens. They came up to the woman menacingly, and she was sure they were going to eat her. In desperation she threw a churn of milk on the floor. This diverted the cats and they began to drink it. When they had finished, the king cat put his tail around the others and ushered them out, leaving the woman relieved at her narrow escape.

So fearful was the image of the cat that some stories tell approvingly of them being killed even if they appear to have done no harm. One such story is of the cat who asked for a pair of shoes. According to the story an old man called Wat decided that he would go into town to buy shoes for his children. His cat asked: 'What about me, Wat?' The old man promised he would get the cat shoes after he had got some for his children. Wat took

the cat in a bag and headed into town. However, he had arranged to meet a man with hounds on the way. The cat heard the sound of the dogs and asked Wat to keep her safe from them. Wat promised he would, but instead he threw the bag with the cat in it to the hounds and they began to chase her. As she ran for her life, the cat called back: 'Ah, 'tis well for you, Wat. If I caught you I would choke you.' The cat's remark is hardly surprising given Wat's treachery, but presumably a talking cat was such an abomination, even in a folk tale, that it had to be destroyed.

Cats appear in quite a few Irish proverbs.[5] Some examples are: *Is ar a shon féin a dhéanann an cat crónán* – 'It's for her own good that the cat purrs'; 'An old cat will not burn herself'; and 'Three fortunes of the cat: the housewife's forgetfulness, walking without a sound, and keen sight in darkness'. Another well-known proverb is: *Briseann an dúchas thrí súilibh an chait* – 'nature breaks out through the eyes of the cat'. The proverb is illustrated by an Irish tale about a man who had his cat so well trained that it could hold a candle for him while he read. A visiting poor scholar bet the man that he could make the cat drop the candle. Accordingly, he released a mouse that ran across the table in front of the cat. The cat's eyes were riveted on the mouse, but it continued to hold the candle. The scholar released another mouse, and this time the cat could control itself no longer. Flinging aside the candle it gave chase. The moral of both the tale and the proverb is that nothing can conceal its true nature completely.

The most famous Irish proverb about cats describes those who love quarrelling to the bitter end as 'fighting like Kilkenny Cats'.[6] According to popular legend, the name arose when Hessian soldiers were quartered in Kilkenny during the 1798 rebellion. They amused themselves by tying two cats together by their tails and throwing them over a line to fight. Their commanding officers disapproved of this practice and banned it, but it continued in secret. One day as a fight was in progress, the soldiers heard an officer approaching. One of the soldiers took out his sword and cut down the cats, leaving only their tails. The officer enquired as to where the cats had gone. The soldier replied that they had devoured each other, so furious was their fighting, and that only their tails remained! The true origin of the proverb, however, most likely lies in Kilkenny history. A peculiarity of Kilkenny's development is that it was run by two corporations and not one. One corporation controlled Englishtown, and the civic life of the city. The other controlled Irishtown, and was ruled by the Bishop of

Ossory. Naturally, two authorities in such close proximity were continually at loggerheads, and became notorious for fighting with each other over every tiny difference of opinion – hence 'fighting like Kilkenny Cats'. The disputes were ended only when the two corporations were incorporated into one body in 1844.

There are also many legends of cats in other countries.[7] In Brittany a silver or 'money' cat (*chat d'argent*) could serve nine masters and make them all rich. In the Isle of Man a traditional story explains how the Manx cat lost its tail. According to the story, invaders to the island cut off the tails of the island's cats to decorate their helmets. Manx mother cats became anxious to protect their kittens from harm, and so bit off their tails at birth, until eventually the kittens were born tailless. In Scotland there were many stories of the ferocious Fairy Cat. Jet black in colour except for a white star on its chest, the Fairy Cat was as large as a dog, had enormous fangs, and was surrounded by sparks wherever it went. In Scotland it was also believed that a storm could be averted by throwing the cat out of the house. This was because it would attract any bolts of lightning present, due to the evil spirits it contained. A widely held belief throughout Europe was that witches were able to turn into cats nine times in their lives.

MYTHS AND LEGENDS

The most famous cat in Irish myth and legend is undoubtedly Pangur Bán, the cat belonging to an anonymous ninth-century Irish monk. In a celebrated poem found in the margins of a manuscript in the monastery of St Paul in Carinthia in Austria, the monk praises Pangur's skill, comparing his prowess in catching mice with his own skill in hunting for the meanings of words. Its clever metaphors have charmed readers ever since its rediscovery:

| *PANGUR BÁN* | PANGUR BÁN |
|---|---|
| *Messe agus Pangur Bán* | Both myself and Pangur Bán, |
| *Cechtar nathar fria shaindán* | Each have trades we call our own |
| *Bíth a menmasam fri seilgg,* | Hunting words my only vice, |
| *Mu menma céin im shaincheirdd.* | He, my white cat, hunts for mice. |

| | |
|---|---|
| *Caraimse fos, ferr cach clú* | I do not care for fame or glory, |
| *Oc mu lebrán, léir ingnu;* | Just a book with well told story. |
| *Ní foirmteach frimm Pangur Bán* | Pangur does not envy that, |
| *Caraid cesin a maccdán.* | He's content to be a cat. |
| | |
| *Ó ru biam, scél gan scís* | 'Tis a sight to gladden hearts, |
| *Innar tegdais, ar n-óendís,* | When we at home, though each apart, |
| *Táithiunn, díchríchide clius* | Ceaselessly our skills employ |
| *Ní fris tarddam ar n-áthius.* | And so find no greater joy. |
| | |
| *Gnáth, húaraib, ar gressaib gal* | Often with a sudden snatch, |
| *Glenaid luch inna línsam;* | A helpless mouse his net will catch. |
| *Os mé, du-fuit im lín chéin* | I too spread my net out far, |
| *Dliged ndoraid cu ndronchéill.* | To capture meanings deep and hard. |
| | |
| *Fuachaidsem fri frega fál* | Against the wall he sets his sight, |
| *A rosc, a nglése comlán;* | With fixed eye, both round and bright. |
| *Fúachimm chéin fri fégi fis* | My feeble eye is also fixed |
| *Mu rosc réil, cesu imdis.* | On spying wisdom's subtle tricks. |
| | |
| *Fáelidsem cu ndéne dul* | What delight my cat does feel, |
| *Hi nglen luch inna gérchrub;* | When his sharp claws make mice squeal. |
| *Hi tucu cheist ndoraid ndil* | Getting a precious answer right, |
| *Os mé chene am fáelid.* | Gives me just the same delight. |
| | |
| *Cia beimme a-min nach ré* | Though we sit close by all day, |
| *Ní derban cách a chéile* | We never harm each other's trade. |
| *Maith le cechtar nár a dán;* | Each content to work alone, |
| *Subaigthius a óenurán.* | Happy with skills he's made his own. |
| | |
| *Hé fesin as choimsid dáu;* | Sure and swift is Pangur's aim. |
| *In muid du-ngní cach óenláu;* | Each and every day he trains. |
| *Du thabhairt doraid du glé* | My own training strives to find |
| *For mu muid céin am messe.* | Out of darkness a clear mind. |

It has been suggested that the name Pangur comes from Old Welsh *pangur*, meaning a fuller or finisher of woollen cloth, as they are likely to be covered in the white dust of fuller's clay.[8] Cats also appear in the earliest Irish myths, often with a humorous aspect.[9] For example, a physician of the Tuatha Dé Danann called Miach uses a cat's eye to replace one lost by a young warrior in battle. Although his sight is restored, the young man finds the replacement to be a mixed blessing: 'For when he wanted to sleep and take his rest, it is then the eye would start at the squeaking of the mice, or the flight of the birds, or the movement of the rushes; and when he was wanting to watch an army or a gathering, it is then it was sure to be in a deep sleep.' A similar character appears in Welsh myth as one of Arthur's men, Gwrddnei Cat Eye, who could see by night as well as he could by day. In one of the stories of Fionn Mac Cumhaill and the Fianna, a member of the Tuatha Dé Danann called Abarthach comes to their aid by killing Caitcheann, the King of the Cat-Heads.

Monstrous cats also appear in Irish myths.[10] In one story a famously bad-tempered bard called Sencha was moved to satirise the cats of Ireland because the egg for his breakfast had been stolen by mice. He reserved his wrath in particular for the king of the cats called Irusan, a cat of monstrous size, who dwelt in a cave near Knowth on the River Boyne. 'Irusan,' he said, 'let your tail hang down for the mouse leers and jeers at your kind.' Hearing of these words, the great cat, who was the size of a bull, set out for the court where Sencha was staying. Irusan grabbed Sencha in his claws and made off with him on his back, the bard desperately trying to compose praise poems to mollify him all the while. Sencha was saved from an unpleasant fate only when St Kieran of Clonmacnoise rushed at the great cat and struck it dead with an iron bar. According to another legend, St Senan of County Clare was menaced by a monstrous cat which dwelt at Scattery Island. First, the cat devoured a smith called Narach, but the saint was able to bring him back to life. Then the cat advanced on Senan himself, 'its eyes flashing flame, with fiery breath, spitting venom'. As the beast opened its huge jaws, however, Senan made the sign of the cross and it immediately collapsed. The huge cat was then harmless, and was finished off by being thrown into Doolough near Mount Callan. Another folk tale has the hero Cúchulainn faced with seven fairy cats with poisonous tails. One drop of the poison is enough to penetrate fatally to the heart, but Cúchulainn is undaunted. With one sweep of his sword he swipes off all seven tails and the cats flee in terror.

Another regular feature of Irish myths is that people turn, or are turned, into cats.[11] For example, according to one legend, the goddess Clíona turned her sister Aoibheall into a white cat because they were both in love with the same chieftain. Clíona and the chieftain got married and lived happily together for a long time. Eventually, however, the chieftain found out the truth and demanded that Clíona restore her sister's human shape. Unfortunately, it was too late to do anything, and in his rage the chieftain banished Clíona from his sight. In one folk tale a princess turns her maid into a 'big yellow cat' so she can steal a comb from the king's son. Once the maid has accomplished this task, however, the princess turns her back into her human form again.

Cats were first worshipped in Egypt as incarnations of the fertility goddess Bastet, who was generally portrayed with a cat's head as a result.[12] It is thought that the association with cats happened because Bastet was previously linked to lions, and when cats were domesticated the focus switched to them instead. Cats were kept in Bastet's temples and even mummified when they died. Another name for Bastet was Bast or Pasht, which is said to be a possible origin of the word 'puss'. Bastet was usually depicted carrying a sistrum, a four-stringed rattle used to ward off evil spirits, and it is thought that this led to the traditional association of cats with fiddles, such as in the nursery rhyme 'The Cat and the Fiddle'. The Egyptians are also responsible for the association between cats and the number nine. Nine was a sacred number to the Egyptians because it is three times three, and their great centre at Heliopolis was sacred to nine different gods, each associated with cats in some way. Due to its nocturnal nature, skill at hunting, and round, reflective eyes, the cat also became associated with night time and the moon. For example, the Egyptian sun god Ra descended into the underworld each night as a cat to do battle with the Great Serpent Apep, only to re-emerge each morning victorious. Occasionally Apep won for a time (causing eclipses), but Ra always triumphed in the end.

The cat also played a role in the mythology of various European countries.[13] To the Greeks the cat became associated with the hunter goddess Artemis, and with Hecate, the goddess who ruled over the dead. The Romans associated cats with the goddess Diana. The cat therefore became a symbol of death, pursuing mice as the symbol of the souls of the dead. As cats spread into northern Europe they became associated with Freya, the Norse goddess of love and fertility. Freya had been traditionally depicted as travelling in a chariot drawn by lynx, but this was later changed to cats as they became more familiar. These links with darkness, the moon, and feminine powers are what gave the cat its indelible associations with witchcraft and magic. Unfortunately, these associations later led to its persecution in Christian Europe as an animal of sorcery and the devil.

RELATIONS WITH HUMANS

The cat was one of the last animals to be domesticated by humans, and it is said that this shows itself in the relative independence that they still retain. The exact origins of the domestic cat are unclear, but there are three likely contenders: the African Wildcat (*Felis libyca*), the Forest Wildcat (*Felis Silvestris*) and the Jungle Cat (*Felis claus*), all very similar species about the same size as their domestic cousin.[14] The cat was first domesticated by the ancient Egyptians around 2600 BC, when wildcats were attracted into growing Egyptian towns by the presence of rats, mice and birds. Taking advantage of this, the Egyptians domesticated the cats to protect the extensive granaries along the River Nile from vermin. Possibly influenced by priests of the goddess Bastet, the Egyptians later began to keep cats solely as pets. The usefulness of cats in keeping vermin under control led to their use on board trading ships. As a result of this, they spread far and wide. The arrival of the Romans into Egypt also aided the spread of the cat, as Roman legionaries took them back to Europe. In Britain the earliest remains of cats and kittens have been found at Iron Age sites in Danebury in Hampshire and Gussage All Saints in Dorset.

In Ireland the earliest evidence of domestic cats comes from a site at Scariff Bridge near Trim in County Meath, dating from about the second century AD.[15] Excavations at the site unearthed cat bones, and it is considered probable that cats were introduced into Ireland in the first centuries AD from Roman Britain. In Gaelic Ireland cats were considered useful for keeping their owner's house and grain store free of vermin, and were also valued as pets.[16] In fact, in the Old Irish Brehon Laws a cat was considered to be worth no less than three cows, if it could both purr and guard the barn and corn mill against mice. Cats seemed to be preferred as pets by women, and especially favoured cats were allowed to sleep indoors in a basket, or even on a pillow beside their mistress. Just as today, cats were noted for their love of milk, and a favourite Old Irish saying declared *cuirm lemm, lemlacht la cat* – 'I like beer, as the cat likes milk'. Again just like today, cats were noted for their skill at stealing food from kitchens, but the Brehon Laws made allowances for their nature. If food had been carelessly left out without proper supervision the cat was not considered liable. However, if the cat had been devious enough to take food from a secure place of storage or a vessel, then the cat's owner had to replace the food. Cats also appear in a similar light in the medieval Welsh laws of Hywel Dda: 'The price of a cat is four pence. Her qualities are to see, to hear, to kill mice, to have her claws whole and to nurse and not devour her kittens. If she be deficient in any of these qualities, one third of her price must be returned.'

Another similarity to modern times which is clear from early Irish literature is that domestic cats came in a variety of colours. The most famous cat in Irish literature, Pangur Bán, was white, but other pet cat names suggest different colours: *Bréone* or 'little flame' suggests an orange- or marmalade-coloured cat, while *glas nenta* or 'nettle grey' may mean a tabby. The Brehon Laws also refer to white-breasted black cats. The affection felt for cats in early Ireland is also reflected in pet names such as *Méone* ('little meow') and *Cruibne* ('little paws'). Cats later appeared in the *Book of Kells*, which frequently shows them in its illustrations, representing human souls and also chasing rats and mice.

The early Christians regarded cats positively as animals that brought good luck, and in fact a widespread (if cruel) practice in Europe was to inter cats in the walls of houses to protect against evil influences.[17] This was a practice that supposedly took place in Dublin. However, the early positive attitude gave way over time to increasing hostility, as the old associations of cats with pagan goddesses and magic became regarded as evidence of links to witchcraft and devil worship.[18] The sexual habits of cats, with multiple couplings and the screeching of the female during the act itself, were seen as further evidence of its ungodliness and satanic nature. The supposed evil nature of cats became official Roman Catholic Church doctrine in the tenth century, when Pope Gregory IX announced a link between black cats and the devil. The persecution of cats became widespread as a result. It has been speculated that this persecution contributed to the devastation caused by the Black Death (or bubonic plague) in twelfth-century Europe, as it led to an explosion in the number of rats, the carriers of the deadly disease.

The hostility reached its height when Pope Innocent VIII in the thirteenth century ordered the killing of every cat in Christendom, on account of their supposed satanic powers. Part of the reason for this extraordinary vendetta was a belief in the existence of an underground network of witchcraft dedicated to the cult of the goddess Diana, who was traditionally depicted with a cat. The persecution of cats went hand in hand with the increasing persecution of witches, and both were burnt in their thousands. The link of cats with witchcraft was also reinforced in the popular mind by the frequent habit of women living on their own having cats as pets. Often the mere fact of having a cat as a pet would be enough to convict a woman of witchcraft, and in northern Europe supposed witches were forced to confess to night-time flights across the sky with Freya and her cats. Witches were also believed to be able to turn themselves into cats or to keep familiars (evil spirits who acted as servants) who looked like cats, or else to converse with the devil in the form of a cat. Ireland was not immune from these trends, and there were several high-profile Irish cases of this nature. For instance, Dame Alice Kytler, a celebrated fourteenth-century witch in Kilkenny, was said to have a demon lover who visited her in the guise of a cat. Similarly, in the eighteenth century, the tale of the witches of Island Magee described them being visited by the devil in the shape of a cat. These beliefs about cats and witches survived the Reformation in Protestant countries, and the last witch trial in England was held as late in 1712. Even after the hysteria about witchcraft finally died away, the association of cats with the devil lingered on. For example, in France cats were regularly burnt, until recent times, on the midsummer bonfires of the St John's Day festival as symbols of the devil. The more the unfortunate cat was seen to suffer the better, as it was thought that their suffering made the devil suffer too. Western attitudes began to turn only towards the end of the nineteenth century, when cats began to be increasingly kept as pets, and cat lovers started to outnumber those who were hostile. Today the attitude in Europe and America towards cats is overwhelmingly benign and they have largely lost any negative associations to become one of our most loved animals.

Yet it would be misleading to describe the modern picture as wholly positive, in Ireland in particular. In 2004 the DSPCA estimated that there were up to two million feral cats in Ireland (one million in Dublin alone) due to a lack of any systematic programme of neutering.[19] According to the DSPCA many Irish businesses and farms are happy to have colonies of feral cats around to keep down vermin, but when cat numbers get out of control the solution is too often that of poisoning, shooting or drowning.

Hopefully as attitudes become more enlightened these problems of cruelty will decline, but for the moment the Irish view of cats is far from completely positive.

### SIMILAR ANIMALS

### Pine Marten – *Cat Crainn* – *Martes martes*

In Ireland the pine marten was associated in the popular mind with 'wild-cats', and its Irish name *cat crainn* means 'tree-cat'. Although it is true that the pine marten is somewhat cat-like in appearance, it is not related to cats, but belongs to the family Mustelidae, which includes otters, stoats and badgers. In County Clare (one of its main strongholds) the pine marten was said to be an uncanny animal, and it was distinguished by people from the 'marten cat', which probably meant a feral cat. Most of the place names referring to the cat in Ireland probably refer instead to the pine marten. Examples include Craignagat (*Creag na gCat* – Rock of the Cats), County Antrim, and Poulnagat (*Poll na gCat* – Hollow of the Cats), County Westmeath. In the early Irish Brehon Laws pine martens are only referred to in the event of being kept as pets. There is confusion among the sources as to how it should be classed, with some texts linking it to the dog, and some to the cat in terms of the legal penalties that apply for offences commited by it. In the Irish legend *Táin Bó Cuailnge*, or *The Cattle Raid of Cooley*, Queen Meadhbh had a pet pine marten around her shoulders, which the warrior Cúchulainn killed with a slingshot. The pine marten is also linked to the Gaelic hero Fionn Mac Cumhaill. His first heroic act while still an infant was to strangle a pine marten when it approached the hollow ivy-clad tree where the young Fionn lay, attracted by the smell of Fionn's food of wild pig meat. The pine marten was skinned and the pelt wrapped around Fionn as a blanket. In fact, the pine marten was valued for its fine pelt, and there was a considerable trade in the export of pine marten skins from Ireland in the Middle Ages. Indeed, trapping pine martens for their fur was still carried out by Irish trappers until the twentieth century. At the same time, however, pine martens were considered a pest by gamekeepers, and their numbers fell, due to persecution, until it was one of Ireland's rarest mammals, largely confined to the west of Ireland. With greater forestation and legal protection, its numbers have been increasing in Ireland again in recent times.[20]

Squirrel – Iora – *Sciurus*

Bee – Beach – *Apis mellifera*

Whale – Míol Mór – *Cetacea*

Seal – Rón – *Phoca/Halichoerus*

# Hare – Giorria – *Lepus*

*The hare is noted in Irish folklore for its swiftness, alertness and agility, but was also regarded as a fairy animal associated with deception and witchcraft. In myth the hare was linked to Celtic goddesses of fertility, both of spring and of the harvest.*

## Folk Beliefs and Customs

A very widespread belief among Irish country people was that witches would go abroad in the form of a hare in order to steal milk, especially on May Day.[1] The most common version of the story tells of a dairy farmer who became suspicious when the milk yield of his cattle diminished considerably. He began to stay up at night to watch the cows, and soon saw a hare come and drink the milk from them. The farmer's dog gave chase to the hare, but succeeded only in drawing blood from its hindquarters as it fled. The farmer followed on, and coming to a nearby house he asked the old woman who lived there if she had seen the hare. Despite the woman's denials, the farmer noticed that she was bleeding from her leg, and so realised that the hare had been the woman in disguise. For this reason any hares found among the cattle on May Day would often be killed by farmers. The farmer could sometimes prevent the theft from taking place. For example, it was the custom to sprinkle the fields with holy water on May Morning, and one tale tells how a farmer accidentally sprinkled a hare hiding in the grass. As soon as the holy water touched the hare, it turned into an old woman crouched down in terror, caught in the act. The belief that hares were old women or witches in fairy form is, perhaps, the reason why many people would not eat them. Indeed, in County Kerry many people believed that hare meat should not be touched, because the souls of their grandmothers were supposed to enter into them.

The hare was also associated in folklore with the end of the harvest.[2] Traditionally one sheaf of corn was left uncut, and it was believed that a hare always hid in it, only making a dash for safety at the very last minute.

Finishing the harvest was called 'putting the hare out of the corn', and the farmer who was late with the harvest was told: 'we sent you the hare'. Similar practices at the end of the harvest were found throughout Europe. In Ireland, finishing the harvest was also called 'putting out the hag (or *cailleach*)'. The story was that the hag hid (often in hare form) in the last sheaf, and was driven from farm to farm as the farmers finished the harvest, until she reached the field of the last man in the parish to cut his corn. In many parts of Ireland the last sheaf was itself called the hag or *cailleach* for this reason. Another popular belief was that hares were the cause of harelips in children, especially if one crossed the path of a pregnant woman. The misfortune could be avoided, however, if the woman tore the hem of her dress, and thus transferred the fissure to the material instead of the child's lip. In County Clare it was generally thought unlucky to meet a hare when setting out in the morning, while it was also believed, rather bizarrely, that hares fed upon dead human flesh, perhaps from being often 'started' in graveyards.

Hares were involved in several folk cures, and, perhaps because of their speed, their feet were considered especially potent.[3] The Roman author Pliny stated that the foot of a hare was a cure for gout, while in England up to modern times it was thought that the right foot of a hare kept in a left-hand pocket kept away rheumatism. Writing in 1665 the diarist Samuel Pepys stated that his hare's foot had kept him from colic. It was similarly thought in Ireland that the paw of a hare hung around the neck on May Day would cure ailments such as cramp and rheumatism. It was also thought in Ireland that a tuft of fur from a hare would staunch bleeding, and that a cure for freckles was to bathe the face in the blood of a hare. In England the hare's or rabbit's foot was generally considered lucky, especially by sailors, and it was used at birth to brush the baby's face and so ward off evil spirits.

There are several Irish proverbs about hares that emphasise its speed and alertness.[4] To say *Tabhair do phóg do chois an ghiorria* ('kiss the foot of the hare') meant to say goodbye to something forever; while 'the sleep of the hare' meant to sleep with one eye open. According to an Irish proverb, the three traits of the hare were a lively ear, a bright eye, and a quick run against the hound. Another popular saying about the hare went: 'A hopper of ditches, a cutter of corn, a brown little cow without any horns.' An old belief dating from Classical times was that the hare always sought shelter under the sow-thistle (*Sonchus oleraceus*), because the plant's properties gave it strength and calmed its nerves.

### MYTHS AND LEGENDS

Hares appear sometimes in Irish folk tales and myths, usually in the context of hunting.[5] According to one legend, Mannanán, the Gaelic god of the sea, led King Conchubar of Ulster to the hiding place of the maiden Deirdre by running before his hounds in the form of a hare. Part of the training of the Gaelic hero Fionn Mac Cumhaill was to keep hares in a field by successfully running before them, whichever way they went. Later, hares were among the animals hunted by the Fianna, and one poem tells of a prodigious week's hunting, when a total of 600 hares were killed.

There is evidence that the hare was sacred in Celtic Britain.[6] A well-known remark by Julius Caesar in his work *De Bello Gallico* stated that the ancient Britons regarded the hare as sacred, and taboo as food. Boudicca, the British Celtic warrior queen, was said to have released a hare while invoking Andraste, goddess of battle and victory, before setting out to defeat the Romans in battle. There is also evidence of hares in ritual burials in Celtic Britain. Two pits at Ipswich in Suffolk contained a piece of hare fur each, perhaps indicating a ritual purpose. Small figurines of hares were found at burials in Colchester and Thistleton in Leicestershire.

In Classical mythology the hare was associated with fertility and the goddess Aphrodite, but also with speed as the messenger of the god Hermes.[7] Hares were generally linked to the spring because of the prominence of the 'mad March hares', namely the male hares which compete with each other in sparring matches at this time. In Anglo-Saxon myth the hare was the animal of the spring goddess Eostra, who later gave her name to the festival of Easter. Despite this, there is no direct link between the Anglo-Saxon Eostra and the modern myth of the Easter Bunny, who comes to give chocolate eggs to children every Easter. It appears to be only a very recent custom in Britain and Ireland, as the Easter Bunny is not mentioned among traditional Easter customs, such as decorating eggs and games like egg-rolling. In fact, the custom of the Easter Bunny originated in Germany and the Netherlands, and was introduced into America by German settlers during the early nineteenth century. From there it was exported to these islands, apparently only sometime in the twentieth century, with the modern growth of American cultural influence.

RELATIONS WITH HUMANS

Perhaps surprisingly, in light of Julius Caesar's remarks to the contrary, the evidence shows that hare was one the main species of wild animal eaten by the early Celts.[8] Excavations of various Iron Age sites in northern Gaul, such as Tartigny and Compiègne, show that hare bones appear in more abundance than those of any other wild animal. The Classical writer Arrian referred to the Celts using dogs to flush out hares from hiding and into snares. At Tartigny a man was buried with the remains of a horse, dog and hare. This probably represented his role as a hunter. The hare also appears in Celtic artwork. A stone statue found at Touget in France shows a hunter god holding a hare and accompanied by his hound. A fourth-century BC ceramic flagon from Matzhausen in Germany depicts hunting scenes, including a hound chasing a hare.

Hares were traditionally hunted in early Ireland.[9] An illustration from the *Book of Kells* shows a hound chasing a hare, while a ninth-century high cross at Castledermot, County Kildare, shows a hunting scene on one of its panels, where huntsmen pursue hare along with deer and wild boar. The old Irish tale *Táin Bó Fraích* describes a great hunt organised by the legendary King Ailill and Queen Maedhbh of Connaught that included hares, among other animals. The Brehon Laws only mention the hare in the context of keeping one as a pet, and equate any offences committed by it with those committed by a domestic hen. It has been suggested that this rather strange link may be due to the fact that hares make nest-like structures on the ground known as 'forms', similar to a hen's nests.

Although hares are no longer hunted for food in Ireland, they are still used for coursing.[10] Hare coursing involving greyhounds is considered a traditional sport in Ireland. It is organised by the Irish Coursing Club, established in 1916, although the sport goes back a century or more in Ireland. Coursing differs from hunting in that the object is not to catch or kill the hare, but to test the skill of the greyhounds against each other as they vie to catch it. The hare is then allowed to go free – none the worse for the experience, according to supporters of coursing, but stressed and traumatised, according to opponents. Hare coursing is legal in the Republic of Ireland, and about thirty to forty coursing licences are issued each year. There are two kinds of hare coursing, open and enclosed. Open hare coursing is done in the countryside where beaters flush hares out into the open for the hounds to chase. The hounds do not have to be muzzled for this form of coursing. Enclosed coursing is done on a coursing field with hares that have been caught some weeks previously. The captured hares are given time to get used to captivity and to get to know the coursing field, with its 'escape' at one end – openings large enough for the hare to get through, but not for the dog. Each field is approximately 400 m long, and the hare is given about a 100 m start before the greyhounds are released. Hares are very agile creatures, and the entertainment comes from watching them dodge and weave to escape the greyhounds who are muzzled. The greyhound that first forces the hare to turn wins the course. Once the hare reaches the 'escape', it is not coursed again, but later tagged and released back into the wild. At the time of writing, hare coursing remains suspended in Northern Ireland, pending review on conservation grounds.

Despite the fact that it may be used for hare coursing, and be hunted under licence, the hare is a protected species in Ireland.[11] There are two species of hare in Ireland: the native Irish mountain hare (*Lepus timidus hibernicus*), a distinct subspecies of the mountain hare (*Lepus timidus*); and the brown hare (*Lepus europaeus*), which was introduced into parts of Northern Ireland in the nineteenth century, probably for hare coursing. The hare may cause some damage to young forestry plantations, particularly those of broadleaf species, but is otherwise fairly harmless. As one of the few indisputably native members of the Irish fauna, the Irish mountain hare has a special place in the Irish countryside, and it deserves every effort to be made for its conservation.

# Rat — Francach — *Rattus*

*The rat is generally despised as vermin for its destruction of crops and for carrying disease. As such it is a symbol of ill fortune, evil and sickness. At the same time, however, there is a grudging respect for an animal that is every bit as cunning, exploitative and opportunistic as humans themselves.*

## FOLK BELIEFS AND CUSTOMS

As they were loathed and feared so much, it is not surprising that most of the folklore surrounding rats concerns the different ways in which they might be expelled.[1] Rats were a particular problem on ships. One widespread and rather gruesome story tells of a ship owner on Waterford Quay, who had a very valuable cargo of yellow meal. This attracted a huge number of rats to infest the ship, and the problem was so bad that the ship owner put a notice in every newspaper in Ireland, offering a reward to the person who could banish the rats. The day before he had to set sail, and still fearful that his cargo would be eaten before he reached its destination, the despairing ship owner was approached by a man about his advertisement. The man simply took the stump of an old razor out of his pocket, and stuck it down between the planks of the deck, with the sharp edge facing upwards. He then took out a book and began to read. Before long every single rat on the ship appeared on deck, and slit its throat going over the razor. By the time all the rats were killed, the deck of the ship was slippery with blood. The man then collected his reward and left the ship, never to be seen again.

A very long standing belief was that Gaelic poets were able to banish or destroy rats through the power of their verse. For example, according to local tradition the poet Peaid Buí Lynch of Ballyvourney, County Cork, had the power to charm rats, and could either send them to a person or send them away. If they were being sent far away, and had to have lodging somewhere for the night, the poet would send them to someone he did not like as they would cause damage. One time the rats were sent to a Dermot O'Leary in Kilgarvan. When the poor man awoke the following morning, he found that the rats had eaten his boots into tatters! The fabled talent of Irish poets

159

to rhyme rats to death is even mentioned by Shakespeare. His play *As You Like It* contains the remark: 'I was never so berim'd since Pythagorus time that I was an Irish rat, which I hardly remember.' Saints were also believed to have the power to banish rats. The red clay of St Colmcille's birthplace in Gartan, County Donegal, was said to have the power to dispel harmful things, especially rats. It was said to have acquired this power from when his mother gave birth to him there, staining the earth red as she did so. According to Gerald of Wales' *History and Topography of Ireland*, a bishop called St Yvor expelled all the rats from an area of southeast Leinster near Wexford. St Canice of Kilkenny was also supposed to have banished rats and mice from his island hermitage.

It was believed that rats could be expelled by writing them a letter asking them to leave, and mentioning a suitable place, such as a grain store, where they might find alternative lodgings. The letter should be deposited in a place where they would be sure to see it. In Scotland this was done by serving a writ of ejection on them. The following words were stuck on the wall where they could be read: 'Ratton and mouse, lea' the puir woman's house; Gang awa' owre by to 'e mill; And there ane and a' ye'll ger your fill.' A similar belief was held in the Ardennes region of France where the message telling the rats to leave had to be placed both under the door the rats had to take and on the road they had to follow at sunrise. Another common belief both in Ireland and Europe was that rats had foreknowledge of disaster, and so rats suddenly leaving a house ironically meant misfortune. In the same way, it was a very bad omen if rats left a ship, especially if the ship had not even left port. In County Wexford rats were considered a sign of war. According to legend, in Kilmore before

the war of 1641 rats suddenly ran though all the houses, where there had been none before.

Occasionally the rat is portrayed in a more humorous, mischievous light.[2] One Irish tale tells of how the rat and the cat were once great friends. One day, however, when they visited a fair, the rat got the cat drunk on whiskey. After they got home the cat fell asleep in the chair and fell into the fire. The rat was slow pulling the cat out so it got badly burnt. While the poor cat was the worse for wear, the rat and all his relatives had great fun around the house, chasing each other and breaking all the crockery. In desperation, the woman of the house doused the cat with a few buckets of water to rouse it, and the unfortunate cat, hungover, half-burnt and half-drowned, finally got the strength to chase away the rats. From that day forth, the tale tells, the cat and the rat were mortal enemies.

The Irish name for rat (*francach*) derives from the belief that rats first came to Ireland from France.[3] This term appears to have first been used after the Norman invasion, probably indicating a dramatic increase in their numbers in post-Norman times. However, the rat had been in Ireland since early Christian times, when it was simply known in Irish as *luch*, the same word used for the mouse – to distinguish them, the rat was sometimes called *luch mór* ('big mouse'), while the mouse was *luch beag* ('small mouse'). The rat appears in the place names Lachtnafrankee (*Leacht na Francaigh* – slab of the rats), County Waterford, and *Oileán na bhfrancach* (rat island), a field name in County Cork. It is likely these names refer to the black rat rather than the brown rat, as the brown rat is a relatively recent arrival to Ireland.

MYTHS AND LEGENDS

The best known legend involving rats is that of the Pied Piper of Hamelin, most famously described by the Brothers Grimm in their 1816 collection of folk tales, *Deutsche Sagen*. According to the legend, the German town of Hamelin was overrun with rats in 1284, and the townsfolk were in despair as nothing seemed to get rid of them. One day a mysterious man came into the town, carrying a fife or small pipe and wearing a coat of many different colours – hence the name the Pied Piper. He claimed to be a rat catcher, and that for a fee he could rid the town of all its rats. Although the fee was high, in desperation the citizens of the town agreed to pay it. The Pied Piper then produced his pipe and began to play, and immediately every rat in the town came out from where they were hiding and gathered around him. When he was sure they were all gathered together, he led them, still playing his pipe, into the nearby River Weser where they were all drowned.

Once the rats were gone the townspeople regretted promising to pay the piper such a high price, and began to make excuses as to why they should not pay. In the end, bitter and angry, the Piper left Hamelin in disgust. The townsfolk thought they had seen the last of him, but the Pied Piper returned on 26 June, the feast of St John and St Paul, dressed in a hunter's costume and with a dreadful look on his face. This time when he played his pipe, all the children of the town stopped what they were doing and ran to follow him. The Pied Piper led them all to a nearby mountain called the Koppen and entered a cave. Neither he nor the 130 children were ever seen again.

RELATIONS WITH HUMANS

The rat is the original 'invasive species' to take advantage of man's activities in order to spread itself across the globe. There are two species of rat in Ireland, the Black Rat (*Rattus rattus*), and the Brown Rat (*Rattus norvegicus*). The black rat probably originated in India or the Malay Peninsula and spread along trade routes to Europe.[4] It first arrived in Britain during Roman times, and seems to have arrived in Ireland in the early Christian period. Its remains have been found at an early Christian site in Rathmullen, County Down. An illustration from the *Book of Kells* also shows a cat chasing what looks like a rat, as it is far too large to be a mouse. The black rat seems to have become widespread in Ireland by the eleventh and twelfth centuries. Indeed, the *Chronicum Scotorum* records a *plág lochad* that affected the Leinstermen and Norse settlers in 1013. Although the term *plág lochad* could refer to a plague of either rats or mice, it was probably rats in this case, presumably coming from ships arriving at ports along the east coast. The black rat is believed to be responsible for the spread of the bubonic plague or Black Death which devastated Europe during the Middle Ages, as it harboured fleas carrying the plague virus *Yersinia pestis*. The bubonic plague arrived in Ireland in 1348, and recurred at intervals in Irish towns until the 1650s. After the arrival of the larger brown rat, the black rat was pushed out of almost all its range. It is now believed to survive permanently only on Lambay Island, off north County Dublin. Modern container shipping and improved pest control on board ships mean that the seafaring black rats are increasingly scarce.

The brown rat, larger and heavier than the black rat, is now by far the commonest Irish rat, having outcompeted it to become Ireland's number one pest.[5] The brown rat probably originated in eastern Asia or China, and was spread by man along trade and commercial routes in a similar fashion to the black rat. It arrived in Britain and Ireland in the early eighteenth century (about 1722) aboard ships originating in Russia and eastern Europe. By 1730 it had become a serious pest in Dublin. The arrival in Ireland of the brown rat caused consternation, and exaggerated accounts of their depredations circulated, as the following report from a Dublin newspaper of the time shows. After describing how rats ate a woman and child in Merrion, the writer went on to say: 'People killed several which are as large as Katts and Rabbits. This part of the country is infested with them. Likewise we hear from Rathfarnham that the like vermin destroyed a little girl in the field. They are to be seen like Rabbits and so impudent that they suck the cows.'

Brown rats will eat almost anything, and are major pests of stored food, fruit, seeds, cereals, root crops and silage. Their best known activity is scavenging around rubbish dumps for whatever rotten meat, fish, bones and bread is available. What makes the brown rat so disliked by humans, however, is not just that it is a pest of food, but that it harbours several nasty diseases. These include Toxoplasma, Salmonella, Leptospira (which causes Weil's disease), Yersinia and Cryptospora. Leptospira in particular is a hazard, as almost 50 per cent of rats carry it and excrete it in their urine into fresh water, causing a hazard to anglers, canoeists and other users of waterways. In fairness, the picture is not wholly negative, as juvenile rats are a major food source for other native animals and birds, such as barn owls, foxes, badgers and cats. Without them, the barn owl in particular would find life difficult. Controlling rats is difficult because they are very wary of new or strange foodstuffs, and can learn quickly to associate certain smells and tastes with poison. Another problem is that the rat can build up resistance to poisons over generations – not a long time, as females can produce three to five litters a year. This means that newer, more effective poisons have to be constantly found if rats are to be controlled. There is no outright victory in sight for humans in this ongoing struggle between rats and chemists, and so it is that the animal that has literally plagued mankind for millennia shows no signs of leaving us in peace.

# Mouse – Luch – *Mus/Apodemus*

*Although, like its larger cousin the rat, the mouse is widely disliked as a pest, it is also regarded with a degree of affection as a charming and relatively harmless creature. The mouse also had a role in some folk cures, even if its real usefulness was doubtful.*

## Folk Beliefs and Customs

The mouse was used in a number of folk cures, both in Ireland and across Europe, some of which are a bit strange to modern eyes.[1] According to the Roman author Pliny, boiled mice in their food would cure infants of incontinence (whatever else it might do to them!). This method was used as a cure in Ireland until modern times, and was used as a cure for whooping cough as well. Mice were also used as a cure for baldness in Ireland, in a manner unpleasant for all concerned. The cure was to fill a pot with the unfortunate mice and leave it under the hearth for a year. The resulting brew was then applied to the scalp. For the more impatient, the wait was only six days if the pot was put at the back of the hearth and a fire lit in front of it. It was also thought that killing a mouse was a cure for chapped lips, as this complaint was said to be caused by a mouse urinating on them. In Ireland the juice of a boiled field mouse was also considered effective as a love potion. Another method was to stick pins into the body of a mouse until they got rusty, then stick them into a puffball for three days, rub them against a purple orchid, and finally stick one of them into the clothes of the intended. If all this was done, the person involved would follow you all over the world.

Superstitions about mice are found in many other European countries.[2] Mice were widely thought to be manifestations of the soul in Germany and other parts of Europe, and a common belief was that the soul of a sleeping person could leave its body and wander far and wide in the form of a mouse, especially a white one. However, if the person was woken before the 'soul-mouse' returned, they would lose their soul. In Germany, instead of leaving a tooth for the tooth fairy, children traditionally put their milk-teeth down a mouse-hole, saying: 'Mouse, give me your iron tooth; I will give you my bone tooth.' Doing this was also said to prevent toothache. Among Manx fishermen it was considered unlucky to say the word 'mouse' while on a

boat. In Wales it was believed to foretell death if a mouse nibbled any part of a person's clothing.

The mouse appears in an old Irish proverb for something impossible: *An rud nach bhfuil is nach mbeidh, nead ag an luch i bhféasóg an chait* – 'Something that isn't and will never be, the nest of a mouse in a cat's whiskers.' The mouse appears in some Irish place names, such as Gortnalughogue (*Gort na luchóg* – the field of mice), County Donegal, and Inchnalughogue (*Inse na luchóg* – the meadow of the mice), County Clare.[3]

MYTHS AND LEGENDS

According to an Irish legend, mice first came into existence thanks to a miracle of St Martin.[4] The saint placed some food under a tub and warned his companions to leave it there until the following day. However, an inquisitive person could not resist lifting the tub during the night to have a look underneath, whereupon a plague of mice rushed forth. Martin threw his glove after the mice in order to control them, and this glove turned into the first cat. A similar tale was widely told in Ireland about St Colmcille. In this version of the story, mice first came into existence as an indirect result of St Colmcille wishing to feed the poor. Jesus granted the saint his wish by giving him some cooking fat and instructing him to put it in a pot for twenty-four hours. At the end of this period, something wonderful would appear to feed the poor. Colmcille carried out these instructions, but as he did so his serving girl stole a small piece for herself and put it in a bowl. When the twenty-four hours were up a herd of succulent young pigs appeared out of the pot. All that came out of the bowl, however, was a plague of mice. Because of its origins in theft, it was said from then on that the mouse will only get what it can steal, and anything stolen belongs to the mouse. Mice also appear as a plague in the Welsh tale *Manawydan, son of Llyr*, when King Llywd magically transforms his company into mice so that they can destroy the crops of his rival Manawydan.[5] The ploy goes wrong on the third night when the queen and ladies of the court join in the destruction. The queen is captured by Manawydan and Llywd has to pay a heavy price for her release.

The mouse appears in a charming legend regarding St Colmán Mac Duach, a bishop of Connaught. According to the tale the saint had three pets, a fly, a cockerel and a mouse. The cockerel used to crow at midnight to call him to prayer, the fly used to walk along the page of the psalter to mark it for Colmán while he sang psalms, and the mouse used to nibble his ear to waken him if he started to doze off.[6] Other Irish saints were not so kindly towards mice. In his account of Ireland, Gerald of Wales relates the story of an island in the sea west of Connaught consecrated by St Brendan.[7] A miraculous trait of this island was that human corpses did not decay there, and so could be left in the open to be seen by their relatives. Another trait of the island was that it contained no mice, and any mouse brought there would immediately head for the sea and throw itself in. If it was prevented from doing this, it died on the spot.

## Relations with Humans

There are two species of mice in Ireland, the Wood Mouse (*Apodemus sylvaticus*), sometimes called the Field Mouse, and the House Mouse (*Mus musculus*).[8] As their names suggest, the wood mouse lives in woods and open countryside and rarely occupies buildings, while the house mouse lives mostly in and around buildings, avoiding open habitats. Although it is not technically native to Ireland, the wood mouse has been in Ireland for about 8,000 years, after it was introduced (no doubt accidently) by Mesolithic settlers. The earliest known remains of the wood mouse in Ireland are of a tooth which was found on a Mesolithic site dating back 7,600 years in Clondalkin, County Dublin. It seems that the wood mouse was also brought over in Viking longships, as Irish wood mice are genetically closer to mice from the Hebrides, Iceland and Norway than those from Britain. The house mouse originated in Central Asia, and spread via the Middle East to Europe about 4,000 years ago, due to its close association with human settlements. Like the wood mouse, it probably began life as a seed eater, but started to exploit the rich opportunities for food and shelter provided by human settlement. It seems to have reached Ireland in the early centuries AD, and was well established by the seventh century.

Mice were considered a major pest in early Ireland.[9] In the Old Irish Brehon Laws, the house mouse was classed as a significant destroyer of food, usually food stored in the barn, mill or drying kiln. One early text also refers to mice eating the standing corn in the field in some parts of Ireland. Gerald of Wales, writing in 1185, described mice in Ireland as 'infinite in number and consum[ing] much more grain than anywhere else, as well as eating garments even though they be locked up carefully'. Today both kinds of mice can be pests wherever foodstuffs such as grain, animal feed, hay and straw are stored. The house mouse is now an omnivore which will eat anything that is digestible, including soap and even electrical insulation. In addition, the house mouse carries Leptospirosis or Weil's disease, a serious illness of the kidney and liver in humans, which is a major health threat. For these reasons, mice are considered a pest to most people, and ongoing efforts are made to control them with poisons. However, like the rat, the mouse can develop resistance to poisons, so control methods must evolve constantly. On the positive side, mice form a significant part of the diet of many of our native mammals and birds, including kestrels, owls, foxes, stoats, pine martens, badgers and domestic cats. As well as being a pest, therefore, they make a significant and valuable contribution to our native fauna, and do not deserve to be seen in quite the same negative light as their cousin, the rat.

## SIMILAR ANIMALS

### Pigmy Shrew – *Luch Féir – Sorex minutus*

Although the shrew is often mistaken for a mouse, it is not a rodent but a member of the insectivora or insect eaters, and is in fact more closely related to the hedgehog. The pygmy shrew is the smallest of Ireland's mammals, and is noted for its energetic pursuit of prey, and its high-pitched squeaking as it hurries along. Perhaps for this reason it was widely held in Ireland to be a relative of the stoat (which it also is not). According to the Roman author Pliny, the bite of a shrew was venomous, and the best cure was to split asunder the animal itself and apply it to the affected area. Pliny also believed that a shrew would die immediately if it ran across the rut made by the wheel of a cart. This belief survived in Britain until modern times, and was probably prompted by the regular sight of the short-lived shrew lying dead on country roads. A widely held belief in Ireland was that a cow that had been walked or run upon by a shrew would develop terrible swellings and die immediately if action was not taken. Any cow displaying such symptoms was said to be 'shrew-struck'. The only remedy was to burn the body of a shrew and apply the ashes to the swellings.[10]

# Squirrel – Iora – *Sciurus*

*The squirrel was regarded as an elusive and nimble creature of the treetops, and admired for its grace and beauty. Its fine red fur was also highly valued for clothing throughout the Middle Ages.*

## Folk Beliefs and Customs

The squirrel does not feature much in folklore, as its life in the trees removed it from the lives of most country people. Nevertheless, some popular notions about its behaviour developed over the centuries.[1] According to the Roman author Pliny, the squirrel could foretell the weather, as it closed off the entrance to its nest (or drey) when the wind was going to blow in that direction. It would then make another entrance on the side away from the wind. The Greek poet Oppian said that red squirrels shaded themselves from hot sunshine by making a shadow for themselves with their tails. The squirrel has also always been regarded approvingly for its industrious habit of storing up food for the winter. There are not many Irish place names that refer to the squirrel, but Carrickirragh (*Carraig na hIorua* – rock of the squirrels) in County Donegal is one.[2]

## Myths and Legends

The squirrel is mentioned in some Celtic and Norse legends, where it features as a creature skilled in running through the treetops.[3] In an Irish tale, *The Pursuit of Gruaidh Ghriansholus*, the Gaelic hero Cúchulainn travels in his chariot so lightly and swiftly that he is described as being 'like a squirrel leaping amongst the leafy trees of the wood'. In Norse myth the World Tree Yggdrasil was inhabited by a squirrel called Ratatosk, who spent its time scurrying up and down the tree, carrying insulting messages from the dragon called Nidhogg, who lived in its roots, up to the eagle, who sat in its topmost bough. In Roman times squirrels were regarded by women as beloved play animals. Pictures of squirrels have been found on urns and marble fountains in Athens, and on Roman mosaic floors in Switzerland.

## RELATIONS WITH HUMANS

There are two species of squirrel in Ireland, the Red Squirrel (*Sciurus vulgaris*), and the Grey Squirrel (*Sciurus carolinensis*).[4] The red squirrel is generally presumed to be native, but it is possible that it was first introduced thousands of years ago by early settlers to Ireland for its pelt. In any case, the present red squirrel population is descended from animals introduced from England in the nineteenth century. The red squirrels of Britain and Ireland are actually a subspecies called *Sciurus vulgaris leucourus* that have a lighter-coloured tail than the red squirrels on the continent. The grey squirrel is a much more recent arrival, having only been introduced from North America in 1911 to Castle Forbes in County Longford. A wicker hamper containing eight or twelve squirrels was given as a wedding present from the Duke of Buckingham to one of the daughters of the house. After the wedding breakfast, the hamper was opened on the lawn 'whereupon the bushy tailed creatures quickly leapt out and scampered off into the woods where they went forth and multiplied'.

The earliest Irish reference to the squirrel dates from AD 655. It is also mentioned in the early Irish Brehon Laws, where it was classed with the domestic cat with regard to legal penalties. Squirrel fur was known in Europe as 'vair', and its use was restricted in the Middle Ages to the

nobility. In medieval times there were sufficient numbers of squirrels in Ireland to support an export trade in pelts that continued until the mid-seventeenth century. The last evidence of this trade was a mention of the taxes levied on squirrel skins for export in an Irish statute of 1662. Writing in 1625, O'Sullivan Beare states that: 'the skin is warm when added to clothes, and it also makes an unseamed purse highly esteemed by noble people, when it is adorned with silk lining inside and gold, silver or silk ribbons, as is the custom in Ireland'. Red squirrel numbers plummeted during the course of the eighteenth century because of woodland clearance, and by the end of the century they were even thought to be extinct in Ireland. They were reintroduced from England during the nineteenth century, and had re-established themselves in every county in Ireland by the twentieth century. Its fortunes changed again with the arrival of the grey squirrel, which is pushing the red out of most of its old habitats, to the extent that its survival in Ireland is once more under threat.

The grey squirrel is native to the eastern United States, but has been introduced to several parts of Europe, Australia and South Africa, where it has successfully established itself. It has colonised the eastern half of Ireland since its introduction in 1911. There is no doubt that it will establish itself in every part of the country, but for the moment it is not found west of the Shannon or in most parts of Munster. While the grey squirrel has already become a fixture of many suburban areas and parks as a more visible and approachable alternative to the shy red, it has also become a major woodland pest. Its habit of stripping the bark of trees, especially broadleaves, to get at the sugar-rich sap makes it hated by many foresters. By far the most controversial aspect to the grey squirrel, however, is the fact that it appears to displace the red squirrel wherever it becomes established. In Britain (where the grey was first introduced in 1890) the red squirrel is now missing from most parts of England and Wales, and the pine forests of Scotland are its last remaining stronghold.

In Ireland a similar situation is developing, with the red disappearing from most parts of the country as the grey advances. To arrest this process and safeguard the red squirrel's future, an All-Ireland Species Action Plan was agreed in 2008 between the Environment and Heritage Departments of both the Republic of Ireland and Northern Ireland. The exact reasons for the red's decline are unclear, but there appear to be several factors. These include the grey's ability to compete for food owing to its greater size and boldness, and also its ability to eat acorns when they are unripe. As the grey squirrel is now established in Ireland for good, the only hope of survival for the red lies in conserving its populations from eventual encroachment by the grey. The main way of achieving this is to maintain suitable refuges for the red squirrel in large stands of coniferous woodlands, the only habitat where it has a competitive advantage over the grey. Red squirrels are better able to cope in coniferous forests because they can exploit small-seeded trees such as the Sitka spruce, while the larger grey struggles to find enough to eat. Red squirrels have been translocated already to suitable conifer woodlands in Connemara and Mayo that are surrounded by bog (and so safe from being reached by greys), and the results are being monitored. In the future it is hoped to identify more woodland sites where these translocations can be carried out. As the red squirrel is not yet endangered in Ireland, it is hoped that these measures will be enough to secure its future and ensure the survival of one of Ireland's most beautiful animals.

# Bat – Ialtóg – *Chiroptera*

*B*ats *were traditionally feared as mysterious flying creatures of the night, associated with death, sickness or witchcraft. These fears increased over time due to more modern associations with vampires. However, in recent times there has also been a greater appreciation by those interested in wildlife of the uniqueness of these harmless and fascinating creatures.*

SPECIES NAMES

Leisler's Bat – *Ialtóg Leisler – Nyctalus leisleri*
Long-eared Bat – *Ialtóg Fhad-chluasach – Plecotus auritus*
Horseshoe Bat – *Ialtóg Crúshrónach – Rhinolophus hipposideros*
Whiskered Bat – *Ialtóg Ghiobach – Myotis mystacinus*
Natterer's Bat – *Ialtóg Natterer – Myotis nattereri*
Daubenton's Bat – *Ialtóg Uisce – Myotis Daubentoni*
Common Pipistrelle – *Ialtóg Fheascrach – Pipistrellus pipistrellus*
Soprano Pipistrelle – *Ialtóg Fheascrach Sopránach – Pipistrellus pygmaeus*
Natasius' Pipistrelle – *Ialtóg Nathusius – Pipistrellus nathusii*

FOLK BELIEFS AND CUSTOMS

The bat was regarded with some fear in folklore.[1] In Ireland the appearance of a bat near the house was traditionally taken as a token of impending death to someone in the household. Bats were also falsely believed to be liable to get entangled in a person's hair (unlikely, given their acute sonar), and that death would ensue unless the hair was cut immediately. In northeast Clare it was believed to foretell sickness if a bat flew into a person's face. The mischevious fairy called the pooka, who generally appeared in the shape of a black horse, could also take the form of a bird or bat. In Scotland the bat was associated with witchcraft, and if one was seen to rise into the air and then descend earthwards, it was taken as a sign that the witch's hour had come, when they had power over anyone not protected against them. In England it was generally considered as a bad omen if bats were seen in daytime, especially if they entered the house. Shropshire was an exception, where it was lucky to see a bat in the daytime but unlucky to disturb them or cause them to fly away.

## MYTHS AND LEGENDS

In European lore the bat was regarded as a hybrid between a bird and a rat, and so symbolised duplicity and hyprocrisy. Bats were also associated with witchcraft, death and the devil. However, according to the Roman writer Pliny, carrying a live bat three times around a house and then nailing it outside the window, with the head facing downwards, was an effective charm against evil. In Slavonic legend vampires took on the form of monstrous bats when they arose from their graves to suck the blood of sleeping persons, who then became vampires in their turn. The Irish writer Bram Stoker drew upon this legend when writing his 1897 vampire horror classic, *Dracula*. The link between bats and vampires is strengthened in the popular mind by the existence in Central and South America of the true-life vampire bat called *Desmodus rotundus*. This notorious bat feeds on the blood of livestock by landing near them, approaching on all fours, biting them with their razor sharp teeth in a sensitive spot, and lapping up the blood that flows from the wound. They have also been known to bite humans when the opportunity arises, and their bites can cause nasty infections and diseases. Fortunately, no Irish or European species of bat behaves remotely in this way.[2]

## RELATIONS WITH HUMANS

Bats are definitely native to Ireland. As the only order of mammal capable of true flight, there is no mystery as to how they reached the island. Suitable woodland sites for bats would have been available in Ireland about 9,000 years ago, but due to lack of fossil evidence there is at present no way of knowing when exactly they arrived. However, there is evidence that bats were in Britain about 6,000 years ago, and the likelihood is that they had reached Ireland by that time also. Not much notice seems to have been taken of bats in Ireland until recent times, as they are not a pest. Nor can they be eaten or hunted for sport, or exploited for any other use. There

is no mention of bats in the early Irish Brehon Laws and Gerald of Wales does not mention them in his description of Ireland. O'Sullivan Beare does write about them in his 1625 work *The Natural History of Ireland,* quoting from Classical sources as to their nature. These present the bat as a sort of flying mouse, which avoided daylight on account of its weak eyes, and this seems to have been the general Irish attitude as well. The only controversy surrounding the bat was the debate among Classical authorities of natural history as to whether it should be classed with birds or with mammals.

Modern advances in natural history have revealed what a remarkable creature the bat really is. There is, in fact, nothing wrong with the bat's eyesight, and it seems that it began to fly at night only to exploit the large number of flying insects that emerge after dark, and to avoid competition with the daylight hunting of birds. Bats are one of the oldest and most diverse orders of mammals, with about 970 known living species. The most remarkable feature of the bat, however, is the fact that it uses echolocation to detect its prey. In other words, it emits short pulses of high-frequency sounds (generally too high for the human ear) from its mouth and/or nostrils and, by listening to the sounds that are reflected back, it can locate its prey. Irish bats prefer woodland locations where their prey consists of various species of flying insects. During the day, and during hibernation in winter, bats roost in a variety of locations, such as caves, hollow trees, crevices in the stonework of old buildings and bridges, and in attics and other roof spaces. It is now known that there are nine species of bat native to Ireland, but they were identified only from the nineteenth century onwards, thanks to the knowledge gained by modern natural history.

Perhaps the only chance the layperson has to distinguish between bat species is by observing their flight. With a wingspan of 32 cm, the largest species of bat in Ireland is the Leisler's bat. Its flight is straight, high and fast at the level of the treetops, but it may also be seen flying around streetlamps to catch the insects attracted to the light. Ireland holds some of the largest colonies of Leisler's bat in Europe. Next in size with a wingspan of 23–29 cm is the long-eared bat. As its name suggests, it has very long ears, about three quarters the length of the head and body combined, which it is possible to see as it flies. Its flight is slow and fluttery near to trees and bushes, and it also has a habit of hovering. In terms of appearance, the horseshoe bat is probably the most distinctive species of Irish bat. It gets its name from the horseshoe-shaped flaps around its nose, flaps that help to reflect its echolocation sound beam in the direction it wants. The horseshoe bat flies at a medium speed, with a rapid wing beat and circles a lot with frequent changes in height and direction. It is found only in the west of Ireland from Kerry up to Galway. The whiskered bat gets its name from the fine sensory whiskers around its lips and the corners of its mouth. It has a fluttering flight, flying straight and at a medium height above the treetops. It is also notable for sometimes gliding rather than flying, and making rapid smooth turns in direction. Natterer's bat gets its name from the Austrian naturalist Natterer who first identified it – not any tendency to talk a lot. It is one of Ireland's rarest bats with a moderately fast flight as it manoeuvres around trees. It can also fly slowly and hover before diving to pluck insects directly off foliage. Daubenton's bat is noticeable for usually flying over water. It flies very close to the surface with a flickering wing beat in order to catch flies and midges.

The common pipistrelle and the soprano pipistrelle vie with the pygmy shrew for the title of Ireland's smallest mammal, with a body weight of up to 8 g and a wingspan of 22 cm. The name Pipistrelle probably comes from Latin *pipio* for 'I squeak'. They are so similar in appearance that even naturalists did not realise they were two different species until recently. The common pipistrelle is probably Ireland's most abundant bat, found in every part of the country, but efforts are only beginning to distinguish it from the soprano pipistrelle (whose call is significantly higher in pitch). Their flight is fast, with an irregular flight path, and they hunt along hedgerows, above water and sometimes around street lamps. Their small size means that pipistrelles can be found roosting in places such as window sashes, under weather boards and behind fascia boards. Another pipistrelle recently found in Ireland is Natasius' pipistrelle, which was only recorded here in 1996. It is found in Counties Antrim, Down and Wicklow, and may be a new arrival. It flies very fast and with an irregular flight path in woodland and over water, and when it does fly in a straight line it uses deep wing beats.

All bat species are protected in Ireland, both north and south, so any roosts that are discovered must not be disturbed without prior consultation with the respective Environment Departments – even if the roosts can be rather messy! Bats are a unique part of the Irish fauna and deserve to be better known, if only to dispel some of the groundless fears that have grown up around them. Far from being any threat to humans, the fact is that their prodigious appetite for insects such as midges, caddis flies and crane flies make them a useful addition to our wildlife.[3]

# Bee — Beach — *Apis mellifera*

*The bee was regarded as a blessed and wise animal for its life-giving honey and useful beeswax, and respected for its industry and organisation. It was associated in mythology with goddesses representing abundance and the fertility of the land.*

## Folk Beliefs and Customs

In Ireland bees were believed to have a special wisdom, and were thought to take an acute interest in the affairs of their owners.[1] Bee-keepers, therefore, informed them in advance of projects the family intended to undertake, in the belief that they might have a beneficial effect on the outcome. Also, when a member of the bee-keeper's family died, it was customary to place a black cloth on the hive so that they might join in the mourning. A tale from County Kerry illustrates what would happen if this custom was neglected. After a boy of the household died, the bees were forgotten by everyone in their grief. The bees swarmed on the day of the funeral and were found the next day on the tomb a few miles away. It was particularly important to inform the bees if their master died, since if this was not done they would all die or fly away. It was also said in Ireland that a swarm of bees suddenly leaving the hive meant that death was hovering near the household, and that only the prayers and exorcism of a priest could avert the evil. In Ireland it was also believed that if a bee entered the house it was a sign of good luck to follow. In fact, if they arrived in a swarm from a neighbour's house, they should never be allowed back in case they took the luck for that year away with them. In England it was thought that bees would be unable to live near a house where there was hatred or anger, and that they were very averse to swearing and blasphemy. So great was the love of bees for purity that, according to another English belief, if a girl was a virgin she could pass through a swarm of bees unharmed.

Despite their ability to give honey, bees also have the disadvantage that they sting.[2] In County Offaly clover was used as a cure for bee stings, while in Counties Meath and Westmeath the leaves of mullein were used for this purpose. However, it was also thought that bee stings themselves could provide a cure. In Ireland it was thought that bee-keepers never developed rheumatism, and so a good cure for that ailment was for the affected person to allow bees to sting them. In Ireland chewing beeswax was also thought to be a good cure for blocked sinuses. Some folk beliefs also surrounded the bumblebee.[3] In the Isle of Man the first fisherman to catch a bumblebee in the spring and carry it to the fishing would be sure of good luck. In Scotland the person who caught the first bumblebee of spring would always have plenty of money. Less fortunately, in England a widespread belief was that a bumblebee coming into the house meant either a death was to follow or a stranger was coming. The bee appears in the place name Cornamagh (*Corr na mBeach* – nook of the bees), County Westmeath.[4]

## MYTHS AND LEGENDS

The bee is associated in Irish tradition with a number of Irish saints.[5] St Gobnait, who is associated with Ballyvourney and the Cork/Kerry border region, was said to have been a bee-keeper and to have used the honey to treat illnesses and heal wounds. According to one story from the area, she prevented invaders from carrying off the cattle from Ballyvourney by letting loose the bees from her hives, forcing the invaders to flee. In another version of the tale the beehive turned into a bronze helmet and the bees into soldiers. St Gobnait's bell was also said to have been miraculously formed from a beehive. The name Gobnait is itself supposedly the Irish version of the Hebrew Deborah, which means 'honeybee'. St Declan was also linked to the honeybee, as he was said to be 'industrious like the bee, so like the bee gathers honey and avoids the poisonous herbs, he gathered the sweet sap of grace and Holy Scripture'.

Bees are mentioned in some early Irish stories.[6] The Gaelic hero Fionn Mac Cumhaill's poem in praise of summer speaks of 'Bees with their little strength, carry a load reaped from the flowers'. In the tale *The Destruction of Da Derga's Hostel* the trickster of King Conaire juggled nine swords, nine silver shields and nine apples of gold so skilfully that 'their movement was like that of bees going past each other on a beautiful day'. Similarly, in the story *Táin Bó Cuailnge* the warriors Cúchulainn and Ferdiad throw their spears and knives so quickly and accurately at each other that they 'were flying from them and to them like bees on the wing on a fine summer day'. Many Irish sagas speak of honey and of the making of mead. Mead was drunk at the great, sacred Celtic festivals, and the official name of the assembly hall at Tara is *Tech Midchuarta* or the House of the Mead Circuit. The mythical Queen Maedhbh of Connaught may also be associated with mead, as her name means 'she who intoxicates'. In Germany the Celtic goddess Nantosuelta (whose name means 'winding stream') is depicted in several sites accompanied by a symbol of a house and a hive. She appears to have been a goddess of prosperity and domestic well-being.[7]

Bees also featured in Classical lore.[8] For example, it was supposed that great writers and orators such as Plato, Sophocles, Virgil and Lucan had been fed by bees or had their lips touched by honey in infancy. Bees were regarded as sacred to the goddesses of fertility and the earth such as Demeter, Cybele, Diana and Rhea. According to the Roman naturalist Pliny, bees were thought to be such pure creatures that the person taking the honey from them should be well washed and clean. They also had a particular aversion to thieves and menstruating women! The Greek philosopher Aristotle features in a popular Irish legend that connects him to the bee. The story goes that Aristotle wanted to find out the secret of how bees made honey, and constructed a glass beehive so that he could watch them at their labours. The bees, however, covered the inside of the beehive with wax so that Aristotle's view was blocked. In a rage Aristotle kicked the beehive so that it broke, and all the bees flew out and stung him until he was blinded. The story ends with the statement that only three things were ever beyond the understanding of Aristotle: the secret workings of the bees, the ebbing and flowing of the tides and the mind of a woman.

RELATIONS WITH HUMANS

The western honeybee is native to Europe, Africa and the Middle East, and its stocks of honey have been plundered by man for his own use for many thousands of years.[9] For example, a rock painting in Spain dating from about 6000 BC shows a man taking honey from a nest high up in a tree. The first evidence of apiculture or bee-keeping is found in the Sun Temple at Abu Ghorab in Egypt and dates to about 2400 BC. The temple contains reliefs showing scenes of honey being transferred from hives to large storage vessels. References to bee-keeping are also frequent in Greek and Latin sources. Roman sources refer to beehives being made of hollowed-out logs, wickerwork, bark, wooden boards and earthenware. There is little doubt that the Iron Age Celts of Europe used honey, and probably also had some knowledge of bee-keeping. The Roman writer Diodorus Siculus stated that the Celts washed honeycombs and used the washings as a drink; other classical writers refer to a honey drink which may or may not have been fermented to make mead. In general honey was used by the Celts as a sweetening agent, for preserving and for fermenting with water to make mead. A huge bronze cauldron found in the grave of a Celtic prince in Hallstatt in Austria contained the sediment of 400 litres of mead. A number of pottery containers found on Celtic Iron Age sites may well have been holders for honey or wax.

Experts are divided on whether the honeybee is native to Britain and Ireland, or whether it was brought to both islands by man.[10] The evidence certainly points to bee-keeping being an ancient practice in both places. Evidence of bee-keeping in Iron Age Britain comes from the fact that the head of a worker bee was found preserved in peat at the bottom of an Iron Age dump at Hardwick in Oxfordshire. In Ireland the earliest bee-keeping was probably carried out using hollowed logs as hives, until about the eleventh century when wickerwork basket hives replaced them. The hives were usually placed in the farmyard or orchard of the early Irish farm. Irish tradition has it that the first swarm of honeybees was brought to Ireland from Britain by St Mo Domnóc in the early seventh century, but the linguistic evidence points to bee-keeping being known in Ireland from early pre-Christian times. The Irish language has native words for bee (*beach*), honey (*mil*) and mead (*mid*) that are all related to other Indo-European languages, and indicate an ancient origin. The linguistic evidence also points to a knowledge of bee-keeping in pre-Christian times. The Irish term for the second swarm which leaves a beehive annually is *tarbhshaithe* or 'bull-swarm'. This is the exact equivalent of the Welsh (*taruheit*) and Breton (*tarvhed*) terms, and indicates a common Celtic origin. This need to

QUEEN.

WORKER.

DRONE.

distinguish between the first and second swarms strongly indicates human supervision in the bee colonies. It may be that the stories of bee-keeping being introduced by Christian saints was because Christian monasteries practised it on a far larger scale than previously, and so became associated with bee-keeping in the popular mind.

Honey was an important high-energy food source in early Ireland, especially in winter as it keeps well in storage.[11] As well as being a nourishing food in its own right, honey was used in Ireland as a flavour in cooking, generally by rubbing meat with honey and salt and cooking it over an open fire. Salmon was also baked in honey. The Old Irish tale *Bricriu's Feast* refers to 'wheaten bread baked with honey'. The other important use of honey was, of course, to make mead, which seems to have been regarded as a somewhat higher class of drink than beer, especially favoured by the Gaelic nobility. Honey was also regarded as having important medical properties, although one medical text warns against using honey when there is an infection of the stomach.

The honeybee was considered important enough in early Ireland for the Brehon Laws to have its own law text on bee-keeping, the *Bechbretha*, which dates to the seventh century.[12] The laws on bees were founded on the rather obscure principle that a bee taking nectar from flowers on a neighbour's property was guilty of 'grazing-trespass', in the same way as animals like cattle or sheep were when they grazed grass on a neighbour's land. They could also be guilty of 'leaping-trespass' like domestic fowl when they flew onto a neighbour's land. How this principle worked in practice was that a landowner was legally allowed three years of freedom when starting bee-keeping, during which his bees could 'graze' or forage on his neighbours' lands without liability. On the fourth year, however, the first swarm to issue from the hive had to be given to the neighbour on whose land the bees had done the most foraging. In fifth and later years, subsequent swarms had to be given in turn to other neighbours. Despite its intricacy, the net effect of this law must have been the positive one of spreading bee-keeping more widely. Another important issue dealt with in the *Bechbretha* was the correct way of dealing with stings from bees. In general the rule was that a person who had been stung by a bee (and who had not been interfering with the hives or bees in any way) was entitled to a meal of honey from the bee-keeper. To get the meal, however, the person had to swear that they did not kill the bee that had stung them, as they would then be regarded as having exacted their own punishment already. In the case where a person was unfortunate enough to die as a result of a bee sting, the bee-keeper had to pay a fine of two hives, presumably to the next of kin.

Apart from honey, bees were also valued for their production of wax, and beeswax was used for many purposes in the ancient world.[13] As early as 3000 BC the ancient Egyptians were using beeswax for embalming and modelling. Wax models of cats, eagles and scarab beatles have been recovered from Egyptian tombs. In ancient Greece urns of oil and amphorae of wine were sealed with wax, and since Roman times a mixture of resin and beeswax has been used for affixing official seals to documents, which are then marked with unique signet rings or seals. The Romans also wrote messages on wax tablets, which had an advantage in that they could be rubbed out and reused. Mural decorations in coloured beeswax also appeared in the homes of many wealthy Romans, and some fine specimens were uncovered in Herculaneum. The pagan gods of Rome had wax candles lit in their honour and this tradition continued into Christian times. Even today, the candles used by the Roman Catholic Church for Pascal celebrations, and for the forty days between Easter and the Feast of the Ascension, must have some beeswax content. Until the advent of modern forms of lighting, the well-to-do generally had candles made from beeswax, which had a good light and a pleasant aroma. The poor usually had to make do with cheap tallow candles made from mutton fat, which burnt with a smoky flame and had an unpleasant smell.

In modern Ireland the number of bee-keepers is well over 2,000, with 22,000 colonies of honeybees between them.[14] In general Irish bees have been spared the worst of the host of ills that now plague honeybees worldwide, some of them deeply mysterious, like Colony Collapse Disorder in the United States, in which whole colonies of bees suddenly abandon their hives and simply disappear. The greatest threat to Irish bees remains the parasitic mite varroa, which weakens hives and leaves them vulnerable to viruses. This has been imported into Ireland with European (especially Italian) queen bees, even though such imports are illegal. Ireland has now been recognised as a unique reserve of the indigenous race of the dark European honeybee (*Apis mellifera mellifera*), and efforts are under way among bee-keepers to preserve this resource through selective breeding programmes. The honeybee is at the furthest extent of its natural range in Ireland and depends on a few key plants to survive the cooler months, such as dandelions in the spring, and ivy which flowers in the autumn. Heather is another crucial plant in sustaining bees in many areas where poorer soils mean that there are few other flowers. Native Irish bees are particularly well adapted to Ireland's climate, and they are able to produce a honey surplus even in cool and windy summers. Unlike the Italian bee, Irish bees also know when to stop rearing more young if the weather turns bad, and maintain smaller hives of about 35,000 bees, rather than the European average of 50,000. The Irish bee is also known for its more amiable temperament, which presumably makes life easier for Irish bee-keepers!

## SIMILAR ANIMALS

### Devil's Coach Horse – *Deargadaol* – *Ocypus olens*

Apart from the bee, the other insect to feature regularly in Irish folklore is the Devil's Coach Horse, a distinctive-looking beetle about 25 mm in length and resembling a large black earwig. It is usually better known in Ireland as the *deargadaol* or *daradaol* (even in English-speaking areas), or more confusingly as the chafer or cockroach, although these names more correctly belong to different species. When threatened, the Devil's Coach Horse raises its abdomen in the air and opens its pincers, giving it a menacing appearance. According to Irish tradition, the *daradaol* is cursed as it helped to betray Christ by giving information to his pursuers. One version of the story is that Christ passed through a field and the soldiers following lost track of him. However, the *daradaol* spoke up and told the soldiers that Christ had just passed by. Another tradition was that the *daradaol* guided Judas to Gethsemane. A widespread belief, therefore, was that blessings would come to anyone who killed a *daradaol*. Various traditions existed as to the best way to do this. One method was to crush it under the bare foot, which guaranteed a day, hour or week less in purgatory. Another tradition

Otter – Madra Uisce – *Lutra lutra*

Salmon – Bradán – *Salmo salar*

Snake – Nathair Nimhe – *Ophidia*

Frog – Frog – *Rana temporaria*

held that it should be killed with the nail of the thumb. Less pleasantly, yet another version held that the *daradaol* could only be killed by biting its head off. However, the person brave enough to do this would have the seven deadly sins removed from them. The *daradaol*'s antipathy to Christians is said to be still shown by its habit of raising its tail to curse the beholder. However, the *daradaol*'s powers were not all negative. A widespread folk tale relates how an old man was able to cut the harvest effortlessly for many years using only an old, worn-out sickle. Eventually the old man died, and the sickle was examined to find out its secret. When the handle was pulled off, a *daradaol* ran out of it and disappeared. When tried again, the blunt old sickle was completely useless.[15]

*Water Animals*

# Whale – Míol Mór – *Cetacea*

*The whale was regarded as a great and mysterious monster of the deep that could bring either great benefit or harm. The whale was also valued for the prodigious amount of meat, oil and whalebone it provided; something that has endangered the survival of many species of whale.*

## SPECIES NAMES

Northern Right Whale – *Fíormhíol Mór na Bioscáine – Eubalaena glacialis*
Humpback Whale – *Míol Mór Dronnach – Megaptera novaeangliae*
Blue Whale – *Míol Mór Gorm – Baleanoptera musculus*
Fin Whale – *Míol Mór Eiteach – Baleanoptera physalus*
Sei Whale – *Míol Mór an Tuaisceart – Balaenoptera borealis*
Minke whale – *Míol Mór Mince – Balaenoptera acutorostrata*
Sperm Whale – *Caisealóid – Physeter macrocephalus*
Killer Whale – *Cráin Dubh – Orcinus orca*

## FOLK BELIEFS AND CUSTOMS

The whale features in an Irish folk tale about the invention of the first harp.[1] The story goes that a dead whale was washed ashore near to where a chieftain lived. The whale rotted away until there was nothing left but the skeleton, and when the wind blew through the skeleton it made lovely music. The chieftain's wife was very fond of singing and music, and was so taken with the sound that she made an instrument with strings out of the whale's bones (probably the baleen contained in the mouth). Thus the first harp was invented.

## MYTHS AND LEGENDS

The most famous Irish legend about a whale appears in *The Voyage of St Brendan*, when the monks on their journey came upon a bare and stony island.[2] It was Easter Sunday and they lit a fire. However, as the pot with their meat began to boil, the island started to rock to and fro like a wave. The monks left hurriedly and watched in amazement as the 'island' moved away over the sea. As they watched the light of their fire recede in the distance, St Brendan told them that the island was in fact the foremost fish in the ocean, called Jasconius. The monks came upon Jasconius the following year, again on Easter Sunday, and saw the remains of their pot. They did not light a fire on this occasion, but spent the time on the creature's back praying instead. On another occasion a whale came to the aid of the monks when they were being pursued by a monstrous creature. St Brendan prayed for aid and the whale arose to do battle with the monster. In their struggle, both creatures sank beneath the waves, never to be seen again.

Another significant Irish legend concerned a great whale called Rossualt that was cast ashore at Murrisk in Connaught, and had the power of prophecy.[3] St Columcille was the only person who could interpret its secrets, by observing the way it spouted water out of its blowhole. If it 'vomited' to sea with its tail held high, it portended foundering of boats and ships, and the destruction of sea animals that year. If it spouted up into the air with its tail down, it meant the destruction of the flying animals of the air that year. If it spouted out over the land so that it stank, it meant destruction to human beings and cattle that year. Another version of the tale is given in a poem in the *Metrical Dindshenchus* (or lore of place names), which, even though it differs in the detail, is in agreement that Rossualt's prophecies meant only misfortune.

ROSSUALT'S LAY

A great sea-fish in whale form came
To land ashore in omen grave
Rossualt the name by which it was known
Bringing tidings of many woes.

When with an outpouring vast
The beast spewed forth its stream of waste
Over the lands it faced to the east
There would appear the vilest disease.

When it spouted up to the clouds
the heavens to warfare were aroused
and its spout with downward motion
was plague to creatures of the ocean.

The whale is also linked in Irish legend to Manannán, the Celtic god of the sea.[4] Manannán had a bag made out of the skin of a crane that contained various treasures. When the sea was full the treasures were visible in its middle, but when the tide ebbed the crane-bag was empty. One of the treasures the bag contained was a 'girdle of the great whale's back' – presumably whalebone or baleen.

RELATIONS WITH HUMANS

It does not appear that whales were ever hunted in early Ireland, but stranded whales were certainly exploited for their meat. For example, the *Annals of Connaught* record that in 1246 a whale was stranded at Cúl Irra in County Sligo, which 'brought great relief and joy to the whole territory'.

Under the law, windfalls such as stranded whales belonged to the king, since they were seen as the result of his just rule, but he could grant the whale to the local community if requested to by the head of the local kin (*fine*). As one law tract put it: 'It is through the justice of the ruler that many creatures and many animals from the deep and great seas are cast up on lawful shores.'

The earliest records of organised whaling date from the eleventh century in the Bay of Biscay, but modern commercial whaling began in the eighteenth century, especially in North America. Whales were hunted because their peculiar evolution as seagoing mammals made them the owners of several natural resources that humans wanted. Firstly, large species of whales such as the Northern Right whale and the Sperm whale contain vast amounts of oil in their bodies, for insulation and to maintain buoyancy (each Northern Right whale has about 20 tonnes of whale oil in its body). Before the modern petroleum oil industry, this was the main source of oil for lamp fuel and lubricants. In the mid-eighteenth century over 700 ships from North America alone were hunting sperm whales, so great was the demand for oil. Another important reason to exploit the whale was the long baleen plates known as 'whalebone' that Baleen whales (*Mysticeti*), like the Blue whale, contain in their mouths instead of teeth. These plates of baleen (not a bone at all, but a form of keratin) form a mesh which acts as a filter to catch plankton when the whale engulfs huge amounts of seawater. The whale then expels the filtered seawater and swallows the accumulated plankton. The tough, flexible baleen or whalebone had many uses as a support material for items such as corsets, umbrellas and, in the Middle Ages, crossbows. In early Ireland 'whale's eyelashes', as they were called, were used for the backs of riddles (or sieves), the breastwork of saddles and for making hoops for barrels. Whales, of course, were also attractive to hunters because of the huge amounts of meat and blubber they provided as food. The great size of whales is also due to their sea-based existence, as it means they do not have the same problems with gravity as land-based animals. Consequently, the Blue whale and the Fin whale are respectively the largest and second largest species of animal that have ever existed on earth, dinosaurs included.

The species that suffered most from whaling were the Northern Right whale, the Humpback whale, the Blue whale, the Sei whale, the Fin whale and the Sperm whale. Although some have recovered better than others, none has reached again its pre-whaling population. The whaling industry began to decline in the twentieth century, both because the important species of whale had been hunted to near extinction, and because whale oil was no longer as much in demand. Eventually the International Whaling Commission moved to protect most species of whale throughout the twentieth century, beginning with the Right whale in 1935, and including most species by the 1970s. A general ban on whaling was declared in 1985, but small numbers of whales are still allowed to be hunted for food by native peoples in such places as Greenland and the Pacific. In Ireland whaling was never an important industry, but whaling stations did operate on Iniskea and in Blacksod Bay, both in County Mayo, between the years 1908–15 and 1920–2. Irish waters are some of the most important migratory routes for many species of whale, and for this reason Ireland declared in 1991 that all cetaceans (whales and dolphins) would be protected within the Irish fisheries limit of 320 km from the coast, the first sanctuary of its kind in Europe.

The first species to be extensively hunted was the Northern Right whale (and its close cousin the Southern Right whale), which gets its name simply because it was the 'right' species of whale to hunt. This was on account of the large amount of oil it contained, its slow speed, and the fact that it floated when killed. Today it is probably one of the most endangered whales, with a world population of a few thousand. It formerly passed Ireland in large numbers as it migrated from its wintering grounds in the Bay of Biscay to its summer feeding grounds off Spitzbergen in Norway. However, only two sightings of Right whales have been recorded off Ireland since 1970, and the population in the eastern Atlantic may be heading for extinction. The Humpback whale (so-called because it arches its back before it dives) also passes Ireland as it migrates from the Carribean to Iceland, but it is still scarce in the eastern Atlantic, with only a few sightings off Ireland since 1966. Its numbers are recovering better than the Right whale, however, with as many as 5,000 whales in the western Atlantic. Humpbacks are famous for having the most complex set of sounds of all whales, and the male produces the long sequence of repeated phrases (probably in order to attract females) that have become generally known as 'whalesong'.

The Blue whale, Fin whale and Sei whale are all fairly fast swimmers, and only became a major target for whalers in the nineteenth and twentieth centuries as steamship technology enabled whalers to pursue them. At about 26 m long, the Blue whale is the largest animal that has ever existed, and can weigh as much as twenty-five African elephants. It was driven close to extinction by whaling, and the current world population is still very low at somewhere between 2,000 and 5,000. There have been few sightings in Irish waters of Blue whales in recent years. The Sei whale, like the Blue whale, was hunted almost to extinction, but has recovered rather better. Its population in the northern hemisphere is now estimated at about 17,000 and it is believed to account for some of the unidentified whales passing through Irish waters as it makes its way from its winter grounds off Spain and Portugal to its summer grounds off the coast of Norway. The Sei gets its name for the Norwegian word for the pollock fish, as it arrives near Norway at the same time as the pollock, both in search of plankton. The Fin whale was also almost wiped out, but its numbers have grown again to about 50,000 in the north Atlantic, and it is now regularly spotted off the south and west coasts of Ireland. The Fin whale gets its name because of its relatively large dorsal fin, about two thirds of the way down its body. Unlike other whales the Fin whale is largely sedentary and there are estimated to be about 700 fin whales 'resident' off the Irish coast at present. Another Baleen whale is the Minke whale, which has a similar-shaped dorsal fin to the Fin whale, but at 10 m long is considerably smaller than the 20 m Fin whale. The minke whale was also hunted in the twentieth century as larger whales became scarce (it gets its name from a famous whaler), but its population has since grown to 80,000 in the north Atlantic. This is the whale most likely to be seen from land in Ireland, as it comes close to the coast in late summer and autumn, and may even occasionally be seen in places such as Dublin Bay. They can feed on small fish, and so are likely to be spotted where shoals of fish have also attracted gulls and other seabirds.

The Sperm whale and the Killer whale (or Orca) are both members of the Toothed Whales (*Odontoceti*), which means they are predators, feeding on fish and squid and, in the case of the killer whale, even their smaller cousins, dolphins and porpoises. The teeth of such whales were considered valuable in early Ireland as decorative items. The Sperm whale was one of the first species to be hunted by whalers, on account of the large amount of oil it contains in its squarish head. This oil was incorrectly known as *spermaceti* or whale sperm, because it solidifies to a white waxy substance after death. As well as providing oil and blubber, Sperm whales were the source of a substance known as ambergris. Ambergris is a deposit in the whale's intestine that was used as a fixative in the manufacture of perfumes and cosmetics. Sperm whales were commercially hunted since the eighteenth century, especially from North America, and the hunting of them was only finally banned in 1985. The most famous whale in literature, Moby-Dick, was a sperm whale, and the author, Herman Melville, based his novel about the great white whale on several real-life accounts of sperm whales. *Moby-Dick* itself was based on stories of a real whale called Mocha Dick,[5] a giant white sperm whale notorious for its violent attacks on ships, which lived off the island of Mocha in Chile. Sperm whales can occasionally be completely white in colour, so Mocha Dick's white colour is not impossible. Melville's novel was also based on the famous incident of the whaleship *Essex*, which was attacked and sunk by a sperm whale in the Pacific in 1820. The event was notorious as the crew who escaped the sinking in lifeboats resorted to eating each other in order to survive.[6]

Sperm whales migrate from the equator to the north pole during the year and may be seen passing in the waters off Ireland in late summer and autumn. They may also occasionally enter coastal waters. There are probably about 20,000 Sperm whales in the North Atlantic at present. The Killer whale is notable for its black-and-white patterned body, and for the male's large upright dorsal fin that frequently appears above the water as it swims. They do not migrate much, but instead range over a wide territory in groups (called pods), including estuaries and shallow bays. Killer whales, known for their intelligence, are ruthless hunters of fish and other cetaceans. One tactic of Killer whales is for a pod to herd a shoal of fish, such as herrings, into tight shoals near the surface before stunning them with tail slaps. They have never been hunted in any substantial numbers by man and are considered to be fairly common. Killer whales are regularly seen off Irish waters, and are probably the third or fourth most frequently sighted whale there. They can also sometimes enter fresh water, and in early November 1977 a Killer whale hunted salmon in the River Foyle for five consecutive days.

The waters off Ireland's south and west coasts are some of the best places in Europe to see whales. Whale watching is becoming a major tourist attraction worldwide, especially on the east and west coasts of America, with Humpback whales a favourite. Ireland is well placed to develop this industry, and whale-watching boats trips are becoming a staple of the tourist industry in the west of Ireland. Ireland is also a good place to see whales from land, from headlands and cliffs along the coast, although this requires a lot more patience. Hopefully the days of being hunted are largely over for the whale, and human's interest in them will increasingly become one of observing these magnificent creatures in their natural habitat.[7]

SIMILAR ANIMALS

Common Porpoise – *Muc Mhara* – *Phocaena phocaena*
The English name porpoise is a corruption of the Latin *porcus* (pig) and *piscis* (fish), and refers to the fact that the porpoise has blubbery but edible flesh. The porpoise frequents estuaries and coastal bays more than other cetaceans, making it easier to hunt. The Irish name *muc mhara* similarly means 'pig of the sea', and is a reference to the fact that they were regularly hunted in Ireland since ancient times. For example, the *Annals of Ulster* record that Norsemen carried out a great slaughter of porpoises in AD 828 on the coast of County Louth. A legal commentary in the early Irish Brehon Laws on the entitlements of a maritime king also refers to him getting his share of catches of salmon, seal and porpoise. As late as the eighteenth century porpoise meat was exported to England. Porpoises are the most common cetacean in Irish waters, but their numbers are threatened in the long term by pollution, overfishing taking their food supply, and from becoming entangled in fishing nets. Porpoises can be regularly seen from places such as the Old Head of Kinsale and Cape Clear, County Cork, Slea Head, County Kerry, Howth Head, County Dublin and Bray Head, County Wicklow. They can be identified by their small size (about 1.5 m long) and the small triangular dorsal fin halfway along the back.

Common Dolphin – *Deilf* – *Delphinus delphis*
The Common dolphin is the second most widely seen cetacean around the Irish coast. Dolphins were associated with sea deities in both Celtic and Classical mythology. Dolphins appear in imagery associated with the Celtic North Sea goddess Nehalennia, protectress of sea travellers and traders, and the British water goddess Coventina. In Classical mythology the dolphin was regarded as the King of the Fishes and was sacred to Apollo, Neptune (or Poseidon) and Venus (or Aphrodite). They were seen as lovers of music, and as kinder and more sensitive than humans. In Roman mythology they were also seen as symbolising the journey of the human soul across the sea

to the Isles of the Blessed. Similar imagery may be involved in the image of a boy riding a dolphin depicted on the Celtic Iron Age ritual cauldron found at Gundestrup in Denmark. Today, large numbers of dolphins are killed in tuna fishing nets and bottom-set gill nets, and it is doubtful if the scale of losses can be sustained in the long term. Dolphins can be regularly seen from places such as the Old Head of Kinsale and Cape Clear, County Cork, Slea Head, County Kerry, Loop Head, County Clare, Dublin Bay and off Rosslare, County Wexford. The Common dolphin is about 2–2.4 m long, and the dorsal fin is long, slender, sickle-shaped and halfway along the back.

Bottle-nosed Dolphin – *Deilf Bolgshrónach* – *Tursiops truncates*
The Bottle-nosed dolphin is one of the most common cetaceans in Irish waters and gets its name from its distinctively large, rounded beak. As well as its broad snout, the Bottle-nose has a mouth which curves up at the end, giving it the appearance of a mischievous grin. This is the species most seen in captivity, and is therefore what most people probably have in mind when they picture a dolphin. Lone individuals often socialise with humans and may take up residence in areas close to human settlement. The most famous example of this in Ireland is 'Fungi', the dolphin who has lived around Dingle Bay in County Kerry for many years. Like other dolphins, Bottle-noses are vulnerable to pollution and becoming entangled in nets. Bottle-noses are found in places such as the Shannon Estuary, Galway Bay, Clew Bay and Killary Harbour, County Mayo, Bantry Bay, County Cork, and Dingle Bay, County Kerry. The Bottle-nosed dolphin, at about 3–4 m long, is much larger than the Common dolphin. The dorsal fin is long, slender, sickle-shaped and halfway down the back.

Pilot Whale – *Míol Phíolótach* – *Globiocephela melaena*
Although it is called a whale, the Pilot whale should be more accurately called a dolphin. The Pilot whale gets its name from its habit of swimming in formation behind a leader, and Pilot whales are highly gregarious animals. The Pilot whale is also known as the blackfish on account of its black or dark grey colour. Unfortunately the Pilot whale's very sociable habits make it vulnerable to mass strandings, as members of the same group or 'pod' will refuse to leave their stranded companion, and so risk becoming stranded themselves. For example, in November 1965 sixty-three individuals were

stranded in Kerry, and mass strandings of several hundred individuals are not unknown. This trait also makes them easy to hunt, and in places such as the Hebrides and the Faroe Islands boats were used to drive the whales onto the shore. The social bond between the whales is so strong that they will then stay close to shore even as their fellow whales are being killed. The Pilot whale is one of the most common species of cetacean seen in Irish waters, mainly off the west coast, and there were estimated to be about 780,000 in the central and northern Atlantic in 1989. The male pilot whale is about 5.7 m long, while the female is about 4.5 m long. The dorsal fin is sickle-shaped and located slightly forward of halfway down the back.[8]

# Seal – Rón – *Phoca/Halichoerus*

*The seal, with its mournful cries and human expression, was regarded in Irish tradition as a mysterious and otherworldly animal, being often the souls of the dead returned in another form. Despite this, it was seen as a valuable source of meat and of oil, which was used as a cure for stiff and painful joints.*

## Folk Beliefs and Customs

The most widespread Irish tradition about seals was that they represented the souls of dead people who had returned in seal form.[1] One belief was that they were the people who had been left out of Noah's Ark, and as a result they had been changed into seal form. Another belief was that they were the drowned children of the giant Balor. Related to these ideas was the notion of fairy beings called 'silkies' who were seals by day and humans by night.[2] Many stories told of how they could be seen on the seashore at night, dancing in their human form after casting off their sealskins. In human form they were noticeable for their webbed hands and feet, and they were forced to obey anyone who secured their oily sealskins. A popular story based on these ideas tells of a young man who saw a number of seals coming ashore and casting off their skins to appear as beautiful young women. The young man stole one of the skins, and the girl to whom it belonged had to follow him home. Despite this, she was happy to live in human form, and forgot about her life in the sea. Indeed, shortly afterwards the young man married her and they had three children together. One day many years later, the youngest child found a strange bundle hidden in the loft and brought it to his mother. It was the woman's sealskin, and when she saw it she at once remembered her own people and her life in the sea. She said goodbye to the children, slipped on the sealskin and returned once more to the sea, never to return. According to tradition, several families in the west of Ireland (such as the Kinealys from Connemara) and Scotland were said to have descended from this seal-woman, and they were duty bound never to assist in the killing of a seal. In County Kerry it was said

that one of the signs that a person was descended from the 'people of the sea' was that he or she could never sleep, day or night.

Seals were valued in Irish coastal communities both for their meat and for their oily fat, which was considered an excellent cure for stiff joints and rheumatism.[3] Killing seals, however, with their humanlike cries and expressions, caused unease, as many stories in Ireland tell of strange consequences for those who attempted to hunt them.[4] For example, one story from County Galway tells of a man who regularly enjoyed hunting seals. He then had two daughters, but when each was born they had webbed claws like a seal, instead of human hands. In County Kerry a story relates how a fisherman killed a seal and brought it to the quayside to skin it. Before he could begin, he heard a voice from the sea calling: 'Brother! Where is my brother?' It was another seal rising on the waves, calling out in vain for the one that had been killed. A story from County Donegal tells of fishermen from Teelin going to a cove west of Slieve League with the intention of killing seals. They found a seal at the top of the cove, but just as one of the men went to hit it on the head, the seal spoke and said: 'Don't strike, don't strike my old grey cap!' From that day on the fishermen of Teelin ceased to kill seals. It was believed in County Donegal that seals were people from Scotland under enchantment, so killing them could have repercussions. One such story tells of a fisherman finding a seal in a cave and starting to strike it. The seal cried out: 'Mac Ruaidhri, Mac Ruaidhri, don't hit me any more!' Frightened by this, Mac Ruaidhri and the three men with him left quickly and went home. Some time later, the four men were caught in a storm and blown over to Scotland. Seeking shelter they arrived at a cottage that had a man with a bandaged head inside. When

Mac Ruaidhri asked him what was wrong, he replied: 'Can't you recognise your own handiwork? Don't you remember the day you hit me in the cave, and if you take my advice you'll leave this house now because if my people catch you, you'll never leave!' Mac Ruaidhri and his men departed rapidly and never hunted seals from that day on.

Seals were sometimes thought to forecast the weather.[5] For instance, in Inis Oirr in the Aran Islands, County Galway, the appearance of a seal on a certain rock signified that a week of dry weather was to come. In County Donegal, on the other hand, it was thought that seals coming up on to the beach meant a storm was on the way, while for seals to be crying out was also a sign of a storm. An Irish proverb for a time so long ago that no one remembers it is: ó bearradh na rónta – 'when seals were shorn'.[6] The seal appears in some Irish place names.[7] The best known of these is Roundstone (Cloch na Rón – stone of the seals) in Connemara, County Galway. Other names include Lisronagh (Lios Rónach – seal fort), County Tyrone, Ringrone (Rinn Róin – seal point), County Cork, and Shinrone (Suí an Róin – seat of the seal), County Offaly.

## MYTHS AND LEGENDS

The seal features in some Irish legends, often coming to the aid of a saint in some way.[8] St Mochua was sustained at one point by a seal that brought him four salmon so he could be fed. St Patrick was also said to have possessed a sealskin, which he used to stand on while he was saying Mass. The skin was credited with working many miracles and was later preserved as a relic of the saint. The seal is also mentioned as a poetic symbol of the sea. A poem in the Metrical Dindshenchus describes the sea as 'the seal's green plain', while seals accompany Tadhg on his journey to the Island of Mannanán, Celtic god of the sea.[9] Another early Irish poem tells of how Mannanán's son Mongán had the power to take on different animal forms, one of which was a seal. In the tale The Exile of the Sons of Uisneach Deirdre in her lament for Scotland mentions 'Assaroe of the seals'.

## RELATIONS WITH HUMANS

Seals have been eaten in Ireland since the earliest times.[10] For example, seal remains were found in a Mesolithic kitchen midden on Dalkey Island in County Dublin, dating back to about 4400 BC. There is also evidence that seals were valued as a source of food in Gaelic Ireland and Scotland. Large numbers of seal bones have been found in Irish maritime sites from the early Christian period. Adomnán's *Life of Columba* also refers to the entitlement of the island monastery of Iona in Scotland to take seal pups from a certain small island near Mull. In the early Irish Brehon Laws a section on the duties and entitlements of a maritime king refers to his right to catches of salmon, seal and porpoise. As well as their flesh, seals would have been considered valuable for their hides and oil. Adult seals were hunted with a special seal spear (*róngáe*).

There are two species of seal normally resident in Irish waters, the Common or Harbour seal (*Phoca vitulina*) and the Grey seal (*Halichoerus grypus*).[11] The easiest way for the layperson to tell them apart is to remember that the Common seal has a somewhat dog-like appearance with an upturned snout, while the Grey seal has a long snout with a 'roman' nose. Despite its name, the Common seal is now the rarer of the two as its numbers declined considerably in the nineteenth century. The largest populations of Common seals in Irish waters are at Strangford Lough, County Down, with about 1,000 seals, and Glengarrif, County Cork, with about 200. The rest are scattered in bays and estuaries right around Ireland. The Grey seal used to be relatively rare in Irish waters, but since the nineteenth century its numbers have grown. There are now estimated to be over 3,000 Grey seals around Ireland. The main breeding sites are the Inishkea Islands, County Mayo, and the Blaskets in County Kerry, with important colonies also on Lambay, Skerries and Dalkey Islands (all in County Dublin), Glengarriff, County Cork, and Wexford Harbour.

The Grey seal was until recently subject to commercial hunting for its flesh, oil and skins. Both species of seals (but the Grey in particular) are regularly blamed for causing serious damage to fisheries, and are intensely disliked by fishermen for this reason. They steal fish caught on lines, damage fish in nets and can also take fish from fish farms. It appears that the damage is caused by a few 'rogue' seals that have learnt to exploit this resource rather than the action of whole colonies. Until modern times these activities meant that seals were regarded as a game species and were regularly hunted. Until the Wildlife Act of 1976 a bounty scheme operated for the Common seal in an attempt to limit their numbers, while Grey seals were hunted along the west coast of Ireland in 'seal safaris'. Both species of seal are now protected and may only be culled under licence. A number of schemes that seek to deter seals from taking fish, and thus reduce or remove the need for culling, are under investigation. Hopefully this will mean that fishermen and seals will have a happier relationship in the future, and allow a more peaceful existence for an animal that is an important and unique part of Ireland's fauna.

# Otter – Madra Uisce – *Lutra lutra*

*The otter was seen in Irish tradition as a kind of 'water-dog', which shared the dog's positive traits of helpfulness and hard work, and is mentioned in legends as coming to the assistance of Irish saints. More pragmatically, the otter was also valued for its fine pelt, and regarded as an animal noble enough to be hunted by royalty.*

## FOLK BELIEFS AND CUSTOMS

According to Irish folk belief, otters slept with their eyes open. A special and rare kind, called the 'king-otter', never slept at all.[1] The king-otter or 'durracow' was claimed to be a male otter of extraordinary size, completely white in colour except for a black cross on his back and black on the tips of his ears. He could only be killed (rather like a werewolf) with a bullet made from silver, and the person who killed him would not live for more than twenty-four hours afterwards. However, anyone who came into possession of a piece of his pelt was very fortunate, as it had the power to guarantee safety at sea to any boat that had a piece on board, safety from fire to any house in which it was kept, and safety from all accidents to any man who had a piece of it in his pocket. Interestingly, a variety of otter with white spots on its coat is apparently not uncommon in Irish waters, so there may be a kernel of truth in the description of the king-otter, if not in its powers!

It was widely believed that the favourite fish by far of the otter was the salmon.[2] It was thought that the otter killed the salmon by grabbing it by the tail and turning its head against the current of the river. The flooding waters were then supposed to kill the fish by choking it. Otters are now a protected species, but in former times they were hunted and trapped, both for their fine fur and because they were considered to be vermin who preyed on fish stocks. Occasionally a hunter would get bitten by an otter as he removed it from a trap. If the wound festered and refused to heal, folk wisdom held that the only remedy was to kill another otter and eat its flesh. The otter was nevertheless respected for its skill in catching fish, and an old

Irish saying stated that the otter was one of three things that never rested – the other two being a steep waterfall and a demon from hell.

The otter appears in some Irish place names.[3] For example, Pouladorane (*Poll an Dobhrán*), County Cork, and Pollnamadraeessky (*Poll na Madra Uisce*), County Longford, both of which mean the den or 'holt' of the otter.

MYTHS AND LEGENDS

The otter appears in several legends as the helper of various saints.[4] The *Life of St Kevin* recounts how the saint used to recite his vespers while standing in the lake at Glendalough. On one occasion the psalter he used for this purpose fell into the lake, but an otter caught it before it got wet. The same helpful otter used to bring a salmon from the lake for the monks every day. However, one of the monks decided to take advantage of this by killing the otter for its skin. The otter somehow knew of the monk's intention and disappeared, and St Kevin was so angered by this that he ordered the monk to leave the community. In the tale 'Mad Sweeney' or *Suibhne Geilt*, Sweeney, a king in early Ireland, insults St Ronan by throwing his psalter into a lake. St Ronan curses the king, who is driven mad and flees to live as an outcast in the woods. St Ronan's psalter is then rescued from the lake for him by a friendly otter. In *The Voyage of St Brendan* the voyagers come upon a monk living on a tiny outcrop of rock in the ocean. The monk is living there by choice as a hermit, and he is helped to survive by an otter that brings him a fish and a bundle of firewood every three days.

Otters are not particularly vocal animals, but they can emit whistles and chattering, chuckling sounds, particularly during courtship.[5] The call of the otter is thus mentioned with affection in several early Irish tales. In his dialogue with St Patrick, the Gaelic hero Oisín lists the sounds of nature that used to soothe his father, Fionn, to sleep, among them 'the call of the otter of Druim-re-coir'. In a poem in praise of Beann Ghualainn, Oisín lists the various animals living there, including the otter, saying 'sweet too were the voices of your otters'.

RELATIONS WITH HUMANS

The early Irish Brehon Laws only refer to otters in the unlikely event of one being kept as a pet, where it is classed with the dog in terms of the legal penalties. This is probably to do with the law covering every eventuality rather than being an indication that otters were kept as pets on any significant scale. There is some evidence of otters being hunted in early Ireland, probably for their pelts. The Old Irish tale *Táin Bó Fraích* describes a great hunt organised at the royal site of the kings of Connaught at Rathcroghan, County Roscommon where the hounds successfully pursued deer, wild boar, hare, fox and otter. Later in the same tale there is a reference to harpers having harp bags made out of otter skin. There are also some indications that otters were occasionally hunted to be eaten. One tale of the Fianna mentions them eating otter; while outside Ireland, the Norse tale *Otter's Ransom* describes how the god Loki killed an enchanted otter for food, and was then forced to pay a ransom to his family. Otter-hunting was also a traditional sport in Britain. King Henry II gave it prominence in 1170, when he appointed a King's Otterhunter, and royal packs of otterhounds were kept by successive kings until 1689. Otter-hunting also continued in Ireland until modern times and there are records of otters having been killed for their pelts from the fifteenth century onwards. For example, almost 350 skins a year were exported from Ireland in the second half of the eighteenth century. Indeed, as late as 1955 there were two otter-hunting clubs in Ireland. Nowadays, however, this beautiful member of our native fauna has full status as a protected species.[6]

## Salmon – Bradán – *Salmo salar*

*The salmon, with its nourishing flesh and athletic feats of leaping upstream, was associated with supreme physical and mental health and long life. It was also associated in myth with kings and poets, and with wisdom and occult knowledge.*

### Folk Beliefs and Customs

The salmon was regarded in Irish folk belief as the epitome of good physical and mental health, and the phrase *sláinte an bhradáin* ('the salmon's health') was synonymous with robust good health.[1] Indeed, every person was supposed to have an internal 'salmon of life' in their body, which overexertion could cause to be expelled, resulting in death if it were not immediately restored. Drowned people were sometimes also said to appear in the form of a large black salmon on a river. According to folklore, St Patrick gave the salmon its great power to leap.[2] The story goes that the saint was passing a river one day where some pagan men were fishing. They decided to make fun of the saint by promising him the next fish they caught. When they did catch the fish, however, they refused to give it to him saying: 'Wait, Patrick, and you'll get the next fish we catch.' Unusually for Patrick he accepted this slight calmly and continued to wait. The next fish the men caught was a plaice, and when it saw the pagan men mocking the saint it joined in, twisting its neck to look over its shoulder scornfully at Patrick. When St Patrick saw that, he said: 'May your head remain as it is!' The plaice has had a twisted head and neck ever since. Then, just as Patrick was leaving, a salmon jumped out of the water and landed cleanly on St Patrick's breast. The saint declared: 'I give you the gift of jumping!' And so, since that day, the salmon can jump better than any fish. The salmon appears in the place name Leixlip, County Kildare. Leixlip is a name of Norse origin, meaning 'salmon's leap', as its Irish name *Léim an Bhradáin* indicates.

MYTHS AND LEGENDS

The salmon appears in several legends associated with long life and knowledge.[3] One such story tells of a man, amazed at the coldness of a particular night, who decides to find out if there was ever so cold a night before. First he meets an otter that is lying in a deep hole on top of a rock. The otter tells him that it has been there so long that his body has worn the hole in the rock, but it has never before seen such a cold night. The man next meets a very old hawk perched on an anvil. The anvil is nearly worn away from the hawk rubbing its beak on it after eating; nevertheless, it too has never seen such a cold night. Finally the man approaches the one-eyed salmon of the Falls of Assaroe in County Donegal. The salmon tells him that he does remember a colder night an extremely long time ago. It was so cold that when the salmon jumped out of the river to catch a fly, it had frozen over when it returned. The salmon lay dying on the ice and a bird came along and plucked out one of its eyes. The blood from the eye melted the ice and so the salmon was able to get back into the water. The one-eyed salmon of the story is actually derived from the mythic lore of the god Ruadh Ró-fheasa, an ancestral deity of the Leinstermen associated with the River Boyne, who could take the form of a one-eyed salmon. The similarity of his name to *Eas Ruadh* or Assaroe led to him later becoming associated with the Donegal location. This story has parallels with an incident in the Welsh tale *How Culhwch won Olwen*. As part of his labours in trying to gain Olwen's hand, the hero Culhwch must perform various tasks, among them the freeing of the warrior Mabon, son of Modron. As Arthur is Culhwch's cousin, he agrees that his knights should undertake this task for him, therefore they go to ask the oldest animal they know of, a bird called an ousel, if it knows where Mabon is. The ousel has not heard of Mabon, but directs them to an older creature, the stag of Rhedenvre. The stag has never heard of Mabon either, but directs them on to an even older creature, the owl of Cwm Cawlwyd. The owl directs them to an eagle, who in turn directs them to the oldest animal of all, the salmon of Llyn Llyw. The salmon knows of Mabon and, carrying the knights on his back, brings them upstream towards Gloucester, where Mabon is imprisoned. Once they have located him, Arthur and his knights are able to storm the prison and free Mabon.

In Irish myths, poets and seers also used the salmon as one of the animals whose shape they took in order to prolong their lives.[4] For example, the legendary seer Fionntan Mac Bóchna, who was said to have lived for thousands of years, achieved this feat by transforming himself into a one-eyed salmon, an eagle and a falcon before returning to his own shape. Similarly, another legendary seer called Tuan Mac Cairill was said to have owed his long life to his various transformations into a stag, boar, eagle and salmon. Eventually as a salmon he was eaten by Caireall's wife, who gave birth to him, and so he resumed human form once more.

The most famous legend concerning salmon is that of the Gaelic hero Fionn Mac Cumhaill and the Salmon of Knowledge.[5] According to Gaelic mythology, the Salmon of Knowledge acquired its wisdom by eating nuts from hazel trees that grew around a sacred Well of Knowledge. Various versions of this well appear in Irish myth – under the sea, or in the otherworld or at the source of Ireland's major rivers. In its form as the Well of Segais it appears as the source of either the Boyne or Shannon rivers. The form of the well is essentially the same in all the different versions. It is surrounded by nine hazel trees of wisdom and poetical inspiration.

The trees continually drop their ripe hazelnuts into the well in a shower that raises a purple wave, and the salmon living in the well eat the nuts. For every nut they eat, a red spot appears on the skin of the salmon, and any person eating one of those salmon would have the gift of knowledge and poetry. The story of how Fionn Mac Cumhaill came to acquire the knowledge of one of the salmon is one of the best known Irish tales. While still a young boy, Fionn came to learn poetry with the old seer Finnéces, who lived by the River Boyne. For seven years Finnéces had been trying to catch the Salmon of Knowledge that he knew came to a place called Féc's Pool. At last he successfully caught the salmon and ordered the young Fionn to cook it, but on no account to eat any of it. However, a blister arose on the side of the salmon, and Fionn innocently burst it, burning his thumb. He sucked his thumb to ease the pain and instantly acquired all the knowledge of the salmon. Instead of being outraged, Finnéces was rather fatalistic about the situation, declaring: 'Fionn is your name, my lad, and to you was the salmon given to be eaten, and truly you are Fionn [playing on the double meaning of Fionn's name, which means both 'fair' and 'wise'].' From that day onwards, whenever Fionn needed to find something out, he had only to put his thumb in his mouth and the knowledge would come to him.

Not surprisingly, the salmon is also associated with Manannán, the Celtic god of the sea.[6] One version of the story of the Well of Knowledge places it in Manannán's land, where five salmon eat the nuts of the hazel trees. One tale tells of the voyager Tadhg approaching Manannán's island, with the 'white-bellied salmon leaping about the currach on every side'. An early Irish poem has Manannán describe salmon to Bran, another voyager to his land, in lyrical terms: 'Speckled salmon leap from the womb / Of the fair sea before you / Like calves, like lambs, so beautiful, / So peaceful in their harmony.' In the same poem Manannán says of his son Mongán, who has the power to adopt various animal forms, that 'he shall be a speckled salmon in a full pool'.

The associations of the salmon with health, and particularly its great ability to leap, made it a symbol of warriors and manly strength.[7] One of the Gaelic hero Cúchulainn's skills was his powerful 'salmon leap', which he put to effective use to best his enemies in various tales. The hero Fionn Mac Cumhaill is also described as a 'golden salmon of the sea' by his son Oisín. In another tale, a princess called Beara is instructed by a druid to make a shirt for her future husband Eoghan out of the skin of a salmon from the River Eibhear. Eoghan puts on the shirt when the couple are betrothed, and the glorious golden shine from it earns him the name Eoghan the Bright. The salmon also has royal associations.[8] The *Annals of Clonmacnoise* record that in the year AD 1061, Áed Ua Conchubair of Connaught destroyed the fort of Kincora, ancestral seat of Brian Boru, and ate the two salmon which were in the king's fish pond there. This was perhaps meant as a deliberate insult to Brian Boru's descendants. A legal text also associates salmon with kings: it states that a king must give a salmon to his judge out of every abundant catch, and that a judge is entitled to the heads of all of the king's salmon. The Irish word for salmon (*bradán*) was also traditionally used in a poetic or figurative sense to mean a king or hero. This fondness of Irish kings for salmon could be turned against them. The Irish king Cormac Mac Airt died after choking on a salmon bone, as a result of a curse placed on him by a druid he had opposed.

RELATIONS WITH HUMANS

Salmon had a high prestige as a food in early Ireland.[9] A ninth-century triad lists the three deaths that are better than life as: 'the death of a salmon, the death of a fat pig, and the death of a robber'. A favourite way of cooking salmon was to rub it with honey and bake it over an open fire. The Brehon Laws do not specifically concern themselves with salmon fishing as opposed to other forms of fishing, but it is clear that salmon was assumed to be one of the main species of fish being caught. It appears that most fishing in Gaelic Ireland was carried out by local farmers, and a person who lived near a salmon river was generally entitled to catch a single salmon a year. The professional fisherman or *iascaire* did exist and, although he had a fairly low status, each king or lord was usually expected to employ a couple in their household. The main method of catching fish appeared to be in weirs of stone walls or fencing erected in rivers and estuaries. The fish were then forced into narrow channels where they could more easily be caught with spears, hooks, and nets, or else trapped in wickerwork baskets set along the weir. An Old Irish tale gives a fanciful account of salmon fishing at the castle of King Gartnáin. According to the tale, fifty fishing nets were in the river below the royal kitchens with ropes attached to them leading up into the kitchen windows. At the end of each rope there was a bell which rang and alerted the steward when a fish had been caught, and four men would then haul in the salmon. A Sligo legend has St Patrick blessing the River Garavogue so that it would yield salmon all year around. The legend has some basis in fact, as the Garavogue is famous as one of the earliest salmon rivers in Ireland, with fresh run salmon entering the river as early as November.

Salmon fishing remains a valued asset in Ireland and salmon angling is an important sport. One of the best known salmon fisheries in Ireland was on the little island of Carrick-a-Rede in County Antrim. For 200 years until the 1990s local fishermen gained access to the island across a bridge of wire rope, where they stretched their nets to intercept the wild salmon as they migrated west along the coast to their home rivers. The 20 m long and 1 m wide bridge still hangs 30 m above the rocky waters below, and crossing it has become a major attraction for tourists. In recent times the potential of salmon as food has been exploited more intensively with the introduction of salmon farms in many coastal areas in the west of Ireland.[10] The first trials of salmon rearing were carried out in the sea at Carna in County Galway in 1974. The Electricity Supply Board (ESB) became the first Irish company to farm salmon commercially, due to their existing expertise in raising salmon for the purpose of restocking rivers. By the mid-1980s the salmon industry was well established, and it is now a business of major commercial importance to Ireland, exporting farmed Atlantic salmon around the world. Controversy surrounds the industry, however, with allegations that sea lice from farmed salmon are infecting wild stocks of salmon and sea trout and contributing to their recent decline. The exact reasons for the collapse of wild stocks are not fully understood, and resolving the controversy will require further study.

# Snake – Nathair Nimhe – *Ophidia*

---

*In Irish tradition the snake was a symbol of poison and evil, and Ireland's status as a snake-free island was taken as a sign of its purity and sanctity. Despite the absence of snakes, Irish myths and legends are nevertheless full of monstrous serpents which have to be defeated and expelled by saints and heroes.*

## Folk Beliefs and Customs

Irish folklore about snakes is naturally rather sparse, but they are mentioned occasionally.[1] For example, it was traditionally believed that hazel was a good protection against snakes, and emigrants to America or Australia might sometimes take hazel rods with them to kill any snakes they would encounter. It was believed in County Galway that the snake hid under a nettle after it tempted Eve, and so gave that plant its sting. It was also thought in Ireland that a nursing mother who had been taken by the fairies might reappear around her house in the form of a venomous snake or a withered old hag. Several place names in Ireland derive from stories about a monstrous serpent or *péist* inhabiting the locality. They include *Poll na bPéist* (the wormhole) on Inishmore in the Aran Islands in County Galway, Altnapastia (*Allt na bPéiste* – cliff of the serpent), County Mayo, and Drumbest (*Droim na bPiast* – ridge of the serpent), County Antrim.

## Myths and Legends

The most famous Irish legends about snakes and serpents relate how the island came to be free of them.[2] The early medieval Irish text *Lebor Gabála Érenn*, or the *Book of Invasions*, gives a very different account to that of popular belief. According to the *Book of Invasions*, it was Moses and not St Patrick who was responsible for ridding Ireland of all poisonous reptiles. The *Book of Invasions* sets out to tell the story of the ancestors of the Irish, who were said to have wandered in many different parts of the Holy Land long before settling in Ireland. During these wanderings they settled in

213

Egypt beside the Israelites and became friendly with them, giving them wine and wheat. While they were there, the son of a man called Nel was bitten by a serpent. Nel took the child, called Gaedheal Glas, to Moses to be cured. Moses made fervent prayer before God, 'and put the noble rod upon the place where the serpent had stung him, so that the lad was cured'. Moses then said: 'I command, by the permission of God, that no serpent harm this child, or any of his seed forever, and that no serpent dwell in the homeland of his progeny.' This then is the reason why there are no serpents in Ireland, and why no serpent does harm to any of the seed of Gaedheal Glas. More details are then given in a following poem:

GAEDHEAL GLAS

Gaedheal Glas or Gaedheal the Green
A suitable name for a man supreme.
How it was given to the hero bold
Is a story seldom told.

As he was bathed on the seashore
Gaedheal son of Nel, the infant pure,
A serpent fastened around him tight,
Wounding him with a venomous bite.

The poisonous wound would not fade
Until Moses fervently prayed.
A green mark could still be seen
And so he became Gaedheal the Green

And so Gaedheal and all his seed
Did Moses bless – a holy deed
That no snake or venomous beast
Would ever a land of Gaedheal's infest.

It seems, however, that Moses did not actually rid Ireland of snakes, but rather directed Gaedheal Glas and his descendants, the Gaels, to a land already free of snakes. This is because the *Book of Invasions* also suggests that the land of Ireland was free of snakes long before Gaedheal Glas arrived. It states that the earliest inhabitant of Ireland was Cesair, the granddaughter of Noah, who fled to Ireland to escape the flood in the hope that 'a place where men had never come 'til then, where no evil nor sin had ever been committed, and which was free from the reptiles and monsters of the world' might be exempt from the flood. Cesair's hope was misplaced, and she was drowned when the flood did indeed reach Ireland. Elsewhere, the *Book of Invasions* explains that the pre-Gaelic firbolgs (*fir bolg* – 'men of the bags') got their name from carrying bags of Irish soil as protection when they were expelled from Ireland and given territory in Greece, which was full of venomous reptiles. This idea of the soil of Ireland offering protection against poison is later repeated by Gerald of Wales, who states it as a well-known fact that no poisonous thing can live in Ireland and that indeed if Irish soil is taken and scattered elsewhere that it will expel poisonous creatures from that vicinity. So powerful is this quality, according to Gerald, that if it is even attempted to bring a snake to Ireland it will die once it reaches the middle of the Irish Sea. Other tales tell of toads brought by accident to Ireland in the holds of ships, which when thrown still living onto the land, turn their bellies up, burst in the middle and die. Gerald says nothing about this having anything to do with St Patrick, however, attributing it to some benign clemency in the air of Ireland, or some hidden force in the soil itself.

The notion of the land of Ireland having some inherent quality that repelled snakes was replaced in the popular mind by the story that the patron saint of Ireland, St Patrick, was responsible for expelling all the snakes from Ireland. The story is first told by the English monk Jocelyn in

his 1185-6 work, *The Life and Acts of St Patrick*. According to Jocelyn, Ireland up to Patrick's time was infested with poisonous creatures and demons that 'not only wounded men and animals with their deadly sting, but slayed them with cruel bitings'. Patrick, therefore, bearing the staff of Jesus on his shoulder, commanded all the poisonous creatures to gather on the high promontory known as Cruachan Ailge (Croagh Patrick, County Mayo), and by the power of his word drove the 'whole pestilent swarm from the precipice of the mountain, headlong into the ocean'. He then turned his face towards the Isle of Man and other islands, and by the power of his prayer 'freed these likewise from the plague of venomous reptiles'. Once Patrick had done that, he fasted for forty days on the mountain so that the creatures would not return. This version of events has become the standard explanation for Ireland's snake-free status, and one of Ireland's best known stories. A later story relates how, after expelling all the other demons, the saint had to face the fiercest of all, a she-serpent called the Caorthannach, who was described as the Devil's mother. Patrick pursued her across the country and finally banished her to Lough Derg in County Donegal, to remain there until Judgement Day. A humorous addition to the tale tells of one wily old serpent that successfully resisted the saint. St Patrick decided at last to trick the snake and so made a wooden box and invited the snake into it. The snake, however, said that the box was too small, despite Patrick's insistence to the contrary. In the end the snake got into the box to prove that it was indeed too small, whereupon St Patrick slammed down the lid and cast it into the sea.

As well as the overall story of St Patrick banishing the snakes from Ireland, various legends exist of Irish saints, including Patrick, banishing serpents from specific locations in Ireland and Scotland.[3] A legend from Galway states that Patrick imprisoned an enchanted serpent in a small lake called *Mám Éan* near the Maumturk Mountains. In County Kerry a legend tells of St Cúan confining a serpent to a small lake at the foot of Mount Brandon by putting a cauldron on her head until Judgement Day. In County Cork St Finbar is supposed to have banished a serpent from the lake at Gougane Barra. The track the serpent left behind her as she fled to the sea filled with water and became the River Lee. Best known of all is the story of how St Colmcille banished the Loch Ness monster. According to the *Life* of the saint, Colmcille and his followers wished to cross the lake and so he commanded one of his men to swim across and get a boat that was moored on the other side. When the man was midway across, the monster arose out of the waters and rushed at him with open maw. Colmcille made the sign of the cross and commanded it to retreat, and the monster immediately fled back into the water. Colmcille's *Life* also tells of how he banished toads and snakes from the island of Iona in Scotland.

Attacking and defeating monstrous serpents is also a common theme in tales of great Gaelic heroes like Fionn Mac Cumhaill and Cúchulainn.[4] At one point in a tale of the Fianna, some of the serpents killed by Fionn are listed: 'he killed many great serpents in Loch Cuilinn and Loch Neathach, and at Binn Eadair (Howth) … and a serpent and a cat in Áth Cliath'. In the tale *Bricriu's Feast* Cúchulainn kills a monstrous serpent by putting his hand down the monster's throat and tearing out its heart. In another tale a reference is made to Cúchulainn defeating a pair of two-headed snakes. According to legend, one of the Tuatha Dé Danann called Mac Cecht killed Mechi, the son of the warrior goddess Morrigan. Mechi had three hearts, each of which had a serpent inside it. If Mechi had continued to live the three serpents would have kept growing until they had destroyed every living thing in Ireland. In another story, the son of King Conn Céadchathach (Conn of the Hundred Fights), called Cian, is born with a bulge in his forehead. When it is cut open a worm leaps out and wraps itself around one of Cian's spears. The worm grows into an enormous serpent with a hundred heads that, after wreaking havoc, is eventually killed by the warrior Conán. An exception to the rule occurs in the tale *The Cattle Raid of Fróech* where the hero, Conall Cernach, and a serpent accommodate each other. The serpent was guarding a fort that Conall was raiding, but as he approached, the serpent leapt into Conall's belt instead of harming him. After they had carried off the treasures of the fort, Conall lets the serpent go free. It has been suggested that this incident is a relic of a link between Conall Cernach and the Celtic god of animals Cernunnos, one of whose sacred animals was the snake.

In Celtic mythology in Britain and the continent, the snake had more complex associations than being merely a symbol of evil.[5] Its habit of shedding its skin made it a symbol of death and regeneration, and its phallic shape linked it to fertility. These elements also associated it with healing, and serpents appear alongside images of continental Celtic deities of healing, such as Damona and Sirona. A similar idea appears in Classical mythology where the snake was said to compensate for its poisonous nature by having the ability to discover healing herbs. For this reason it was depicted on the caduceus of Mercury, which is still a symbol of medicine today. The rippling movement of the snake also made it a symbol of water and linked it to Celtic water deities. A depiction of the Celtic water goddess Verbeia in Yorkshire in England shows her with snakes rippling down her arms like streams of water. In Welsh tradition snakes were linked to sacred wells. Gerald of Wales speaks of a Pembrokeshire well whose golden treasure was guarded by a serpent. The link between serpents and water also appears in Norse mythology in the legend of a great sea-serpent called Jormungard that lived in the oceans of Midgard. It was so large that it encircled the earth, biting its own tail. Irish mythology may have had the same concept, as in one early Irish tale a character, hearing a loud noise, wonders if the 'Leviathan that encircles the world has overturned it with its tail'. In any case, the link between serpents and water is certainly reflected in Irish legends, where monstrous serpents nearly always live in lakes or rivers.

SIMILAR ANIMALS

Eel – *Eascann* – *Anguilla anguilla*
The eel was seen in Irish folklore as a mysterious creature, probably on account of its serpent-like appearance and ability to travel over land in search of water. It was believed that dead eels sometimes came back to life again, and that horse-hair left in water for a long time turned into an eel. A more sinister belief was that large eels could be seen going into graves to eat corpses. Eels were also involved in some folk cures. A cure for baldness involved burying an eel in a dunghill until it had broken down into an oily liquid and then rubbing this into the scalp daily. Also, a cure for pains in the knee was to tie an eel skin around it. A folk tale common in Munster tells of a man who caught a large eel and brought it home. During the night, however, a voice was heard outside calling for the eel. The captive eel then spoke up and said that its comrade was outside. When the man went to investigate, he found a similar large eel outside the door. Without any further delay the man opened the door and let the captive eel escape. The eel could also be a positive sign. In Donegal it was believed that if a person praying at a holy well saw an eel coming to the well, it meant the person they were praying for would be cured by the time the person praying got

home. It is interesting to note that eels are associated with holy wells in Wales and Brittany. In Wales the well of St Cybi contained a huge eel whose power protected the well. In Brittany the fairy inhabitant of a spring usually had the form of an eel. The eel also appears in the mythological early Irish tale *Táin Bó Cuailnge*, when the warrior goddess Morrigan attacks the hero Cúchulainn by turning herself into a slippery black eel and coiling around his legs. The Gaelic warriors of early Ireland, the Fianna, are also described as eating eels from the River Shannon in one tale. Eels have been eaten in Ireland since the earliest times. The remains of eels have been found at a Mesolithic site at Mount Sandel in County Derry.[6]

# Frog – Frog – *Rana temporaria*

*The frog is a recent addition to Ireland's fauna and was once as famous for its absence as the snake. The circumstances of its arrival in Ireland are unknown, but it has found a place as a harmless and well-liked part of our wildlife. The frog was used in some Irish folk cures, and was sometimes regarded as a fairy animal.*

## Folk Beliefs and Customs

The frog was used for a number of folk cures in Ireland.[1] The most common of these was to use a frog as a cure for toothache, by rubbing a live frog on the affected tooth, or by chewing a frog's leg. In County Clare it was thought that a child could be cured of whooping cough by bringing it to running water, putting a frog into the child's mouth three times, and then letting the frog swim away uninjured, supposedly taking the whooping cough with it. Similar beliefs existed in England where it was widely believed that thrush or a sore throat could be cured by putting a live frog in a cloth bag and putting it into the patient's mouth. Perhaps folk cures like these are the origin of the expression 'to have a frog in one's throat'! Frogs were also used in love charms. This involved first burying a frog alive in a box and then later digging it up and taking the skeleton apart to select a particular bone. The bone should then be placed in the clothing of the intended, who would fall madly in love with the person who placed the bone. In England it was said to be bad luck if a frog came into the house.

The fairies were believed in Ireland to sometimes take the form of a frog.[2] One story tells of a midwife who kicked a frog with her boot as she walked home. Later that night she heard a knock on the door. Outside was a man with a horse who said 'Come with me' and put a blindfold on her. She was taken to a house where the man removed her blindfold to reveal a woman sick in the bed. The midwife was forced to stay and nurse her until she got better, and then she was sent home with a bruise in her side, so that she might suffer as the fairy woman had suffered while in the form of the frog. A story from County Cork tells of another midwife who was walking home one evening when she saw a frog with a distended belly making its way slowly along. 'God help you,' said the midwife, 'I would help you if I could'. Later that night she was taken to a fairy fort where a pregnant woman came towards her saying: 'Well, you promised you would help.' The midwife stays to help her deliver the baby and is then returned safely home.

In European folklore a common theme is the frog prince who lives in a well and insists on marrying the girl who draws its waters.[3] Similar themes have found their way into some Irish folk tales, such as the County Donegal story of 'The Princess and the Frog'. In the story, a frog promises to retrieve a ball that the princess has lost down a well if she lets him share her food and sleep in her bed. The princess agrees, but when the frog retrieves the ball, she reneges on her promise and runs away. The next day there is a knock on the door of the castle. It is the frog, who declares to the princess: 'You must keep your promise.' The princess is reluctant at first, but then her father, the king, hears the story and tells her she must agree. So for the next two days the princess shares her food and lets the frog sleep in her bed. At the end of two days there comes a flash of lightning and a bolt of thunder, and the frog turns into a handsome young prince who had been enchanted. Naturally enough, he and the princess soon get married and live happily ever after. In Ulster the frog is often called the *puddock* or *pudyach*, which is a word of Scots origin.

MYTHS AND LEGENDS

Like the snake, Ireland was traditionally famous for the absence of frogs.[4] As early as the ninth century, Donatus, the bishop of the Italian town of Fiesole, wrote a rhymed account of Ireland in which he refers to the absence of frogs and snakes: *Nulla venena nocent, nec serpens serpit in herba, nec conquest canit garrula rana lacu* – 'No snakes are creeping there with venomed guile, no raucous frogs disturb the rustling reeds.' Writing in the twelfth century, Gerald of Wales reaffirmed that no frogs were found in Ireland, supposedly on account of the purity of its environment. He went so far as to say that any snake, toad, frog or poisonous reptile brought to Ireland would quickly die, as the Irish environment contained some quality that was inimical to their poisonous nature (even though the common frog is not poisonous). Notwithstanding these remarks, he then recounted a story concerning the discovery of a frog in Ireland:

Nevertheless in our days a frog was found near Waterford in some grassy land, and was brought to Richard Poer, who was in charge there at the time, and many others in assembly, both English and Irish, while it was still living. While the English, and more so the Irish, regarded it with great wonder, Duvenaldus, the king of Ossory, who happened to be there at the time, with a great shaking of his head and great sorrow in his heart at last said (and he was a man of great wisdom among his people and loyal to them): 'That reptile brings very bad news to Ireland.' And regarding it as an indication of what was to be, he said that it was a sure sign of the coming of the English, and the imminent conquest and defeat of his people.

Gerald suggested that the frog had arrived by chance from some passing ship. However, a closer examination of the story suggests a different, more cynical, explanation. It is a quite a coincidence to believe that Norman soldiers would happen to find a frog in some grassy spot, and have the presence of mind to bring it to Richard de Poer, conveniently in assembly at the time with the local Irish and English nobility. It is far more likely that the whole incident was staged as propaganda, perhaps even with a frog carried over especially from Britain. The symbolism of the incident is obvious: Ireland was no longer a sacrosanct place apart, its separateness was over and its future was now linked to Britain. Certainly those at the assembly were quick to draw the conclusion that just as newcomers like the Normans had arrived, so other newcomers like the frog were coming to establish their presence for good. It is also, of course, entirely possible that the whole incident never took place at all, and that the story and the words of Duvenaldus were simply invented and spread for the same propaganda reasons.

In Classical mythology frogs were regarded as a symbol of fertility and associated with the goddess of love Venus or Aphrodite.[5] In more modern times the frog is associated with the French, who are called 'frogs' in English slang.[6] The origin of this is only partly the well-known French delicacy of frogs' legs. The main reason is that three frogs or toads have been depicted on the heraldic device of Paris since ancient times, probably from the fact that Paris used to be a swamp. In pre-Revolutionary France the common people of Paris were called *grenouilles*, or frogs, and the name was later extended to mean all French people (at least by the English).

RELATIONS WITH HUMANS

The absence of any old fossil remains of frogs means most naturalists accept the accounts of early writers, and agree that the frog is not native to Ireland. It is assumed to have been introduced at some stage over the centuries since the Normans arrived. The earliest reference to a frog in Ireland is the story quoted above from Gerald of Wales, about the appearance of one in Waterford soon after the arrival of the Normans. However, this is a very suspect story to take as evidence for the frog's successful introduction. The next reference to the matter is of a much later date, with an account of the introduction of frog spawn to Ireland in 1696 by a Fellow of Trinity College, Dublin. The Edinburgh *New Philosophical Journal* reported in 1735 that a Dr Gwithers, a Fellow of natural history at Trinity, having failed to find the frog in Ireland, and apparently convinced that its absence was contrary to the natural order of things, obtained some frog spawn from England and placed it in a ditch in College Park, 'from which these prolific colonists sent out their croaking detachments through the adjacent country, whose progeny spread from field to field throughout the whole kingdom'. A competing story was given by Dubourdieu writing in the 1802 'Statistical survey of the County Down'. He stated that frogs were first seen in Ireland in Moira, County Down, in the 1750s, and from there 'spread throughout the country with amazing rapidity'.

It is possible to accept these stories as real accounts of introduction without accepting that either introduction was the first one. In an era before Irish natural history had really developed, people may well have taken at face value the traditional assumption that there were no frogs in Ireland, even if frogs had indeed been living unobtrusively in the country for centuries. The problem with both stories is their very late date, which would seem to preclude the widespread dispersal that the frog had attained by the nineteenth century (for example, the fast-moving grey squirrel has been in Ireland for almost a century now and still has not colonised substantial parts of the country). There are also simply too many documentary sources surviving from the eighteenth century onwards to easily believe that the sudden appearance of the frog all over the country could happen without any further accounts or discussion of the process.

So how and when did the frog arrive in Ireland? One explanation sometimes given is that the Normans brought the frog to Ireland as food. This seems implausible, as the kind of frog generally eaten in France – the Edible frog (*Rana esculenta*) – would not survive the cold in Britain or Ireland. It is true that the Common frog (*Rana temporaria*) is often eaten in France and Belgium in the early spring when the Edible frog is not available, but it does not appear to have ever been farmed in special frog ponds in a manner similar to the Edible frog. There is also no evidence of frog farms in Ireland, and it seems unlikely that the Normans would bother to bring it over to Ireland without any attempt at farming it. The truth is that without any definite proof one way or the other, any theories on the matter remain speculation. Nevertheless, it is the author's opinion that there is another simpler and more plausible explanation, namely that the frog arrived accidently along with the many introductions of coarse fish into the country sometime over the centuries since the Normans' arrival.

Because Ireland became an island after the end of the last ice age, the only fish definitely native to Ireland are those that could arrive by sea, such as salmon, trout and eel. It is generally accepted that any truly freshwater fish in Ireland must have been introduced since Norman times. There is evidence that the pike was brought to Ireland by the sixteenth century, and tench and carp by the seventeenth centuries, while bream and rudd must also have been introduced at some point in the last few centuries. All of these fish species were bred on fish farms in England, established since Norman times, and the likelihood is that this is where the introduced Irish fish came from. The traditional method of fish farming was the construction of artificial fish ponds where the fish were reared for both eating and selling on as stock. This is where the relevance for frogs comes in. Such fish ponds would also be excellent habitats for frogs, and it is not hard to see how frog spawn and tadpoles could be collected along with the fish fry for selling on. It seems there were numerous introductions of fish over the centuries, and the accidental importation of frogs in this manner could have happened many times. Therefore, it may be that the frog arrived in Ireland by accident and unnoticed, due to the activities of anglers and fishermen. It probably first happened sometime in the late medieval or early modern period, giving the frog enough time to spread over the country and be a quietly accepted part of the Irish fauna by modern times.[7]

# Irish Animals and Transformation

Stories of human transformation into animal forms play an important role in the legends of the Celts, and regularly occur in many of the best known Celtic myths. Many of these stories follow a theme of successive transformations into different animals, birds and fishes. For example, the famous 'Song of Amairgen' and the story of Tuan Mac Cairill both follow a similar path of animal transformations. Among other things, Amairgen in his famous poem declares: 'I am stag of seven fights / I am hawk on cliff … I am boar in fury / I am salmon in pool.' This pattern is echoed in the story of Tuan Mac Cairill, one of the first inhabitants of Ireland, who survived for many centuries by taking on different animal forms, first as a stag, then as a boar, then an eagle and finally a salmon. It is easy to draw the conclusion that both sequences involve a stay in each of the Classical elements – fire (stag), earth (boar), air (eagle) and water (salmon). These stories echo the beliefs of Pre-Christian Ireland, where a form of shamanism similar to the beliefs of Native Americans and other cultures was practised. The poet or seer drew strength and wisdom by entering an altered or trance state and taking on the forms of the different animals.

Even without believing directly in shamanism, we can use this tradition today. By imagining ourselves as different animals in visualisation techniques we can access inner reserves and insights that might be otherwise hard to bring to mind. Calling on the qualities of the animals through visualisation and imagination can thus be a help to us in our daily lives. The following scheme of twelve animals has been devised with this aim in mind – three in each of the four categories of fire, earth, air and water. The scheme also includes the eagle because, even though as a bird it does not appear in the book, it has a central role in so many of the stories of transformation. Despite this arrangement, there is no set pattern to the scheme, and each person is free to draw upon the imagery of the animals in whatever order they see fit. It may be that one person will find each of the twelve a help in different situations, while another person may only use one or two. It does not matter. The sole aim is to help each of us to face our daily lives more effectively, by enabling us to call upon the rich resource of animal lore left to us by our ancestors.

## HORSE

To the Celts the horse was a symbol of nobility and prestige, valued for its strength, beauty and speed. It carried warriors to battle, the aristocracy about their lands, and travellers to and from distant places. The horse brought new ideas and people as it travelled, carrying messengers and migrants in search of a different life. The horse is proud, noble, swift and intelligent, the fitting companion of kings and warriors. It was also associated with Celtic goddesses of war and fertility like Macha and Epona. Although the horse is not usually aggressive, it is strong and brave, and not afraid to go into battle in a righteous cause. Thus the Grey of Macha pulled the chariot of the hero Cúchulainn, and was not afraid to join him in the fight. Also, in countless legends and stories the hero usually sets out on a quest for fame or justice on a white horse, symbol of the rightness and purity of his intentions. In addition, the horse has a zest for life, and values excitement and speed, so it enjoys the thrill of the sports of racing and hunting every bit as much as the humans involved. We can draw on the qualities of the horse whenever there are situations where we must rise to the challenge of new things, to show courage and a sense of justice, and to act with speed. These qualities especially come into play in any competition and sporting event, where drive and self-assertion should be linked to the ideal of fair play and respect for others. The horse represents the urge for freedom and new experiences, for independence, adventure and the testing of limits. The horse through its behaviour can also show us how to develop a sense of noble-mindedness, idealism and generosity. The horse reminds us that nothing ever stays stagnant or still for long, and that new people and experiences are continually travelling our way.

## STAG

The stag or deer represents the power and potential of the forest. The stag prefers to live roaming in the high peaks and moorland, master of all he surveys, especially his own herd of hinds and fawns. His bellow is heard across the woods and hills as he marks his territory. The stag was a worthy adversary for kings and warriors, and only the finest hunters were successful in the pursuit. In many tales the stag led the hero to the otherworld, acting as the guide to new and more profound realities. In mythology the stag, with its imposing antlers that are renewed each year, stands for creativity, regeneration and security. They allow him to impress others and to project his power. With his branching antlers the regal stag is Lord of the Forest, providing leadership for the growth and well-being of all the creatures in his domain. In Celtic myth he was associated with Cernunnos, the god of the forest and nature, who was depicted as a man with antlers growing out of his head. Courageous under attack, the stag will stand firm against its opponents as it seeks to protect and defend the vulnerable. The stag is proud, noble, steadfast, loyal, swift and dignified. We can call upon the qualities of the stag when we are called upon to lead. Just as the stag is happiest in the high mountains leading his herd, so when leading it is best to take the broader view and rise above petty concerns. Just as the stag led kings and heroes into the otherworld, so we need a vision of another reality if we are to bring others along with us. The stag also reminds us that to lead we need to protect and defend those who follow. Therefore, just as the stag carries his heavy load of antlers, so we must take the burden of leadership on our shoulders. As the stag is able every year to regenerate those antlers, so we too must be a force for renewal and regeneration if we are to lead successfully.

## WOLF

The wolf was the main predator in the Irish countryside, living on its wits in wild places, in mountains and woods. Although it was feared for its ability to kill livestock, it was also respected as a noble animal. But the wolf is not only an aggressive animal. In various stories the wolf shows that it can act in a just way, repaying those who help it. The legendary King Conaire was able to agree with the wolves of Ireland not to hunt them, in return for the wolves taking only one male calf from each herd during the year. When St Molua took pity on a pack of hungry wolves and provided them with a cooked calf, in their gratitude they protected the monastic livestock from other wolves and from robbers. In myths the wolf nurtures heroes and kings, fostering their warrior spirit. It represents the force that seeks out opportunities and is not afraid to take them. The wolf tests the complacent and foolhardy, hoping to benefit as it probes for weaknesses. Understood properly, the wolf is not aggressive for the sake of it, but takes only what it needs to survive and no more. So the wolf takes only from the flock those sheep that are too weak to survive by themselves. The wolf represents the warrior impulse that is not afraid to face danger and does not give up in the face of failure. The wolf is ruthless, cunning, aggressive, competitive, self-liberating, brave and daring. Yet the wolf controls its aggression, focused on its target and acting as part of a pack in a disciplined way, taking orders and obeying commands, like a military operation. If we want to achieve goals that are difficult we can learn from the wolf's discipline and control. It is sometimes necessary to show our teeth if we want to get things done. Sometimes we need to assert ourselves and act to secure what is rightfully ours.

## Cow

The cow is sensuous, dependable and powerful. It is life-giving and supporting through its meat, milk and hide. It is also a symbol of security, fertility and the land. In folklore, the milk and dairy were so precious to the well-being of the household that they had to be protected by powerful charms. The goddess Bóand, or *bo-vinda* meaning 'white cow', gave her name to the River Boyne, whose life-giving waters were seen as her milk. Also in legend, the *Glas Goibhneann*, or the grey cow of the smith god Goibhniu, gave an inexhaustible supply of milk to its owner. In later stories white cows were reputed to have given their pure, nourishing milk to support SS Brigid and Kevin while they were infants. The cow is therefore willing to give the fruits of its labours to sustain those it serves, through its refreshing and health-giving milk. The bull also maintains the herd through its strength, protecting it from all threats and reproducing it through its virility. In addition it is a symbol of wealth and status. So Queen Maedhbh and her consort Ailill measured their wealth by ownership of the magnificent *Donn Cuailnge*, the Brown Bull of Cooley, and his rival the *Finbheannach* or Fair-horned. We can draw upon the qualities of the cow or bull when we need to work hard and steadily to provide security and a stable environment for ourselves and our loved ones. The cow provides us with an example of the qualities of steadfastness, dignity, reliability and responsibility that we need to sustain a decent livelihood. The cow also shows us how to live comfortably and within our means by not seeking too much. Although the cow and bull are sensuous and aware of their physical needs, they are not greedy, keeping good health and fitness by a simple, contented lifestyle.

## BOAR

The pig or boar is acquisitive, and works hard at rooting out food from the earth. Traditionally the pig lived in the woods and wild places, turning acorns, roots and other forest produce into its own succulent flesh. The pig was also especially valued by the poor, as it could eat scraps and rubbish, and find nourishment in the most unpromising places. In legends it is the symbol of the Otherworld Feast, presided over by the sea god Manannán, whose pigs were killed every evening for the feast, but were miraculously restored to life the following day to provide for the next feast. The Champion's Portion, the finest cut of meat reserved for the bravest hero in the company, was usually of pork. Thus the pig's actions do not take from others – he turns over the soil and enriches it and makes use of what others cannot, ultimately for the benefit of all. In the same way we can sometimes create wealth and opportunities for others when we seek it out for ourselves. The pig is not fat and lazy, but puts in the effort to get what it wants, and will fiercely defend what it considers to be its due. The boar is famously courageous and strong and prepared to fight to get its way. Sometimes we have to be determined and seek out what we want and not be afraid to think of our material needs and desires. It is important to remember that to be acquisitive and accumulate wealth is not necessarily a bad thing if we put it to productive use to benefit others as well as ourselves. The pig also takes unashamed pleasure in satisfying its physical needs and enjoying its food; and this is something we might need reminding is not necessarily a bad thing. The pig is literally 'pig-headed' – stubborn, focused, sensuous, likes the finer things, conservative, sensible and hard-working.

## DOG

The dog is the loyal companion to man, and in Gaelic Ireland it was the indispensible help to hunters, warriors and farmers. The dog is not afraid to serve and be at the command of others for the greater good. It is happy to guard and protect the vulnerable, even at a cost to itself. The Irish wolfhound was famous for its bravery in facing its enemy, the wolf. Normally placid and good-natured, the wolfhound was capable of enormous ferocity when defeating its foe. The dog was also noted in folklore for its healing properties – its saliva was believed to cure infections. In legends the baying of hounds foretold death or misfortune. So the sharp-eyed dog is on the lookout for trouble, and can sniff out enemies and warn of their approach. It is also a ruthless hunter, swift in tracking down and catching its quarry. The same qualities can make it good at organising – as the conscientious and dependable sheepdog can control the flock. In other words, it is literally 'dogged'. The hound Bran was forever at the side of the warrior Fionn Mac Cumhaill, helping him hunt down many deer and wild boar, and asking only for love and respect in return. The hero Cúchulainn was proud to serve as the hound of the smith Culainn, an act which gave him his name. He was happy to protect Culainn's home until a hound had been trained to replace the one that he had killed. In the same way we should not be afraid to sometimes emulate the dog and put aside our egos to be of service for the good of others. We can learn from the dog's unflagging devotion, sense of duty and sharp eye for every detail. We can also take inspiration from the dog when facing threats, to have the bravery to speak out and warn others of approaching danger.

## Cat

The cat is independent and values freedom. It is individualistic, aloof, unpredictable, self-contained, intelligent and playful or hostile as the mood takes it. The cat is also famous for fighting its corner when needed. In legend Irusan, the King of the Cats, carried off the poet Sencha when he made a satire against him, and wildcats were noted for being fierce when disturbed. But the cat is also good at catching rats and mice and other vermin, and is happy to be of use to mankind when it suits, just as the white cat Pangur Bán helped his owner, the scholar monk. The cat is comfortable with darkness and the night, when it goes on the prowl, and so traditionally has been associated with witchcraft. It has also been associated with many different goddess figures, such as the Egyptian Bastet and the Roman Diana. The cat was also the companion of wise women or village healers, females who lived on the margins of society and were different from the norm. Contrary to belief, the cat can be a loyal companion, but on its own terms, never in a slavish or submissive way. The cat has a sense of grace and style and is at ease with its own body. It is in touch with its intuition and is not afraid of things that are mysterious or strange. The cat always lands on its feet because it is self-assured enough to deal with any situation, however unexpected. We can draw upon the qualities of the cat to create links to our unconscious mind, imagination and creativity. We need sometimes to copy the cat and do our own thing without fear of what others think, especially things that are creative, unconventional or outside the norm. We should not be afraid to stand out from the crowd or to go it alone. We can also usefully learn from the cat how to balance loyalty to others without sacrificing our independence.

HARE

The hare is one of our swiftest animals, skilled at avoiding the hunter. They were perceived as scatterbrained but clever, quick, nervous and opportunistic creatures. Witches or hags were traditionally believed to take the form of hares in order to steal milk from their neighbours, and to carry out various other forms of trickery and subterfuge. There is also an element of silliness and fun about the hare. Think of the mad March hares battling each other – in reality they are males competing for a mate by posturing and bounding around. The Easter bunny is also a humorous creature, bringing eggs to children despite the impossibility that it could produce them itself! The hare is associated with spring and the fertility of the land, with new life rising up. The hare is also associated with the harvest later in the year, when it was supposed to hide in the last sheaf of the crop to be harvested, again symbolising the land. Hares are restless animals, forever in movement, always active and leaping about and never staying still for long. They are adaptable, good at twisting and turning to escape their pursuers, and able to change direction suddenly and with great speed. With their large ears and eyes they are also good at listening and spotting danger, and with their sharp senses are always alert. The traits of the hare can be useful to us whenever we face situations where adaptability is needed, where 'brains not brawn' is the order of the day. Sometimes we find that quick thinking is required, and a rapid change of direction, to save ourselves from disaster. Only by staying alert and sensing what way the wind is blowing can we avoid defeat. We can draw on the hare's other qualities when we need to enjoy the moment, by being playful and silly and indulging in our sense of fun.

## EAGLE

The eagle is the most majestic of our native birds, living up in the mountains and flying high out over the land in search of its prey. It builds its nest in lofty crags, far above the petty concerns and struggles of the life below. From its high vantage point, the eagle's sharp eyes can spot from a great distance anything that moves. In Classical myth the eagle was associated with the gods of the sky such as Zeus and Jupiter, and represented spiritual power and victory. Traditionally the eagle was said to be able to gaze directly into the sun without harming itself, symbolising its fearlessness. The eagle is also ruthless, able to swoop for the kill in an instant and snatch up its prey in its great talons before it knows what has happened. We can be like the eagle – just, noble, impartial and able to look at things with cool, measured eyes. Sometimes it is necessary to put aside our feelings and rise above issues to see them from afar, with a larger perspective, and a dispassionate, logical mind. Like the eagle, however, this does not mean that we are incapable of strong action; rather it means that we can take difficult and sometimes harsh decisions, forcefully and effectively. The eagle on its journey can also twist and turn in the currents of wind, riding the air to soar to great heights or to swoop down to the ground. Although it is constantly aware of the shifting, changing air, it is always in control of its movements, and never simply a plaything of the wind. In the same way we should be aware of the changing opinions and perceptions of others, and bend to them if necessary, but staying true to our principles, not changing direction simply to suit the prevailing outlook.

## SEAL

The seal is something of an ambiguous animal, as it is both a sea creature and a warm-blooded mammal that comes ashore to rest and breed. So it straddles the two worlds of land and water, fully belonging to neither. Graceful and flexible in the sea, it is ungainly and uncomfortable on land. The seal was seen as a melancholy, otherworldly creature, with its soulful expression and mournful cries that are almost human. These features undoubtedly gave rise to the many Irish legends that seals were fairy or enchanted people, who were seals by day and humans by night. It was also widely believed that seals were the souls of drowned people who could not enter Noah's Ark and took on the form of seals after their death. It was therefore considered wrong by many people to kill seals, however useful their flesh, oil or skin. Like the seal on land, many of the most sensitive, creative people are awkward and ill at ease with the hard, uncaring realities of life. Far from being irrelevant, such people need only the right environment and the understanding of others to develop their talents to the enrichment of everyone. The seal represents those unworldly qualities of the non-materialistic and imaginative that society all too often desperately needs to develop. We can use the seal as an example to develop a sense of compassion, remembering and mourning those who have been lost or hurt by life. On land the seal lies on remote beaches and rocky shores to rest and give birth to its young, and we can follow its example by finding a hidden refuge where we can replenish our spirits and nurture our creativity. But in the water, the seal is able to swim deep down in order to catch fish, and in the same way we can capture inspiration in the depths of the imagination if we have the courage to go down deep enough.

OTTER

The otter is a shy but determined hunter, and like the seal it crosses in and out of the two worlds of land and water. Unlike the seal, however, the otter seems equally at home in both, being adaptable enough to manage the change. The otter is seen as a noble but playful and good-natured animal as it splashes in and out of rivers and lakes, and frolics on the bank nearby. According to folk belief otters slept with their eyes open, so that they were always on guard. In folklore the King Otter was a huge white otter, whose skin protected its carrier from drowning, fire or accident. So the otter protects those it favours. The otter was also said never to rest, diligent in catching fish for both itself and its young. The otter is known in Irish as the *dobharchú* or 'water-dog' and shares some of the qualities of the dog. It is modest, unassuming and loyal to those close to it. It is also efficient at providing for its needs and those who depend on it at the same time. In legends, the otter was a loyal companion to hermits and holy men such as St Kevin, bringing them food and keeping them company. The otter is thus independent but also willing to serve if the principle is right. The favourite fish of the otter was the salmon, which it pursued skilfully and vigorously. We can draw a lesson from the otter's behaviour and pursue wisdom and knowledge with the same diligence. This wisdom is not mystical or esoteric; rather it is shrewd learning acquired through application and experience. We can draw on the qualities of the otter of good humour and adaptability to reach a balance between different parts of our life, such as the personal, emotional side and the practical, hard-headed side of work and responsibility. Like the otter we can be an 'all-rounder', not too stuck in one mode of existence and unafraid to experience the different sides of life.

## SALMON

The salmon represents the cycle of death and rebirth, as it journeys long distances out to sea and returns to its spawning grounds again to reproduce and die. The journey is a mysterious one, as the salmon leaves the sanctuary of the river where it was spawned and takes to the ocean to live a life in uncharted waters. This life cycle requires great determination and stamina, which makes the salmon a symbol of health and strength, and its tasty and nourishing flesh the food of kings. The salmon also has to be wily and cunning to avoid the fisherman's traps and ensure its survival. In Irish mythology the most famous salmon was the Salmon of Knowledge, which acquired its wisdom by eating the nuts of the druidic hazel trees at the source of the Boyne. In turn, eating the flesh of the Salmon of Knowledge gave the Gaelic hero Fionn Mac Cumhaill great wisdom and knowledge of hidden lore. Also in Irish legend was the salmon of Assaroe, which was one of the longest-living creatures, acquiring extensive knowledge over its many years of life. Like the salmon, we can seek hidden knowledge if we are willing to take a spiritual journey to the source of that wisdom. This means facing the realities of our existence and exploring the hidden places in our psyche, which often means returning to the time of our birth and early years, or facing the reality of our eventual death. The lesson of the salmon is that the cycle of birth and death is a part of us all, and facing that truth can bring us to a deeper understanding. If we face these issues bravely and in the right spirit it can make us stronger and more mature. The salmon also teaches us to stay loyal and true to our principles and identity, no matter how far we travel from our origins.

# Postscript: Animal Lore around the World

Throughout this book we have seen how animals are a central part of our lives. As well as the practical benefits they bring of food, clothing, and easier work or transport, they provide us with many examples of behaviour that we can hold up as mirrors to ourselves. We feel a kinship with animals that is unique, however much other elements of nature can uplift us and make us feel whole. Animals are special to us because they are 'flesh and blood' creatures like we are, with recognisable drives and motivations. Crucially we can see that many animals are unique individuals, with personalities of their own, just like us. For this reason it is inevitable that we should project our own fears and desires on to them, and ascribe human motives and characteristics to them. We have seen examples of animals being regarded this way in Ireland, but similar closeness to animals can be found in every corner of the globe.

There are many examples in cultures throughout the world of animals being used to represent human attributes, to provide moral example, and to serve as a warning of negative behaviour. For instance, in Chinese culture there are many examples of animal symbolism.[1] The tortoise, whose longevity and slow movements represent immutability and steadfastness, is one. According to an old Chinese saying the tortoise 'conceals the secrets of heaven and earth', and is naturally also a symbol of long life. Similarly the Chinese for cat is *mao*, which is also the word for an octogenarian. Images of cats are therefore used to indicate the wish for a long life. Famously, of course, in Chinese astrology the zodiac consists entirely of animals, each representing a different human personality. Animals can also be used to portray moral lessons. In Buddhist iconography the 'three poisons' of destructive behaviour are traditionally portrayed as animals, located at the hub of the Wheel of Rebirth. The three animals are the pig representing ignorance (due to its blinkered pursuit of food, however revolting), the rooster representing desire and attachment (due to its possessiveness) and the snake representing hatred and anger (because it can strike out without cause). As long as a person retains one or all of these 'poisons' they will remain trapped in the Wheel of Rebirth, doomed to suffer endless reincarnations.

Animal gods, or gods in the form of animals, are found right across the world, both historically and today. In Hinduism monkeys are revered as sacred animals because one of the most popular deities is Hanuman, the monkey god. He is an incarnation of the god Shiva and is worshipped as a symbol of physical strength, perseverance, and devotion. According to legend Hanuman led an army of monkeys to defeat the demon king Ravana. Another popular Hindu god is Ganesh, the elephant-headed god who is patron of the arts and sciences, of intellect and wisdom. Not surprisingly for a god associated with the elephant, he is worshipped as the Remover of Obstacles. For some animals, such as the majestic lion, it is easy to see why they should become linked to deities. The lion was linked to several Egyptian deities, like Sekhmet, the lion-headed goddess of war and vengeance, and the Sphinx, a creature with the body of a lion and a human head, representing wisdom. Similarly in Mayan mythology, the jaguar, the night-hunting big cat of Central America, was regarded as a sacred animal. In one of the most important Mayan myths, the Sun takes the form of a jaguar on its journey through the underworld each night. However, less obvious animals (at least to Western minds) can also be considered sacred. Such a deity is Anansi, the spider god of West Africa and the Carribean. Anansi is a major figure in West African mythology, a trickster god who makes up in cunning what he lacks in strength. He is credited in legend with managing to force the sky god Nyame to give up his best stories so that mankind could hear them. Anansi achieved this by using his skill to capture various animals demanded by Nyame as his price for the stories.

Shamanism, or shape-shifting between human and animal form, is also a widespread feature of animal lore around the world.[2] For example, the Yakut people of Siberia believed that every wise man or shaman kept his soul hidden in a wild animal such as a boar, elk, bear or eagle. For most of the year the animals were kept safely away in remote mountains, but when the snows melted they came to prowl around the settlements of men. Similarly, in many tribes in Cameroon in West Africa, a person could choose a wild animal such as an elephant, hippopotamus, gorilla, fish or serpent to be a friend or familiar. The chosen animal was of a species known for its strength or ability to hide, especially in water, and was expected to help his human friend with hunting and outwitting his enemies. However, the life of the person was bound up with that of the animal, so if one was killed the other died also. Closely allied to this is the idea of totemism, where a whole tribe or clan is linked to a particular species of animal (or even plant). Totemism is still found in many peoples of the world, such as Native Americans and Australian aborigines. For example, the Wotjobaluk tribe of southeastern Australia held that the life of each man of the tribe was bound up with that of a bat, and each woman with that of the bird, the nightjar. It was not possible to make the link with individuals, but it was strongly believed that the death of a bat would be followed by the death of one of the men of the tribe; the same fate awaited one of the women of the tribe should a nightjar die. Similarly the Bataks of Sumatra are divided into clans, each with a totem animal such as the tiger, ape, crocodile, buffalo and so on. Each clan is forbidden to eat the flesh of its totem animal, because of the belief that the clan is descended from them, and because after death their soul might migrate into one of the animals.

But we do not have to regard animals as sacred to appreciate their value. The fact is that animals are our constant companions, and without animals the world would be a much colder, more boring and lonelier place for humans. Even if we could somehow replace their practical benefits we would still depend on animals to comfort us, to support us and to thrill us with their power and beauty. Whatever technology brings in the future, it will not change the fact that a relationship of some kind with animals is a central part of the human experience, and this will always be so.

Leabharlanna Poibli Chathair Bhaile Átha Cliath
Dublin City Public Libraries

# References

Aspects of the Folklore of Animals

1. Gibbs, L., *Aesop's Fables* (Oxford, 2002); Cooper, J.J., *Brewer's Book of Myth and Legend* (Oxford, 1993), p. 6.
2. http://bestiary.ca/intro.html.
3. Cooper, *op. cit.*, p. 34.
4. *Ibid.*, p. 235.
5. Ó hÓgáin, D., *Myth, Legend and Romance – An Encyclopedia of the Irish Folk Tradition* (New York, 1991), pp. 209, 224, 301, 364–8; Macalister, R.A.S., *Lebor Gabála Érenn*, Part 5 (Dublin, 1956), pp. 111–3.
6. Dinneen, P.S., *Foclóir Gaedhilge agus Béarla* (1927), p. 1196.
7. Beresford Ellis, P., *Dictionary of Celtic Mythology* (London, 1992), p. 119–20.
8. Swift, E., *Jocelyn's The Life and Acts of St Patrick* (Dublin, 1809), p. 61.
9. Gantz, J., *The Mabinogion* (London, 1976), pp. 104–5.
10. Gregory, Lady A., *Complete Irish Mythology* (London, 1994), pp. 215–6.
11. Stokes, W., *Cormac's Glossary* (Calcutta, 1868), p. 83.
12. McManus, D., 'A Guide to Ogam', *Maynooth Monographs*, 4 (Maynooth, 1991), pp. 102–13.
13. Kelly, F., *Early Irish Farming* (Dublin, 1997), pp. 57–66, 75–6.
14. Kelly, F., *A Guide to Early Irish Law* (Dublin, 1988), pp. 8, 10, 100, 132, 147; Kelly, *op. cit.* (1997), pp. 58–9.
15. Kelly, *op. cit.*, (1988), pp. 30, 99.
16. Flanagan, D. & Flanagan, L., *Irish Place Names* (Dublin, 1994), pp. 12–31.
17. *Ibid.*, pp. 12–31; Hayden, T. & Harrington, R., *Exploring Irish Mammals* (Dublin, 2000), pp. 97, 123, 268, 275, 299, 327.
18. Mac Giolla Léith, C., *Oidheadh Chloinne hUisneach* (1993), pp. 105, 111; Gregory, *op. cit.*, p. 120; O'Keeffe, J.G., *Buile Suibhne* (Dublin, 1913), pp. 136–7; Murphy, G., *Early Irish Lyrics* (Dublin, 1998), pp. 12–3.

Horse

1. Ó hÓgáin, *op. cit.*, pp. 251–2; Danaher, K., *Irish Country People* (Cork, 1966), pp. 102–3; O'Sullivan, P.V., *Irish Superstitions and Legends of Animals and Birds* (Cork, 1991), pp. 88–9; Roberts, J., *Irish Blessings, Toasts and Traditions* (Dublin, 1993), p. 31; Lamont Brown, R., *A Book of Superstitions* (Devon, 1970), p. 21; Opie, I. & Tatum, M., *A Dictionary of Superstitions* (Oxford, 1989), p. 445.
2. Ó hÓgáin, *op. cit.*, pp. 251–2; Roberts, *op. cit.*, p. 15; Minihane, P., *Beara Woman Talking: The Lore of Peig Minihane* (Cork, 2003), p. 25; Westropp, P.J., *Folklore of*

*Clare* (Ennis, 2000), p. 42; O'Farrell, P., *Irish Folk Cures* (Dublin, 2004), pp. 45–6.

3. White, C., *A History of Irish Fairies* (Dublin, 2001), pp. 71–2; Westropp, *op. cit.*, p. 30; Ó hÓgáin, *op. cit.*, p. 252; O'Sullivan, P., *op. cit.*, p. 83; Gregory, Lady A., *Visions & Beliefs in the West of Ireland* (Buckinghamshire, 1970), pp. 16, 26; McCullough, J.A., *The Religion of the Ancient Celts* (Edinburgh, 1911), p. 188; Ellis, A.T., *Wales: An Anthology* (London, 1991), pp. 164–5.

4. Danaher, K., *The Year in Ireland – Irish Calender Customs* (Cork, 1972), pp. 88, 172–5, 213–4, 249; Wilde, W., *Irish Popular Superstitions* (Dublin, 1979), p. 68; Ellis, *op. cit.*, pp. 213–4.

5. Gantz, J., *Early Irish Myths and Sagas* (London, 1981), pp. 128–9; Stokes, W., *The Edinburgh Dinnshenchus* (London, 1892), p. 63; Green, M., *Dictionary of Celtic Myth and Legend* (London,1992a), pp. 90–2, 176; Frazer, J.G., *The Golden Bough* (London 1987), p. 471.

6. O'Meara, J., *Gerald of Wales: The History and Topography of Ireland* (Harmondsworth, 1982), p. 110; Ó hÓgáin, *op. cit.*, p. 195, 268.

7. Gregory, *op. cit.* (1994), pp. 373, 379, 535; O'Rahilly, C., *Táin Bo Cúailgne* (Dublin, 1967), p. 218.

8. Gantz, *op. cit.*, pp. 53, 236; Curtin, J., *Hero Tales of Ireland* (London, 1894), pp. 161, 514.

9. Green, M., *Animals in Celtic Life and Myth* (London, 1992), pp. 113–4, 153–6.

10. Macalister, R.A.S, *Lebor Gabála Érenn*, Part 4 (Dublin, 1941), p. 135; Gregory, *op. cit.* (1994), pp. 29, 85–6; Cooper, *op. cit.*, p. 131; Crossley-Holland, K., *The Penguin Book of Norse Myths* (Harmondsworth, 1980), p. 14.

11. Green, *op. cit.* (1992), pp. 153–6; Smyth, D., *A Guide to Irish Mythology* (Dublin, 1988), p. 15; Crossley-Holland, *op. cit.*, pp. 5–6; Cooper, *op. cit.*, p. 131.

12. Hartley Edwards, E., *The Encyclopedia of the Horse* (London, 2000), pp. 30–1.

13. *Ibid.*, p. 32; Budiansky, S., *The Nature of Horses* (London, 1998), p. 64; Green, *op. cit.* (1992), pp. 71, 79, 82; Kelly, *op. cit.* (1997), p. 90.

14. Green, *op. cit.* (1992), pp. 66, 68–9, 71, 73, 80, 82.

15. *Ibid.*, pp. 69-70; Hartley Edwards, *op. cit.*, p. 170.

16. Kelly, *op. cit.* (1997), pp. 88, 90–1, 95–6.

17. *Ibid.*, pp. 89, 95–7; Green, *op. cit.* (1992), pp. 84–5.

18. Kelly, *op. cit.* (1997), pp. 88, 91–2, 100, 352-3, 432–3.

19. *Ibid.*, p. 98; O'Hare, N., *The Irish Sport Horse* (Eastbourne, 2002), pp. 78–9; Hayden & Harrington, *op. cit.*, p. 274.

20. Welcome, J., *Irish Horse Racing* (London, 1982), pp. 1–2; Kelly, *op. cit.* (1997), p. 99; Macalister, *op. cit.* (1941), p. 161; Stokes, *op. cit.*, p. 127; O'Hare, *op. cit.*, pp. 85, 92.

21. Welcome, *op. cit.*, pp. 27, 208; Holland, A., *Steeplechasing – A Celebration of 250 Years* (London, 2001), pp. 54–7, 180–4; http://www.sji.ie.

22. Kelly, *op. cit.* (1997), p. 91; Hartley Edwards, *op. cit.*, p. 180.

23. http://www.kerrybogponies.com; O'Hare, *op. cit.*, pp. 7, 17, 111–3.

DEER

1. Power, P., *Lives of S.S. Declan and Mochuda* (Dublin, 1914), pp. 55, 95–7; Stokes, W., *Lives of the Saints from the Book of Lismore* (Oxford, 1890), pp. 223, 249; Hynes, S.B.E., *Legends of St Kevin* (1928), p. 17.

2. Murphy, G., *Duanaire Finn*, Part 2 (Dublin, 1933), pp. 180–1, 193; Ó hÓgáin, *op. cit.*, pp. 154, 350; Gregory, *op. cit.* (1994), pp. 126–8, 179–81; Mac Neill, E., *Duanaire Finn*, Part 1 (Dublin, 1908), pp. 131–2.
3. Ó hÓgáin, *op. cit.*, p. 231.
4. O'Keeffe, *op. cit.*, pp. 35, 68, 78–9, 145; Murphy, *op. cit.* (1998), pp. 134–7.
5. Green, *op. cit.* (1992), pp. 125, 147, 150, 152, 231–2; Green, *op. cit.*, (1992a), p. 90; Cooper, *op. cit.*, pp. 65, 70.
6. Harbison, P., *Pre-Christian Ireland* (London, 1988), pp. 46, 70; Kelly, *op. cit.*, pp. 273–80; Green, *op. cit.* (1992), pp. 41, 50–3; O'Meara, J., *The Voyage of St Brendan* (Dublin, 1978), p. 47; http://www.wardunionhunt.ie/history.html
7. Hayden & Harrington, *op. cit.*, pp. 329–35.
8. *Ibid.*, pp. 343–7.
9. *Ibid.*, pp. 336–42.

WOLF

1. Flanagan & Flanagan, *op. cit.*, pp. 12–31; Hickey, K., 'Wolf – Forgotten Irish Hunter', *Wild Ireland* (2003), p. 11; Dinneen, *op. cit.*, p. 690.
2. Kelly, *op. cit.* (1997), pp. 38–9, 187; Ó hÓgáin, *op. cit.*, pp. 75, 381; Swift, *op. cit.*, p. 10; Baring-Gould, S., *The Book of Werewolves* (Dublin, 2007), pp. 48, 69–72.
3. Ó hÓgáin, *op. cit.*, pp. 101, 122; Gantz, *op. cit.* (1981), pp. 77–8; Gwynn, E., *The Metrical Dindshenchus*, Part 4 (Dublin, 1924), p. 367.
4. Macalister R.A.S, *Lebor Gabála Érenn*, Part 3 (Dublin, 1940), p. 155; O'Rahilly, *op. cit.*, p. 194.
5. O'Keeffe, *op. cit.*, pp. 40–1, 120–1, 152–3; Murphy, *op. cit.* (1933), pp. 206–7; Gregory, *op. cit.* (1994), p. 290; Stokes, *op. cit.* (1868), p. 87.
6. Green, *op. cit.* (1992), pp. 45, 51, 53, 64, 147, 159–60; Crossley-Holland, *op. cit.*, p. 173.
7. Crossley-Holland, *op. cit.* pp. 33–7, 61, 174–5; Cooper, *op. cit.*, pp. 242, 304.
8. Baring-Gould, *op. cit.*, pp. 14–5, 81–7.
9. Kelly, *op. cit.* (1997), pp. 130, 186–7.
10. Hickey, *op. cit.*, pp. 10–3; Beresford Ellis, P., *Hell or Connaught* (Belfast, 1988), p. 29; O'Rourke, F.J., *The Fauna of Ireland* (Cork, 1970), p. 113.

FOX

1. Ó hÓgáin, *op. cit.*, p. 27; O'Sullivan, P., *op. cit.*, pp. 45–6, 63.
2. Ó hÓgáin, *op. cit.*, p. 33; O'Sullivan, P., *op. cit.*, pp. 64–5; Gregory, *op. cit.* (1970), pp. 174, 178; Westropp, *op. cit.*, p. 46; Lamont Brown, *op. cit.*, p. 97; O'Farrell, *op. cit.*, pp. 50, 139; Gaffney, S. & Cashman, S., *Proverbs and Sayings of Ireland* (Dublin, 2003), p. 85.
3. Kelly, *op. cit.* (1997), p. 125; Stokes, *op. cit.* (1890), pp. 196, 266; Swift, *op. cit.*, p. 201.
4. O'Keeffe, *op. cit.*, pp. 76–7.
5. Green, *op. cit.* (1992), pp. 42, 54.
6. *Ibid.*, pp. 51–2.
7. *Ibid.*, pp. 51, 54; Kelly, *op. cit.* (1997), pp. 130, 188, 282, 425.

8. Hayden & Harrington, *op. cit.*, pp. 273–4.
9. http://www.thefoxwebsite.org/foxhunting; Hayden & Harrington, *op. cit.*, p. 274; http://www.fresco.ie/imfha

STOAT

1. Hayden & Harrington, *op. cit.*, p. 281.
2. Ó hÓgáin, *op. cit.*, p. 33; Gregory, *op. cit.* (1970), pp. 292–3; Westropp, *op. cit.*, pp. 45, 63; O'Sullivan, P., *op. cit.*, p. 57.
3. O'Sullivan, P., *op. cit.* p. 56; Gaffney & Cashman, *op. cit.*, p. 36; Opie & Tatum, *op. cit.*, p. 431; Ó hÓgáin, *op. cit.*, p. 33; Mac a'Bhaird, P., *Cogar san Fharraige* (Dublin, 2002), pp. 71–4; O'Farrell, *op. cit.*, pp. 51, 106; Fenton, J., *The Hamely Tongue* (Newtownards, 1995); Westropp, *op. cit.*, p. 63.
4. Hayden & Harrington, *op. cit.*, p. 281.
5. Murphy, *op. cit.* (1933), pp. 72–5; Stokes, *op. cit.* (1868), p. 126.
6. Green, *op. cit.* (1992), p. 51; Kelly, *op. cit.* (1997), p. 130; Hayden & Harrington, *op. cit.*, pp. 281, 286.

LIZARD

1. Westropp, *op. cit.*, p. 65; O'Farrell, *op. cit.*, pp. 55, 127.
2. Lamont Brown, *op. cit.*, p. 91.
3. Danaher, *op. cit.* (1972), p. 43; O' Farrell, *op. cit.*, pp. 108–9, 129; Opie & Tatum, *op. cit.*, p. 232.
4. Share, B., *Slanguage – A Dictionary of Irish Slang* (Dublin, 1997).
5. Cooper, *op. cit.*, p. 251; http://www.eol.org/pages/7518.
6. O'Rourke, *op. cit.*, pp. 49–52; O'Meara, *op. cit.* (1982), p. 50; O'Sullivan, D.C., *The Natural History of Ireland by Philip O'Sullivan Beare* (Cork, 2009), p. 167.

COW

1. O'Sullivan, P. *op. cit.*, pp. 112–3; Danaher, *op. cit.* (1972), pp. 36, 89, 96; Smyth, *op. cit.*, p. 19.
2. Danaher, *op. cit.* (1972), pp. 85, 146, 172, 239.
3. O'Sullivan, P., *op. cit.*, pp. 113–5, 123; O'Farrell, *op. cit.*, p. 13; Ó hEochaidh, S., Ní Néill, M., Ó Catháin, S., *Síscéalta ó Tír Chonaill* (Dublin, 1977), p. 83; White, *op. cit.*, p. 54; Ó hÓgáin, *op. cit.*, p. 335.
4. Ó hÓgáin, *op. cit.*, p. 29; O'Sullivan, P., *op. cit.*, pp. 114, 116; Ó hEochaidh, Ní Néill, Ó Catháin, *op. cit.*, pp. 352–3.
5. Ó hEochaidh, etc., *op. cit.* pp. 328–31; McCullough, *op. cit.*, p. 189.
6. O'Sullivan, P., *op. cit.*, p. 121.
7. *Ibid.*, p. 124; Lamont Brown, *op. cit.*, p. 95; Roberts, *op. cit.*, p. 40.
8. Stokes, *op. cit.* (1890), pp. 152, 167, 185, 189, 197, 248; Hynes, *op. cit.*, pp. 3–5; O'Sullivan, S., *Legends from Ireland* (London, 1977), pp. 107–8; Mac Neill, M., *The Festival of Lughnasa* (Oxford, 1962), pp. 393–4; Kelly, *op. cit.* (1997), pp. 31–2.
9. Ó hÓgáin, *op. cit.*, pp. 49, 240–1; Wilde, *op. cit.*, p. 70; Dinneen, *op. cit.*, p. 543; Gwynn, E., *The Metrical Dindshenchus*, Part 1 (Dublin, 1903), p. 23; Green, *op. cit.* (1992a), p. 75.

10. Ó hÓgáin, *op. cit.*, p. 50; Gantz, *op. cit.* (1981), pp. 53, 114; Gwynn, *op. cit.* (1903), p. 107; O'Rahilly, *op. cit.*, p. 194.
11. *Ibid.*, pp. 174, 271.
12. Green, *op. cit.* (1992), pp. 52–3.
13. Gantz, *op. cit.* (1981), p. 65; Kendrick, T.D., *The Druids* (London, 1927), p. 89; Frazer, *op. cit.*, p. 663; Green, *op. cit.* (1992), pp. 119–23.
14. Macalister, *op. cit.* (1940), p. 25; Macalister, *op. cit.* (1941), pp. 158–9; Ó hÓgáin, *op. cit.*, p. 60; Gantz, *op. cit.* (1981), p. 54.
15. Kelly, *op. cit.* (1997), pp. 30–6.
16. Green, *op. cit.* (1992), p. 14; Kelly, *op. cit.* (1997), pp. 167–8.
17. Kelly, *op. cit.* (1997), pp. 43–7; O'Sullivan, D. C., *op. cit.*, p. 41.
18. *Ibid.*, pp. 323–30; http://www.ipcc.ie/infobogbutter.html.
19. Kelly, *op. cit.* (1997), pp. 54–7, 336–9; Green, *op. cit.* (1992), p. 41.
20. Kelly, *op. cit.* (1997), pp. 48–50.
21. http://www.tcd.ie/botany/GHI/irishorgs.html; http://www.kerrycattle.ie/history.asp; http://www.dextercattle.co.uk; http://www.irishmoiledcattlesociety.com; Kelly, *op. cit.* (1997), p. 35; Ó hÓgáin, *op. cit.*, p. 231; Gregory, *op. cit.* (1994), p. 22.

## Pig

1. Ó hÓgáin, *op. cit.*, p. 30; Ó Muimhneacháin, A., *Stories from the Tailor* (Cork, 1978), p. 99; Lamont Brown, *op. cit.*, p. 37; Opie & Tatum, *op. cit.*, pp. 262–3, 307–8; O'Sullivan, P., *op. cit.*, p. 104; Danaher, *op. cit.* (1972), pp. 207, 230–2; Gregory, *op. cit.* (1970), pp. 234, 280.
2. O'Sullivan, P. *op. cit.*, p. 102; Minihane, *op. cit.*, p. 68; O'Farrell, *op. cit.*, p. 31.
3. Rosenstock, G., *Irish Proverbs in Irish and English* (Cork, 1999), p. 15; O'Sullivan, P., *op. cit.*, pp. 102, 105; O'Farrell, P., *Irish Proverbs and Sayings* (Cork, 1980), p. 14.
4. Murphy, *op. cit.* (1993), pp. 186–93; MacNeill, *op. cit.* (1908), pp. 130, 143; Gregory, *op. cit.*, (1994), pp. 199, 206–8.
5. Gregory, *op. cit.* pp. 216, 261–4; Frazer, *op. cit.*, p. 327.
6. Gwynn, E. *The Metrical Dindshenchus*, Part 3 (Dublin, 1913), p. 383; Stokes, *op. cit.* (1890), p. 154.
7. Kelly, *op. cit.* (1997), p. 84; Gantz, *op. cit.* (1981), pp. 182–7; Gwynn, *op. cit.* (1924), p. 195; Stokes, W., 'The Rennes Dinnshenchus', *Revue Celtique*, 15 (1895), p. 63; Gregory, *op. cit.* (1994), pp. 36–7, 61; Smyth, *op. cit.*, p. 20.
8. Green, *op. cit.* (1992), pp. 63, 82, 108, 118.
9. *Ibid.*, pp. 46, 91.
10. Gregory, *op. cit.* (1994), p. 56; Macalister, *op. cit.* (1941), pp. 158–9; Ó hÓgáin, *op. cit.*, p. 60; Stokes, *op. cit.* (1868), p. 156; Gantz, *op. cit.* (1976), pp. 169–75; Jones, G., *Welsh Legends and Folktales* (London, 1979), p. 224.
11. Green, *op. cit.* (1992), pp. 218–9; Crossley-Holland, *op. cit.*, p. 52; Cooper, *op. cit.*, p. 221; Frazer, *op. cit.*, pp. 469, 476.
12. Kelly, *op. cit.* (1997), pp. 79, 80, 81, 83, 86–7, 142–3, 154–5, 281–2, 336; Green, *op. cit.* (1992), pp. 5, 10, 41, 46; O'Rourke, *op. cit.*, p. 131; O'Rahilly, *op. cit.*, p. 139.
13. O'Meara, *op. cit.*, pp. 47–8; O'Rourke, *op. cit.*, p. 131; O'Sullivan, D.C., *op. cit.*, p. 79; Fitzgerald, O., 'The Irish "Greyhound" Pig: An Extinct Indigenous Breed of Pig', *History Ireland*, 13, 4 (Dublin, 2005).
14. Fitzgerald, *op. cit.*

Dog

1. Lamont Brown, *op. cit.*, p. 97; O'Sullivan, P., *op. cit.*, pp. 97, 101; Ó hEochaidh, Ní Néill, Ó Catháin, *op. cit.*, pp. 262–3; Danaher, *op. cit.* (1966), p. 97; Minihane, *op. cit.*, p. 51; Westropp, *op. cit.*, p. 30; Gregory, *op. cit.* (1970), p. 279.
2. O'Sullivan, P., *op. cit.*, p. 97; Ó hÓgáin, *op. cit.*, p. 28; Ó Muimhneacháin, *op. cit.*, p. 99; Westropp, *op. cit.*, p. 46; O'Farrell, *op. cit.* (2004), pp. 108–9, 111; Opie & Tatum, *op. cit.*, p. 121.
3. Gaffney & Cashman, *op. cit.*, pp. 13–4; O'Farrell, *op. cit.* (1980), pp. 22, 35, 73; O'Sullivan, P., *op. cit.*, p. 101.
4. O'Rahilly, *op. cit.*, pp. 161–3; Gantz, *op. cit.* (1981), pp. 139–40; Gregory, *op. cit.* (1994), p. 532.
5. Murphy, *op. cit.* (1933), pp. 114–5, 198–203; Gregory, *op. cit.* (1994), p. 127.
6. Gantz, *op. cit.* (1981), pp. 90–1; Gregory, *op. cit.* (1994), p. 407; Squire, C., *Mythology of the Celtic People* (Twickenham, 1998), p. 392; Murphy, *op. cit.* (1933), p. 207.
7. Macalister, *op. cit.* (1940), p. 39; Gwynn, *op. cit.* (1913), p. 33; Stokes, *op. cit.* (1868), p. 111; Cooper, *op. cit.*, p. 76.
8. Gantz, *op. cit.* (1976), p. 46.
9. Green, *op. cit.* (1992), pp. 111–3.
10. *Ibid.*, pp. 198–203; Cooper, *op. cit.*, p. 76.
11. Crawford, P., *The Living Isles* (London, 1985), pp. 187–8; Meadows, G. & Flint, E., *The Dog Owner's Handbook* (London, 2001), pp. 12–4.
12. Green, *op. cit.* (1992), pp. 56–7, 200.
13. Kelly, *op. cit* (1997), pp. 115–6; http://www.irishwolfhounds.org/association.html.
14. Kelly, *op. cit.* (1997), pp. 117–20.
15. *Ibid.*, p. 120.
16. *Ibid.*, p. 144, 148–9.
17. http://www.fresco.ie/imfha; O'Hare, *op. cit.*, pp. 80–1; Hayden & Harrington, *op. cit.*, p. 274.
18. http://www.irishcoursingclub.ie; http://www.encyclopedia.com/topic/dog_racing.aspx.
19. Kelly, *op. cit.* (1997), p. 186; http://www.irishwolfhounds.org/association.html.
20. O'Dwyer, R., *The Irish Red Setter* (Cork, 2007), p. 7; Schweppe, F., *Kerry Blue Terriers* (New Jersey, 1990), pp. 8–9.
21. http://www.ispca.ie/spaying-and-neutering.aspx.

Donkey

1. Ó hÓgáin, *op. cit.*, p. 30; Danaher, *op. cit.* (1972), p. 239; Swinfen, A., *The Irish Donkey* (Dublin, 2004), pp. 145–7.
2. O'Sullivan. P., *op. cit.*, p. 92.
3. O'Farrell, *op. cit.* (2004), pp. 19, 30–1, 46–7, 136; Opie & Tatum, *op. cit.*, p. 122.
4. Swinfen, *op. cit.*, pp. 113–4, 148–9.
5. *Ibid.*, pp. 3–4, 7; Kelly, *op. cit.* (1997), p. 131.
6. Swinfen, *op. cit.*, pp. 20, 23, 25, 31, 33, 36–7, 39, 146; Kelly, *op. cit.* (1997), pp. 130, 132.

GOAT

1. Foley, K., *History of Killorglin* (Killarney, 1988), p. 107; Ó hÓgáin, *op. cit.*, p. 30; MacNeill, *op. cit.*, p. 292.
2. O'Farrell, *op. cit.* (2004), p. 17; Ó hÓgáin, *op. cit.*, pp. 29, 420; O'Sullivan, P., *op. cit.*, p. 79; Opie & Tatum, *op. cit.*, p. 174; Werner, R., 'The Old Irish Goat', *Heritage Outlook* (Dublin, 2009), p. 23; Westropp, *op. cit.*, p. 29.
3. O'Sullivan, P., *op. cit.*, pp. 78–80; Ó Muimhneacháin, *op. cit.*, p. 63.
4. Hayden & Harrington, *op. cit.*, p. 348.
5. Stokes, *op. cit.* (1890), p. 160; http://www.skerries.dublindiocese.ie/goat.html.
6. Green, *op. cit.* (1992), pp. 18, 43, 83, 95, 110; Kelly, *op. cit.* (1997), p. 78; Crossley-Holland, *op. cit.*, pp. 80–1.
7. Cooper, *op. cit.*, pp. 5, 12, 72, 111, 211.
8. Kelly, *op. cit.* (1997), pp. 77–9; Hayden & Harrington, *op. cit.*, p. 349; Green, *op. cit.* (1992), pp. 17, 42.
9. Hayden & Harrington, *op. cit.*, pp. 349–50; Halliday, J. & J., *Practical Goat Keeping* (London, 1982), p. 7; Werner, *op. cit.*, p. 25.
10. Hayden & Harrington, *op. cit.*, pp. 349–50, 353; Werner, *op. cit.*, pp. 22–5.


SHEEP

1. O'Sullivan, P., *op. cit.*, pp. 80–1; O'Farrell, *op. cit.* (2004), p. 25; MacNeill, *op. cit.*, pp. 292, 300.
2. White, *op. cit.*, p. 54; Opie & Tatum, *op. cit.*, pp. 31, 348.
3. Danaher, *op. cit.* (1972), p. 188; Stokes, *op. cit.* (1890), p. 248; Hynes, *op. cit.*, p. 3.
4. Macalister, *op. cit.* (1941), pp. 122–3; Gregory, *op. cit.* (1994), pp. 89, 192, 277–8.
5. Stokes, *op. cit.* (1895), pp. 274–5; Gwynn, *op. cit.* (1913), pp. 325–9.
6. Green, *op. cit.* (1992), pp. 83, 123–4.
7. *Ibid.*, pp. 227–8.
8. Cooper, *op. cit.*, pp. 153, 232.
9. Kelly, *op. cit.* (1997), pp. 66–7, 70–1, 72–4; Green, *op. cit.* (1992), pp. 5, 10–1, 15, 30, 32.
10. Kelly, *op. cit.* (1997), pp. 66–7, 69, 75–7.
11. http://www.tcd.ie/Botany/GHI/irishorgs.html.


BADGER

1. Ó hÓgáin, *op. cit.*, p. 34; O'Sullivan, P., *op. cit.*, p. 58; Dinneen, *op. cit.*, p. 785.
2. O'Sullivan, P., *op. cit.*, p. 58; Westropp, *op. cit.*, p. 63; Ó hÓgáin, *op. cit.*, p. 34; O'Meara, *op. cit.* (1982), p. 48.
3. Westropp, *op. cit.*, p. 136.
4. O'Sullivan, P., *op. cit.*, p. 59; Westropp, *op. cit.*, pp. 1, 2, 27.
5. O'Keeffe, *op. cit.*, pp. 78–9; Stokes, *op. cit.* (1868), p. 83; Ó hÓgáin, *op. cit.*, p. 399.
6. Green, *op. cit.* (1992), pp. 42, 51–4; Kelly, *op. cit.* (1997), pp. 131, 282; Gregory, *op. cit.* (1994), p. 131; Westropp, *op. cit.*, p. 63; Mac Giolla Léith, *op. cit.*, p. 99; Hayden & Harrington, *op. cit.*, pp. 295–7; O'Rourke, *op. cit.*, p. 124.

HEDGEHOG

1. Ó hÓgáin, *op. cit.*, p. 34; Danaher, *op. cit.* (1972), pp. 14, 111; Westropp, *op. cit.*, p. 64; Gregory, *op. cit.* (1970), p. 293; O'Farrell, *op. cit.* (2004), p. 86; Rosenstock, *op. cit.*, p. 15.
2. Hayden & Harrington, *op. cit.*, p. 28.
3. Cooper, *op. cit.*, p. 124; Lamont Brown, *op. cit.*, p. 96.
4. O'Meara, *op. cit.* (1982), p. 49; Grzimek, B., *Animal Life Encyclopedia*, Vol. 10 (London, 1972), pp. 204–5, 214; O'Sullivan, P., *op. cit.*, p. 60.


RABBIT

1. Ó hÓgáin, *op. cit.*, pp. 34, 91; Ó hEochaidh, Ní Néill, Ó Catháin, *op. cit.*, p. 325; O'Sullivan, P., *op. cit.*, p. 74; Opie & Tatum, *op. cit.*, p. 193; Brown, M. & Richardson, V., *Rabbitlopaedia: A Complete Guide to Rabbit Care* (Gloucestershire, 2000), p. 13.
2. Hayden & Harrington, *op. cit.*, p. 85.
3. Brown & Richardson, *op. cit.*, pp. 7–10; Kelly, *op. cit.* (1997), p. 133; Hayden & Harrington, *op. cit.*, p. 87; O'Rourke, *op. cit.*, p. 137.
4. Hayden & Harrington, *op. cit.*, p. 90.


CAT

1. Jay, R., *The Kingdom of the Cat* (London, 2000), p. 78; Westropp, *op. cit.*, pp. 46, 62; O'Sullivan, P., *op. cit.*, p. 109; Mac a'Bhaird, *op. cit.*, p. 72; Minihane, *op. cit.*, p. 25; Opie & Tatum, *op. cit.*, p. 62.
2. Lamont Brown, *op. cit.*, pp. 37, 97; Danaher, *op. cit.* (1972), p. 259; O'Sullivan, P., *op. cit.*, p. 109; Minihane, *op. cit.*, p. 65; O'Farrell, *op. cit.* (2004), p. 109; Bluett, A., *Ireland in Love* (Cork, 1995), p. 18; Opie & Tatum, *op. cit.*, p. 62; Moore, J., *The Mysterious Cat: Feline Myth and Magic through the Ages* (London, 1999), p. 121.
3. Gregory, *op. cit.* (1970), pp. 169, 257, 291; White, *op. cit.*, p. 76; Becker, H., *Seaweed Memories* (Dublin, 2000), p. 156; Ó hÓgáin, *op. cit.*, p. 34.
4. Ó hÓgáin, *op. cit.*, p. 27; Mac a'Bhaird, *op. cit.*, p. 13; O'Sullivan, P., *op. cit.*, pp. 108–9.
5. O'Sullivan, P., *op. cit.* p. 111; Gaffney & Cashman, *op. cit.*, p. 82; Ó hÓgáin, *op. cit.*, p. 28.
6. Gaffney & Cashman, *op. cit.*, p. 35; Egan, P.M., *The Illustrated Guide to the City and County of Kilkenny* (1885), pp. 28–9.
7. Moore, *op. cit.*, pp. 37, 115–6; Jay, *op. cit.*, pp. 60, 70–1.
8. Kelly, *op. cit.* (1997), p. 123.
9. Gregory, *op. cit.* (1994), pp. 23, 153; Gantz, *op. cit.* (1976), p. 259.
10. O'Sullivan, P., *op. cit.*, pp. 19–20; Westropp, *op. cit.*, pp. 26–7; Curtin, J., *Myths and Folktales of Ireland* (New York, 1975), p. 129.
11. Ó hÓgáin, *op. cit.*, p. 91; Curtin, *op. cit.* (1975), p. 129.
12. Heath, S., *Why Does My Cat ...?* (London, 1993), p. 31; Jay, *op. cit.*, pp. 38, 58, 60.
13. Jay, *op. cit.* pp. 56–7, 66.
14. Mays, M., *Moggies: A Book for Owners of Non-Pedigree Cats* (Havant, 1997), pp. 6–7; Heath, *op. cit.*, pp. 28, 31; Jay, *op. cit.*, pp. 6–7; Green, *op. cit.* (1992), p. 25.

15. Mitchell, F., *Shell Guide to Reading the Irish Landscape* (Dublin, 1986), pp. 136–7.
16. Kelly, *op. cit.* (1997), pp. 122–3, 145; Moore, *op. cit.*, p. 34; Jay, *op. cit.*, p. 74.
17. Heath, *op. cit.*, p. 32; Westropp, *op. cit.*, p. 40.
18. Heath, *op. cit.*, p. 32; Jay, *op. cit.*, pp. 66, 76–7, 80–2, 87–8; O'Sullivan, P., *op. cit.*, p. 107.
19. McKittrick, D., 'Animal Experts warn Ireland Plague of Feral Cats is Spreading', http://www.independent.co.uk (2004).
20. Westropp, *op. cit.*, p. 62; Kelly, *op. cit.* (1997), p. 130; O'Rahilly, *op. cit.*, p. 173; Hayden & Harrington, *op. cit.*, pp. 276, 279; Flanagan & Flanagan, *op. cit.*, pp. 12–31.

HARE

1. Ó hÓgáin, *op. cit.*, p. 34; Wilde, *op. cit.*, p. 56; Danaher, *op. cit.* (1972), p. 117; Gregory, *op. cit.* (1970), pp. 55, 288–9; Opie & Tatum, *op. cit.*, p. 190.
2. Danaher, *op. cit.* (1972), pp. 190–1; Frazer, *op. cit.*, pp. 452–3; Ó hÓgáin, *op. cit.*, p. 34; Westropp, *op. cit.*, pp. 46, 61.
3. Opie & Tatum, *op. cit.*, pp. 193–4; Lamont Brown, *op. cit.*, p. 95; O'Farrell, *op. cit.* (2004), pp. 32, 84; Roberts, *op. cit.*, p. 40.
4. Rosenstock, *op. cit.*, pp. 14, 25; Gaffney & Cashman, *op. cit.*, p. 85; O'Sullivan, P., *op. cit.*, p. 75; Grigson, G., *The Englishman's Flora* (Oxford, 1996), p. 393.
5. Gregory, *op. cit.* (1994), pp. 79, 117; Murphy, *op. cit.* (1933), p. 193.
6. Green, *op. cit.* (1992), p. 112.
7. Cooper, *op. cit.*, p. 120; Danaher, *op. cit.* (1972), pp. 75–8.
8. Green, *op. cit.* (1992), pp. 38, 44, 50–1, 113.
9. Kelly, *op. cit.* (1997), pp. 117, 130–1, 282, 299.
10. http://www.irishcoursingclub.ie.
11. Hayden & Harrington, *op. cit.*, pp. 91–6, 101–2.

RAT

1. O' Sullivan, S., *op. cit.*, pp. 88–9 ; Ó hÓgáin, *op. cit.*, pp. 34, 95; Ó Muimhneacháin, *op. cit.*, pp. 84–5; Opie & Tatum, *op. cit.*, p. 323; O'Meara, *op. cit.* (1982), p. 81; O'Sullivan, P., *op. cit.*, pp. 70, 73; Frazer, *op. cit.*, p. 531; Lamont Brown, *op. cit.*, p. 94.
2. O'Sullivan, P., *op. cit.*, pp. 70–1.
3. Hayden & Harrington, *op. cit.*, p. 138; Kelly, *op. cit.* (1997), p. 244.
4. Hayden & Harrington, *op. cit.*, pp. 139–41; Kelly, *op. cit.* (1997), pp. 243–4.
5. Hayden & Harrington, *op. cit.*, pp. 133–7; O'Rourke, *op. cit.*, p. 149.

MOUSE

1. Opie & Tatum, *op. cit.*, p. 276; O'Farrell, *op. cit.* (2004), pp. 40, 64, 112; Bluett, *op. cit.*, pp. 14, 16.
2. Frazer, *op. cit.*, pp. 39, 182; Lamont Brown, *op. cit.*, p. 94; Opie & Tatum, *op cit.*, p. 322; Rosenstock, *op. cit.*, p. 19.
3. Hayden & Harrington, *op. cit.*, p. 123.

4. Ó hÓgáin, *op. cit.*, p. 34; Mac Cionnaith, M., *Seanchas Rann na Feirste* (Dublin, 2005), p. 72.

5. Gantz, *op. cit.* (1976), pp. 92–6.

6. Ó hÓgáin, *op. cit.*, p. 381.

7. O'Meara, *op. cit.* (1982), pp. 61–2.

8. Hayden & Harrington, *op. cit.*, p. 124.

9. Kelly, *op. cit.* (1997), pp. 236, 243; O'Meara, *op. cit.* (1982), p. 49.

10. O'Sullivan, P., *op. cit.*, p. 60; Opie & Tatum, *op. cit.*, p. 354.

SQUIRREL

1. Grzimek, *op. cit.*, pp. 245–6.

2. http://www.logainm.ie.

3. O'Rahilly, C., *The Pursuit of Gruaidhe Griansholus* (London, 1924), pp. 46–7; Crossley-Holland, *op. cit.*, p. 15; Grzimek, *op. cit.*, pp. 245–6.

4. Hayden & Harrington, *op. cit.*, pp. 107–8, 114–7; O'Rourke, *op. cit.*, pp. 29, 139; http://www.rte.ie/radio/mooneygoeswild/schoolwatch/greysquirrel.html; Kelly, *op. cit.* (1997), p. 130; O'Sullivan, D.C., *op. cit*, p. 83; http://www.npws.ie/en/media/Media,6435.en.pdf.

BAT

1. Ó hÓgáin, *op. cit.*, p. 34; Westropp, *op. cit.*, p. 46; Wilde, *op. cit.*, p. 71; Opie & Tatum, *op. cit.*, p. 14.

2. Cooper, *op. cit.*, pp. 29, 295; Opie & Tatum, *op. cit.*, p. 14; http://www.nationalgeographic.com/animals/printable/common-vampire-bat.html.

3. Hayden & Harrington, *op. cit.*, pp. 39–82; O'Sullivan, D.C., *op. cit*, p. 109.

BEE

1. Ó hÓgáin, *op. cit.*, p. 31; Opie & Tatum, *op. cit.*, pp. 18, 21; O'Sullivan, P., *op. cit.*, p. 125; Lamont Brown, *op. cit.*, p. 98.

2. Allen, D., & Hatfield, G., *Medicinal Plants in Folk Tradition* (Cambridge, 2004), pp. 162, 251; O'Farrell, *op. cit.*, pp. 83, 98.

3. Opie & Tatum, *op. cit.*, p. 47

4. http://www.logainm.ie.

5. http://www.dioceseofkerry.ie/pages/heritage/gobnait.html; Power, *op. cit.*, pp. 20–1.

6. Gregory, *op. cit.* (1994), pp. 71, 472; Gantz, *op. cit.* (1981), p. 94; Kelly, *op. cit.* (1997), p. 113; Green, *op. cit.* (1992), p. 35.

7. *Ibid.*, pp. 211–2.

8. Cooper, *op. cit.*, p. 31; Opie & Tatum, *op. cit.*, p. 18; O'Sullivan, S., *op. cit.*, pp. 131–2.

9. Kelly, *op. cit.* (1997), pp. 108, 110; Green, *op. cit.* (1992), pp. 34–5.

10. Kelly, *op. cit.* (1997), p. 109–11.

11. Green, *op. cit.* (1992), p. 35; Kelly, *op. cit.* (1997), p. 113.

12. Kelly, *op. cit.* (1997), pp. 108, 111–2, 145–6, 155–7.

13. Brown, R., *Beeswax* (Somerset, 1981), pp. 11, 13.
14. http://www.irishbeekeeping.ie; http://www.tcd.ie/Botany/GHI/irishorgs. html.
15. O'Sullivan, P., *op. cit.*, p. 126; Westropp, *op. cit.*, p. 66; Minihane, *op. cit.*, p. 61; Ó hÓgáin, *op. cit.*, p. 36; O'Sullivan, S., *op. cit.*, p. 86.

WHALE

1. O'Sullivan, S., *op. cit.*, p. 41.
2. O'Meara, *op. cit.* (1978), pp. 34–6, 54; Stokes, *op. cit.* (1890), p. 258.
3. Stokes, W., *The Bodleian Dinnshenchus* (London, 1892), p. 41; Gwynn, *op. cit.* (1913), pp. 428–9.
4. Mac Neill, *op. cit.* (1908), pp. 118–20.
5. http://www.melville.org/mobyname.htm; http://animals.nationalgeographic. com/animals/mammals/sperm-whale.html
6. Philbrick, N., *In the Heart of the Sea: The Tragedy of the Whaleship* Essex (London, 2001), pp. 80–3
7. Kelly, *op. cit.* (1997), pp. 284–5; Hayden & Harrington, *op. cit.*, pp. 142–240.
8. Kelly, *op. cit.* (1997), pp. 283–4; Hayden & Harrington, *op. cit.*, pp. 201–8, 213–8, 233–6; Green, *op. cit.* (1992a), p. 84; Cooper, *op. cit.*, p. 77.

SEAL

1. Ó hÓgáin, *op. cit.*, p. 32; Mac Neill, M., *op. cit.*, p. 8.
2. White, *op. cit.*, p. 64; Danaher, *op. cit.* (1966), pp. 122–3, 126; Westropp, *op. cit.*, p. 31.
3. Mac a'Bhaird, *op. cit.*, p. 103; O'Farrell, *op. cit.* (2004), p. 83.
4. Gregory, *op. cit.* (1970), p. 293; Danaher, *op. cit.* (1966), p. 124; Ó hEochaidh, Ní Néill, Ó Catháin, *op. cit.*, p. 219; Mac a'Bhaird, *op. cit.*, p. 14.
5. Becker, *op. cit.*, p. 144; Mac a'Bhaird, *op. cit.*, pp. 71, 75.
6. Rosenstock, *op. cit.*, p. 25.
7. Flanagan & Flanagan, *op. cit.*, pp. 12–31.
8. Stokes, *op. cit.* (1890), p. 287; Swift, *op. cit.*, p. 131.
9. Gwynn, *op. cit.* (1924), p. 147; Gregory, *op. cit.* (1994), p. 95; Murphy, *op. cit.* (1998), pp. 98–9; Mac Giolla Léith, *op. cit.*, p. 111.
10. Hayden & Harrington, *op. cit.*, p. 315; Kelly, *op. cit.* (1997), pp. 282–4.
11. Hayden & Harrington, *op. cit.*, pp. 310–1, 315–9.

OTTER

1. Ó hÓgáin, *op. cit.*, p. 32; Westropp, *op. cit.*, p. 62; O'Rourke, *op. cit.*, p. 125.
2. O'Sullivan, P., *op. cit.*, pp. 60–1.
3. Hayden & Harrington, *op. cit.*, p. 299.
4. Ó hÓgáin, *op. cit.*, pp. 74–5; O'Keeffe, *op. cit.*, p. 9; O'Meara, *op. cit.* (1978).
5. Hayden & Harrington, *op. cit.*, p. 300; Gregory, *op. cit.* (1994), p. 301; Murphy, *op. cit.* (1933), pp. 372–3.
6. Kelly, *op. cit.* (1997), p. 130; Gantz, *op. cit.* (1981), pp. 116–7 ; Gregory, *op. cit.* (1994), p. 147; Crossley-Holland, *op. cit.* p. 137; Hayden & Harrington, *op. cit.*, p. 304.

SALMON

1. Ó hÓgáin, *op. cit.*, pp. 32, 254.
2. O'Sullivan, S., *op. cit.*, pp. 39–40.
3. Ó hÓgáin, *op. cit.*, p. 32; Gantz, *op. cit.* (1976), pp. 165–6.
4. Ó hÓgáin, *op. cit.*, p. 224; Macalister, *op. cit.* (1940), p. 43.
5. Rees A. & Rees B., *Celtic Heritage* (London, 1961), p. 250.
6. Gregory, *op. cit.* (1994), pp. 88, 95–6; Murphy, *op. cit.* (1998), pp. 94–5.
7. Gregory, *op. cit.* (1994), pp. 211–2, 305–6, 358, 400; Gantz, *op. cit.* (1981), p. 215.
8. Kelly, *op. cit.* (1997), pp. 291–5; Smyth, *op. cit.*, p. 34.
9. Kelly, *op. cit.* (1997), pp. 285–95; Green, *op. cit.* (1992), p. 35.
10. http://www.bim.ie.

SNAKE

1. Vickery, R., *A Dictionary of Plant Lore* (Oxford, 1995), p. 174; Williams, N., *Díolaim Luibheanna* (Dublin, 1993), p. 131; Bluett, *op. cit.*, p. 46; http://www.logainm.ie.
2. Macalister, R.A.S., *Lebor Gabála Érenn,* Part 2 (Dublin, 1939), pp. 34–5, 60–1, 122–3, 185–7; Macalister, *op. cit.* (1940), p. 147; O'Meara, *op. cit.* (1982), pp. 50–1; Swift, *op. cit.*, pp. 225–7; Mac Neill, M, *op. cit.*, p. 399; Cooper, *op. cit.*, p. 215.
3. Mac Neill, M., *op. cit.*, pp. 105, 127; O'Sullivan, S., *op. cit.*, p. 152; Ó hÓgáin, *op. cit.*, p. 93; Stokes, *op. cit.* (1890), p. 180.
4. Gregory, *op. cit.* (1994), pp. 68, 206; Gantz, *op. cit.* (1981), pp. 169, 126, 248; Ní Shéaghdha, N., *Toruigheacht Diarmaid agus Gráinne* (Dublin, 1967), pp. 59–63.
5. Green, *op. cit.* (1992a), pp. 194–5; Cooper, *op. cit.*, p. 257; Crossley-Holland, *op. cit.*, p. 33; Gantz, *op. cit.* (1981), p. 75.
6. Ó hÓgáin, *op. cit.*, p. 32; O'Farrell, *op. cit.* (2004), pp. 64, 86; Mac a'Bhaird, *op. cit.*, pp. 104–5; McCullough, *op. cit.*, p. 186; O'Rahilly, *op. cit.* (1967), p. 194; Harbison, *op. cit.*, p. 20; Gregory, *op. cit.* (1994), p. 147.

FROG

1. O'Farrell, *op. cit.* (2004), p. 134; O'Sullivan, P., *op. cit.*, p. 125; Westropp, *op. cit.*, p. 42; Opie & Tatum, *op. cit.*, pp. 169–70; Bluett, *op. cit.*, p. 14; Lamont Brown, *op. cit.*, p. 92.
2. O'Sullivan, P., *op. cit.*, p. 125; Minihane, *op. cit.*, p. 95.
3. McCullough, *op. cit.*, p. 187; Mac Cionnaith, *op. cit.*, pp. 12–3.
4. Praeger, R.L., *The Way That I Went* (Cork, 1997), p. 178; O'Meara, *op. cit.*, pp. 50–2.
5. Cooper, *op. cit.*, p. 102.
6. *Ibid.*, p. 103.
7. O'Rourke, *op. cit.*, pp. 43, 47; Praeger, *op. cit.*, p. 180; Fitzsimons, M. & Igoe, F., 'Freshwater Fish Conservation in the Irish Republic', *PRIA,* 104B, 3 (2004), pp. 17–8; Fitzmaurice, P., 'The Effects of Freshwater Fish introductions into Ireland', *EIFAC Technical Paper 42 (suppl. 2)* (1984), pp. 449–57; Currie, C., 'The Early History of the Carp and its Economic Significance in England', *The Agricultural History Review,* 39, 2 (1991), pp. 105–6.

POSTSCRIPT

1. Eberhard, W., *A Dictionary of Chinese Symbols* (London, 1986), pp. 58, 294–5.
2. Frazer, *op. cit.*, pp. 683–91.

# Bibliography

Allen, D. & Hatfield, G. (2004): *Medicinal Plants in Folk Tradition*, Timber Press, Cambridge

An Roinn Oideachais (Dept. of Educ.) (1978): *Ainmneacha Plandaí agus Ainmhithe*, Oifig an tSoláthair, Dublin

Baring-Gould, S. (2007): *The Book of Werewolves*, Nonsuch Publishing, Dublin

Becker, H. (2000): *Seaweed Memories*, Wolfhound Press, Dublin

Beresford Ellis, P. (1975): *Hell or Connaught*, The Blackstaff Press (1988), Belfast

— (1992): *Dictionary of Celtic Mythology*, Constable & Co. London

Bluett, A. (1995): *Ireland in Love*, Mercier Press, Cork

Brown, M. & Richardson, V. (2000): *Rabbitlopaedia: A Complete Guide to Rabbit Care*, Ringpress Books, Gloucestershire

Brown, R. (1981): *Beeswax*, Bee Books New & Old, Somerset

Budiansky, S. (1998): *The Nature of Horses*, Phoenix Illustrated, London

Cooper, J.J. (1993): *Brewer's Book of Myth and Legend*, Helicon Publishing, Oxford

Crawford, P. (1985): *The Living Isles*, British Broadcasting Association, London

Crossley-Holland, K. (1980): *The Penguin Book of Norse Myths*, Penguin, Harmondsworth

Currie, C. (1991): 'The Early History of the Carp and its Economic Significance in England', *The Agricultural History Review*, 39, 2, pp. 97–107

Curtin, J. (1890): *Myths and Folktales of Ireland*, Dover Publications (1975), New York

— (1894): *Hero Tales of Ireland*, Macmillan Press, London

Danaher, K. (1966): *Irish Country People*, Mercier Press, Cork

— (1972): *The Year in Ireland – Irish Calendar Customs*, Mercier Press, Cork

Dinneen, P.S. (1927): *Foclóir Gaedhilge agus Béarla*, Irish Texts Society, Dublin

Eberhard, W. (1986): *A Dictionary of Chinese Symbols*, Routledge & Kegan Paul, London

Egan, P.M (1885): *The Illustrated Guide to the City and County of Kilkenny*, Kilkenny

Ellis, A.T. (1989): *Wales: An Anthology*, Fontana Paperbacks (1991), London

Fenton, J. (1995): *The Hamely Tongue*, Ulster Scots Academic Press, Newtownards

Fitzgerald, O. (2005): 'The Irish "Greyhound" Pig: an Extinct Indigenous Breed of Pig', *History Ireland*, 13, 4

Fitzmaurice, P. (1984): 'The Effects of Freshwater Fish Introductions into Ireland', *EIFAC Technical Paper 42 (suppl. 2)*, pp. 449–57

Fitzsimons, M. & Igoe, F. (2004): 'Freshwater Fish Conservation in the Irish Republic', *PRIA*, 104B, 3, pp. 17–32

Flanagan, D. & Flanagan, L. (1994): *Irish Place Names*, Gill & Macmillan, Dublin

Foley, K. (1988): *History of Killorglin*, Killorglin History & Folklore Society, Killarney

Frazer, J.G. (1922): *The Golden Bough*, Macmillan Press (1987), London

Gaffney, S. & Cashman, S. (2003): *Proverbs and Sayings of Ireland*, Wolfhound Press, Dublin

Gantz, J. (1976): *The Mabinogion,* Penguin Books, Harmondsworth

— (1981): *Early Irish Myths and Sagas,* Penguin Books, Harmondsworth

Gibbs, L. (2002): *Aesop's Fables,* Oxford World Classics, Oxford

Green, M. (1992): *Animals in Celtic Life and Myth*, Routledge, London

— (1992a): *Dictionary of Celtic Myth and Legend,* Thames and Hudson, London

Gregory, Lady A. (1902; 1904): *Complete Irish Mythology,* The Slaney Press (1994), London

— (1920): *Visions & Beliefs in the West of Ireland,* Colin Smythe (1970), Buckinghamshire

Grigson, G. (1958): *The Englishman's Flora*, Helicon Publishing (1996), Oxford

Grzimek, B. (1972): *Animal Life Encyclopedia,* Vol. 10, Van Nostrand Reinhold, London

Gwynn, E. (1903; 1906; 1913; 1924; 1935): *The Metrical Dindshenchus,* Dublin

Halliday, J. & J. (1982): *Practical Goat Keeping*, Ward Lock Ltd, London

Harbison, P. (1988): *Pre-Christian Ireland,* Thames and Hudson, London

Hartley Edwards, E. (2000): *The Encyclopedia of the Horse*, Dorling Kindersley, London

Hayden, T. & Harrington, R. (2000): *Exploring Irish Mammals*, Town House and Country House, Dublin

Heath, S. (1993): *Why Does My Cat …?*, Souvenir Press, London

Hickey, K. (2003): 'Wolf – Forgotten Irish Hunter', *Wild Ireland* (2003)

Holland, A. (2001): *Steeplechasing – A Celebration of 250 Years*, Little, Brown, London

Hynes, S.B.E. (1928): *Legends of St Kevin*, CTSI Pamphlet No. 959

Jay, R. (2000): *The Kingdom of the Cat*, Apple Press, London

Jones, G. (1955): *Welsh Legends and Folk Tales,* Puffin Books (1979), London

Kelly, F. (1988): *A Guide to Early Irish Law*, Dublin Institute for Advanced Studies, Dublin

— (1997): *Early Irish Farming,* Dublin Institute for Advanced Studies, Dublin

Kendrick, T.D. (1927): *The Druids,* Methuen & Co. Ltd, London

Lamont Brown, R. (1970): *A Book of Superstitions*, David and Charles Ltd, Devon

Mac a'Bhaird, P. (2002): *Cogar san Fharraige*, Coiscéim, Dublin

Macalister, R.A.S (1938–41; 1956): *Lebor Gabála Érenn,* Parts 1–5, Irish Texts Society, Dublin

Mac Cionnaith, M. (2005): *Seanchas Rann na Feirste,* Coiscéim, Dublin

McCullough, J.A., (1911): *The Religion of the Ancient Celts*, T & T Clark, Edinburgh

Mac Giolla Léith, C. (1993): *Oidheadh Chloinne hUisneach*, Irish Texts Society, Dublin

McManus, D. (1991): 'A Guide to Ogam', *Maynooth Monographs,* 4 (1991)

Mac Neill, E. (1908): *Duanaire Finn*, Irish Texts Society, Dublin

MacNeill, M. (1962): *The Festival of Lughnasa*, Oxford University Press, Oxford

Mays, M. (1997): *Moggies: A Book for Owners of Non-Pedigree Cats*, Kingdom Books, Havant

Meadows, G. & Flint, E. (2001): *The Dog Owner's Handbook*, New Holland Publishers, London

Minihane, P. (2003): *Beara Woman Talking: The Lore of Peig Minihane*, Mercier Press, Cork

Mitchell, F. (1986): *Shell Guide to Reading the Irish Landscape*, Country House, Dublin

Moore, J (1999): *The Mysterious Cat: Feline Myth and Magic through the Ages*, Judy Piatkus Ltd, London

Murphy, G. (1933): *Duanaire Finn*, Part II, Irish Texts Society, Dublin

— (1998): *Early Irish Lyrics*, Four Courts Press, Dublin

Ní Shéaghdha, N. (1967): *Toruigheacht Diarmaid agus Gráinne*, Irish Texts Society, Dublin

O'Dwyer, R. (2007): *The Irish Red Setter*, Cork University Press, Cork

O'Farrell, P. (1980): *Irish Proverbs and Sayings*, Mercier Press, Cork

— (2004): *Irish Folk Cures*, Gill & Macmillan, Dublin

O'Hare, N. (2002): *The Irish Sport Horse*, Harkway, Eastbourne

Ó hEochaidh, S., Ní Néill, M. & Ó Catháin, S. (1977): *Síscéalta ó Tír Chonaill*, Dublin

Ó hÓgáin, D. (1991): *Myth, Legend and Romance - An Encyclopaedia of the Irish Folk Tradition*, Prentice Hall Press, New York

O'Meara, J (1978): *The Voyage of St. Brendan*, Dolmen Press, Dublin

— (1982): *Gerald Of Wales: The History and Topography of Ireland*, Penguin Books, Harmondsworth

O'Keeffe, J.G. (1913): *Buile Suibhne*, Irish Texts Society, Dublin

Ó Muimhneacháin, A. (1978): *Stories from the Tailor*, Mercier Press, Cork

O'Rahilly, C. (1924): *The Pursuit of Gruaidhe Griansholus*, Irish Texts Society, Dublin

— (1967): *Táin Bó Cúailnge*, Irish Texts Society, Dublin

O'Rourke, F.J. (1970): *The Fauna of Ireland*, Mercier Press, Cork

O'Sullivan, D.C. (2009): *The Natural History of Ireland by Philip O'Sullivan Beare*, Cork University Press, Cork

O'Sullivan, P.V. (1991): *Irish Superstitions and Legends of Animals and Birds*, Mercier Press, Cork

O'Sullivan, S. (1977): *Legends from Ireland*, B.T. Batsford Ltd., London

Opie, I. & Tatum, M., (1989): *A Dictionary of Superstitions*, Oxford, University Press, Oxford

Philbrick, N. (2001), *In the Heart of the Sea: The Tragedy of the Whaleship* Essex, Penguin Books, London

Power, P. (1914): *Lives of S.S. Declan and Mochuda*, Irish Texts Society, Dublin

Praeger, R.L. (1997): *The Way That I Went*, The Collins Press, Cork

Rees, A. & Rees, B. (1961): *Celtic Heritage*, Thames and Hudson, London

Roberts, J. (1993): *Irish Blessings, Toasts and Traditions*, Mercier Press, Cork

Rosenstock, G. (1999): *Irish Proverbs in Irish and English*, Mercier Press, Cork

Schweppe, F. (1990): *Kerry Blue Terriers*, TFH Publications, New Jersey

Share, B. (1997): *Slanguage – A Dictionary of Irish Slang*, Gill & Macmillan, Dublin

Squire, C. (1912): *Mythology of the Celtic People*, Tiger Books International (1998), Twickenham

Smyth, D. (1988): *A Guide to Irish Mythology*, Irish Academic Press, Dublin

Stokes, W. (1868): *Cormac's Glossary*, Calcutta

— (1890): *Lives of the Saints from the Book of Lismore*, Clarendon Press, Oxford

— (1892): *The Bodleian Dinnshenchus*, London

— (1892): *The Edinburgh Dinnshenchus*, London

— (1895): 'The Rennes Dinnshenchus', *Revue Celtique*, 15 (1895)

Swift, E. (1809): *Jocelyn's 'The Life and Acts of St Patrick'*, Hibernia Press, Dublin
Swinfen, A. (2004): *The Irish Donkey,* Lilliput Press, Dublin
Vickery, R. (1995): *A Dictionary of Plant Lore*, Oxford University Press, Oxford
Welcome, J. (1982): *Irish Horse Racing*, Gill & Macmillan, Dublin
Werner, R. (2009): 'The Old Irish Goat', *Heritage Outlook* (2009)
Westropp, P.J. (2000): *Folklore of Clare,* Clasp Press, Ennis
White, C. (2001): *A History of Irish Fairies*, Mercier Press, Cork
Wilde, W. (1853): *Irish Popular Superstitions*, Irish Academic Press (1979), Dublin
Williams, N. (1993): *Díolaim Luibheanna*, Sáirséal-Ó Marcaigh Teoranta, Dublin

# Index